The Turkey Hunter's Bible - 2nd Edition

Copyright © 2014 John E. Phillips

Table of Contents

CHAPTER 1 - KNOWING WILD TURKEYS

Before Christopher Columbus landed on the banks of the New World, man was already hunting and domesticating the wild turkey, a hardy survivor today of changing times and habitat. Naturally wary, the wild turkey has been very successful in living a life of adaptability.

THE ADAPTABILITY OF WILD TURKEYS

The wild turkey's expertise in living and multiplying in the face of encroaching civilization is partly due to the turkey's excellence at the game of hide-and-seek. Also the wild turkey:

- possesses keener senses of hearing and seeing than man,

- has the ability to run at 12.5-miles per hour,

- covers a vast amount of ground by constantly walking an average of 30,000-steps in a day's time,

- takes off from the ground like a helicopter,

- flies as fast as the speed limit on highways for short distances and

- negotiates easily flight paths through trees.

The growth of turkey populations also has been aided by their uniqueness and self-sufficiency. The wild turkey feeds on nuts, seeds, insects, berries and other small fruits and animals, eating more than 354-species of plants and 313-kinds of small animals. A turkey can eat up to a pound of food per meal with his powerful gizzard that can crush the hardest foods. In snow, the turkey can scratch up to a foot deep to find food.

1

Wild turkeys, which gather in small flocks, are led in the spring by a dominant male known as a gobbler or a tom and often has a harem of female hens. A definite pecking order is set up within the flock. When the dominant male turkey is killed, the flock adapts by another tom moving up to the dominant position in the pecking order.

The wild turkey's mating and reproduction systems make them particularly strong and disease-resistant. Usually only the dominant gobbler breeds. A great number of eggs will be laid with only a few infertile. Gobblers prepare for mating season by feeding heavily and then living on their breast sponges -- masses of thick, cellular tissue -- during mating season when they do not have to take time to eat. If a hen's eggs or nest, which is built on the ground, are destroyed, and she then mates with a bird other than the dominant gobbler, a large proportion of the eggs will not develop.

Hens do the nesting. They are cautious and aggressive in protecting the nests from all predators --including raccoons, skunks, foxes and coyotes, which particularly have become a problem in many areas of the nation. Turkey eggs, which are almost twice the size of chicken eggs are a pale, creamy-tan color with brown speckles. The shell of a turkey egg takes in oxygen and gives off carbon dioxide. The female turkeys turn the eggs to enable the poults (baby turkeys) to get oxygen. These hens remain on the nests 23-hours per day during incubation.

Then on the twenty-fourth day, the poults make noises and vibrations in the shells. This pipping noise made by the poults inside the eggs and the mother hen outside encourages the poults to burst through the shells. Turkey poults, which are able to move immediately after birth, quickly adapt to the harsh environment outside their shells and imprint immediately on their mother --following her away from the egg area which will attract predators. Biologists have observed that poults will walk all day following their mother on their birth day.

Although somewhat strong at birth and committed to outwitting predators, turkey poults are vulnerable to spring storms and cold and wet weather. They must be kept warm and dry, which is the reason for the high mortality rates of turkeys in springs that have floods and plenty of wet weather.

By the seventh day of life, turkey poults are still adapting to their environment by scratching stones and seeds on the forest floor to feed themselves and beginning to fly. The poults then are able to fly to their roosts by their fourteenth day of life. In August, turkey poults are two-thirds grown with males and females still looking alike. But by November or December each year, the male poults, now known as jakes which are toms less than one year old, leave their mothers and sisters to form bachelor flocks.

THE HISTORY OF THE WILD TURKEY

The Indians of North America, as well as the colonists, found wild turkeys exciting to hunt and useful when caught. Indians were utilizing many of what we consider today new tactics for hunting wild turkeys when the first colonists landed in America. They called to turkeys, flushed them, ran them with dogs and horses, shot them on their roosts and trapped them in trenches by baiting before taking the birds with their bows and arrows.

Where were the first turkeys, which are indigenous only to North America, found? The ancestral range of the turkeys living on our continent in the early days included about forty states. The Indians of Virginia and North Carolina, as well as the Aztecs of Mexico, farmed and raised wild turkeys that had been domesticated.

Evidence suggests the wild turkey and the domesticated turkey were both important foods for the native American Indian. The Indians' techniques for hunting were probably similar to today's bow hunter's tactics such as finding an area where the turkey fed, watered and then determining the path of travel between the roost and feeding region.

Indians not only ate turkeys but also used them for decoration, clothing, sewing and ceremonial items. Historians say the Crows, a Rocky Mountain tribe, used the leg bones of turkeys to make ceremonial whistles, which were highly prized possessions. Prehistoric pottery of the Mexican Indians --both petroglyphs (rock pickings) and pictographs (paintings) --showed turkey images, causing historians to believe the turkey held an important place in this civilization.

Cortez probably took the Mexican turkey back to Spain around 1519 where it was domesticated and spread across Europe, later returning to North America with the Pilgrims in the 1600s. An estimated 10-million turkeys lived in the New World when the first permanent colony was settled and established at Plymouth, Massachusetts, in 1620. Early settlers brought caged specimens of domestic turkeys with them but still preferred the meat of the wild turkey, which were very plentiful at the time. The diaries of these colonists often made reference to flocks made up of more than 5,000-turkeys.

With the arrival of the white man in America, market turkey hunting became popular. Commercial hunters tried to develop ways to take the greatest amount of meat using the least amount of powder, shot and effort. Among their tactics for taking turkeys was lining. A trail of corn was laid out in a straight line as bait for turkeys. Turkeys would crowd shoulder to shoulder along the line with their heads down, eating the corn. The hunter would call to them, the turkeys would raise their heads to investigate, the gun would sound, and many turkeys would be bagged. Wild turkey was a cheap staple in many frontier meat markets. At this time, turkeys by anyone's standards were a bargain.

The demand for the meat of the turkeys, the efficiency of the hunt and the vast usefulness of the turkey all played major roles in making the turkey almost extinct in much of its historic range. Too, the growth of cities, agriculture, human populations and domestication diseases of the turkey eventually aided the turkey's demise.

In the 1600s, the thought of protection of the turkey was unheard of and seemed ridiculous and unnecessary since the wild turkey supply seemed inexhaustible. But much like the buffalo of the western frontier faced poachers and loss of habitat, wild turkeys experienced the same problems. After the Civil War in the 1860s until the early 20th Century, market hunting was at its height. The turkey was gone from Connecticut by 1813, from Massachusetts by 1851, from Ohio by 1880 and from Michigan by 1881. By the end of World War II, what originally had been a population of 10-million or more turkeys had been reduced to only 30,000-birds in the entire United States. The saga of the wild turkey was yet another chapter in the shameful greed and insatiable appetite of the new nation.

In the early 20th Century, President Theodore Roosevelt, who was known as an outdoorsman and hunter, asked Congress to set aside wildlife refuges and begin a planned, scientific way to help America's dwindling wildlife. As a result in 1935, the Cooperative

Wildlife Research Unit Program was established. Then in 1937, Congress passed the Federal Aid in Wildlife Restoration Act, the Pittman-Robertson Act, that legislated a hunter tax and thereby directly aided the American turkey. Men and women paid a tax on each and every hunting and outdoor equipment item, and this money was used to aid wildlife and wildlife restoration. This act, along with increased knowledge and awareness of the plight of the wild turkey, helped the turkey to come back.

Alabama, Virginia, Louisiana, Texas and Missouri were the first states with wild turkey research programs. They located existing populations of turkeys, provided information for hunting seasons and selected areas for restocking. Unfortunately, many of the early projects did not succeed because game farm turkeys were used. These birds were not self-sufficient, had lost their instincts to survive in the wild and also carried poultry diseases.

But continued efforts and new methods of transplanting turkeys changed all this. Wild turkeys of the West were not as overhunted as those of the East. In the 1940s and 1950s, some populations in the West actually increased. Numerous factors also helped other turkey populations. The cannon-projected net trap, originally used for taking waterfowl, was utilized for transplanting wild turkeys. Improved forest management, better law enforcement, increased concern for conservation and new methods for the care and transplanting of wild turkeys helped increase their numbers. Biologists even transplanted turkey into habitats beyond their ancestral range. For instance, Michigan swapped 200-eastern turkeys to Ontario for twenty moose. Increased knowledge of the turkey's history, decimation, biological makeup, breeding habits and necessities of habitat all worked to bring back the turkey to its original ranges.

By 1958, enough birds had come back through restocking and protection that they again could be hunted in many parts of the United States. However, in sections of Alabama, Louisiana and some other southern states turkey season never had been closed. Now the wild turkey is present in fifty states and in Canada and Mexico.

Support, protection and conservation of the wild turkey continues. The National Wild Turkey Federation (NWTF) was incorporated in 1973 as a nonprofit conservation and education organization. The NWTF established the NWTF Research Foundation in 1981 to solicit funds and use these for wild turkey research nationwide. In 1986, the NWTF and the U.S. Forest Service signed an agreement to provide money and volunteers to maintain and improve wild turkey habitat and conduct research on Forest System lands. By 1988, the national flock of wild turkeys was at one-fifth of its original number. In 2010, an estimated 7 million turkeys live nationwide.

THE BIOLOGY OF THE WILD TURKEY

An adult male turkey is about 4-feet tall with brilliantly colored plumes of metallic green, copper and bronze. Body feathers have black tips, and a tuft of bristle-like feathers called a beard hang from the male's breast. Turkey feathers insulate and cover. Their down feathers, which are closest to their bodies, are covered and shielded by vein feathers or contour feathers. The male bird also has spurs on his legs.

The head and the neck of the male turkey are featherless. A tom's head can be many colors including purple, blue, white and/or red, depending on the gobbler's mood, the amount of blood flow or lack of it near the surface, the time of the year and the location

4

where the bird lives. The growth on the front of the head is called a snood or a dewbill. The pouchlike area at the front of his throat, a wattle, usually is the penetration target for the hunter. Small, fleshy, reddish growths of skin at the base of the throat are called caruncles.

The hen is smaller than the tom. Like most species of birds, the hen appears duller in color and has fewer bristles on the breast than the male does.

All turkeys are good runners, even when melting snow covers the ground. Audubon once followed a flock of wild turkeys on horseback without being able to overtake them while they were running. However, one advantage hunters of turkeys all over the United States have is that these birds are poor fliers-- except for short distances-- because turkeys lack blood vessels in their breast muscles.

THE SPECIES AND SUBSPECIES OF TURKEYS

There are two living species of turkeys-- the turkey of North America (*Meleagris gallopavo*) and the smaller and more colorful ocellated turkey (*Meleagris ocellata*) of southern Mexico and Central America. Turkeys may have received their common name in any one of several ways. Some people think the Indian name for the bird, which was furkee or firkee, may have been changed in pronunciation to turkey. Others believe the North American turkey's scientific names, *Meleagris*, which means guineafowl, and *gallopavo*, which is derived from gallus (cock) and pavo (peafowl), support a theory that the turkey was confused with the guineafowl (*Nunida meleagris*) at one time. Since the guineafowl was thought to have originated in the country of Turkey, perhaps that is why the turkey came to be called a turkey. Species: North American Turkey- *Meleagris gallopavo*

Various factors have caused a mixing of breeds of wild turkey. Interbreeding sometimes occurs between subspecies when their native habitats overlap. An example of this occurrence is the wild turkey in northern Florida. The Osceola (Florida turkey) is native to southern Florida. The eastern race of turkeys is native to northern Florida. A strain of turkey that is neither pure Osceola or Eastern will live where the ranges overlap, and this occurrence is not unusual.

Another factor is the transplantation of birds to historic and non-historic ranges. For example, where Rio Grandes, easterns and Merriams have been released in California, they have produced a colony of turkeys called the California turkey, a hybrid of the three subspecies.

The wild turkey species, *Meleagris gallopavo*, includes the subspecies of the eastern, the Osceola, the Merriam and the Rio Grande in the United States and the Gould mainly in Mexico. The Mexican turkey, which is now extinct, was the ancestor of our domesticated birds. Many of the characteristics that identify the different subspecies are subtle and mostly limited to differences in graduations of color. The identification of the subspecies is usually dependent on the region in which the turkey lives.

Eastern Turkey

The eastern wild turkey, *Meleagris gallopavo silvestris*, has been restocked successfully across much of the United States. This turkey of the East, some parts of the Midwest and the South has as its habitat mainly farmlands and hardwood forests, an area that produces much in the way of mast crops. The species designator, silvestris, translates to woodlands. Pennsylvania, New York, Missouri and many of the southern states have large numbers of easterns, and Missouri is known nationwide for its vast turkey hunting opportunities.

According to the NWTF, this most sought-after species holds the record for the heaviest turkey -- at 35.81 pounds -- and the best atypical turkey with eight beards and 199.9-points. Also, many sportsmen believe the eastern wild turkey is the most difficult type to take. Distinctive in appearance, the eastern turkey's tail tips can be chocolate color or buff. The primary wing feathers are barred with white divided by a black bar of similar width.

Rio Grande Turkey

This gobbler, *Meleagris gallopavo intermedia*, is found throughout the arid Southwest. Texas, Oklahoma and California typically have the largest birds, and Texas probably has the most Rio Grandes. Rio Grandes also are found in Kansas, New Mexico and Mexico.

The Rio Grande looks much like a combination of the eastern and western strains, which probably is the reason for the subspecies name, intermedia. The tail tips of this turkey can range from yellowish-buff in color to nearly pure white. The tail feather tips are almost always lighter than those of the eastern or the Osceola and are darker than the Merriam or the Gould.

The home of the Rio Grande ranges from the mesquite-dotted rangelands of Texas to the eastern-looking Kansas habitats with alternating farmland and hardwood ridges. Oklahoma's habitat is open farmland by tree-lined waterways. Obviously, the Rio Grande wild turkey is very adaptable. When hunting the Rio Grande in the West, because of the lack of foliage, finding a good place to hide and to take a stand are much more critical to your success in bagging a tom than getting close to the birds.

Merriam Turkey

The *Meleagris gallopavo merriami* (Merriam) turkeys are taken from a wide range of territory including South Dakota, California, Washington, Colorado, Minnesota, New Mexico, Nebraska and Wyoming. This bird originally lived in the mountainous areas of Arizona and New Mexico, but restocking has caused the range of the Merriam to be greatly extended.

The Merriam, named to honor zoologist, C. Hart Merriam, is sometimes called the mountain turkey because much of its range is the ponderosa pine belt to the foothills that surround the mountains. The Merriam is a migratory turkey in some areas. Summer birds stay high on the mountain to take advantage of the pine tree roosts, cooler air and a better water and food supply. When snow falls, these turkeys move to the foothills that support transition woodlands. Biologists have estimated the trip between a Merriam's summer and winter habitats may be as far sixty miles. Because of the high altitudes in which a hunter must hunt Merriams, you must be in top-notch physical condition to be able to manage the hunt itself. The Merriams look much like the other subspecies of turkeys, only their tail feathers are much whiter.

Osceola Turkey

Because this subspecies, *Meleagris gallopavo osceola*, is found in the peninsula of Florida, it sometimes is called the Florida Turkey. Other regions of Florida have wild turkeys, but they are either easterns or hybrids of the easterns and the Osceolas. The Osceola has the most restricted range of all the subspecies.

The Osceola bears the name of the 19th century Seminole Indian Chief, Chief Osceola, who was undefeated in his war against the Americans. Because of the swamps, mosquitoes and rugged terrain of Florida, the Seminole nation was unconquered. To take an Osceola gobbler, hunters have to face these same elements as well as almost tropical heat.

The Osceola resembles the eastern turkey in coloration, but its body is smaller. Also the barring of the wing feathers is slightly different. The Osceola's wing color is predominantly black.

Gould Turkey

This turkey, the *Meleagris gallopavo mexicana*, is found predominantly in the northern range of Mexico in the Sierra Madre Mountain, although small groups of these birds also live in the area where New Mexico, Arizona and Mexico meet. State and federal game management officials hope these birds can come back to a good number in this part of their historic range, since the estimated Gould population in the U.S. only was 150-birds in 1989.

To make this hope a reality, the Arizona Game and Fish Department, the USDA Forest Service, the Bureau of Land Management, the U.S. Fish and Wildlife Service, the state and federal governments of Mexico, the Southeastern Cooperative Wildlife Disease Study of Athens, Georgia, and the NWTF have worked together to trap Gould turkeys in Mexico. Then they have moved them into the Galiuro Mountains, a wilderness area in the Coronado National Forest.

The Gould turkey also is a migratory bird between a summer and a winter range. This bird resembles the Merriam gobbler in that the tips of its tail feathers are also white but not as intense. The wide band that borders the tail feathers is wider than in the Merriam, and the rump patch of the Gould usually is slightly smaller than the Merriam.

Species: The Ocellated Turkey

The ocellated turkey, *Meleagris ocellata*, is a separate species of turkey, rather than a subspecies. These birds are found on the Yucatan Peninsula of Mexico and in the adjoining Central American countries of Guatemala and Belize. The ocellata is a jungle bird.

Male and female ocellatas are similarly colored with an iridescent green body with gold, copper, bronze and red flashes of light. The ocellated turkeys have been said to be the most beautiful birds in the world. Interestingly, neither sex has a beard, but the males do have spurs. This bird is smaller than the gallopavo, and males average around 12-pounds, while some have reached 18-pounds.

TIPS ON HUNTING THE SUBSPECIES OF THE NORTH AMERICAN TURKEY

Because of differences in habitat, breeding and hunting pressure of the different subspecies of the North American wild turkey, Meleagris gallopavo, I have discovered some keys to hunting the various kinds of birds. All the experts agree the main differences between hunting eastern and western gobblers are terrain and the amount of hunting pressure the birds have experienced. More gobblers live in the West, and these birds may be easier to call and take since they are not as familiar with hunters and/or calls as eastern turkeys are. However, as soon as hunting pressure is applied, the easy western gobblers can and will become just as difficult to call and bag as their eastern cousins.

Generally eastern birds prefer farmlands and woodlands for their habitat. Although Rio Grande turkeys often roost in small water oak trees in the desert, the ground under the trees will be so clean the birds can see for great distances. You must set up much further back from the Rio Grande turkeys than you do easterns. However, your calls will carry much further because of the lack of foliage to absorb sound. You also can see the birds at greater distances since the land is so barren. Rio Grandes also flock together in much larger flocks than easterns. Rios even flock together in the spring because so few roost sites are available in the West.

In the West, a hunter's eyes are more critical to hunting turkeys than his ears, but in the East, the opposite is true because of the proximity of the hunter to the birds and the habitat. In the East, sportsmen call very little and softly to be effective because of the intense hunting pressure. But in many parts of the West, the wild turkeys, such as the Rio Grandes and the Merriams, may have been called very little. Generally a hunter can call louder and more often to western turkeys because of the lack of hunting pressure. A hunter can get excited about and hooked on hunting turkeys when they have hunted the western birds. Also, the turkeys of the West are much more vocal in the afternoon and even up until an hour after dark. So they are much easier to roost and more fun to listen to than the Easterns.

Because of hunting pressure and smaller populations of birds, eastern turkeys are usually more difficult to hunt and require more skill, knowledge and preparation to bag a bird. Therefore, many hunters consider them more challenging and their favorite birds to hunt.

The wild turkey is one of the smartest birds around. Because you must hunt him on his turf, the key to bagging him is to outsmart him. Perhaps this is what makes the hunt for a wild turkey so appealing and bagging the bird such a victorious experience. When you have outsmarted a gobbler, looked him in the eye and pulled the trigger, you have won another victory of endurance and smarts.

CHAPTER 2 - EQUIPPING THE TURKEY HUNTER

The knights of the round table never went to a tournament without first checking their equipment. Each piece of armor, every lance, their maces and their swords all were cleaned, polished, sharpened and prepared for the tournament. Any weakness in their armor not only would mean their defeat but also could cause them to lose their lives.

Turkey hunters of the spring and fall who pit their skills and equipment against the bronze baron of the roosts must be as thorough as the knights of old in inspecting their equipment. Because the turkey hunter must run, hide, shoot, call and outsmart the bronze baron in the bird's living room, and this wild turkey knows the woods better, is more conscious of danger and can see and hear better than the hunter, having the proper equipment in good working order is a key ingredient to bagging a gobbler. If you pick up the gauntlet to challenge a bronze baron, you will need this equipment.

MEDICINE

Although often turkey hunters must sneeze, cough, clear their throats and wipe their runny noses, these seemingly minor irritations will spook toms. To prevent these ailments from occurring when you are chasing a gobbler, take a decongestant like Tylenol Sinus before the hunt. If you have any type of allergy, hay fever, a cold or a cough, a decongestant is a must before you go into the woods.

The spring turkey hunter must use a quality insect repellent. You will have a difficult time concentrating on turkeys if mosquitoes or flies buzz in your ears or around your face. More turkeys have been spooked by hunters swatting bugs than for any other reason.

Another advantage of wearing insect repellent is it will ward off ticks and red bugs. When you are on a stand waiting for a gobbler to show up and see a tick crawling up the back of your neck, you naturally want to grab, pinch and squash that tick before the tiny mite can bury its nose deep in your skin. However, when a tom in front of you is screaming out a gobble so loud he causes the leaves on the tree you are sitting under to quiver, you have to fight the urge to pick the tick.

I use two types of insect repellent to prevent this situation. An Avon bath oil, Skin So Soft, has a very sweet, feminine smell. But many of the servicemen in the armed forces apply this product to their skin to prevent them from encountering biting insects around the world. I have found by wiping Skin So Soft all over my body, I rarely if ever get bitten by ticks or red bugs.

To put up a second barrier of defense, I also use a commercially made insect repellent with 25-percent DEET or more. I spray this on my clothing, my boots, the bill of my cap, my headnet and my gloves. But be careful when using this type of repellent, because if you fail to let it dry before you use your shotgun, the repellent may take the finish off the gun.

UNDERCLOTHES

Had you ever thought how uncomfortable a suit of chain mail or body armor was for the knights of old? Could you imagine riding a horse with jointed armor moving up and down on your legs and back and around your neck? Without the proper underclothes, a knight would have been terribly uncomfortable and less than functional. For the turkey hunter, underclothes also can be a critical key to success.

Although the gladiators of the Middle Ages were dependent on their trusty steeds for transportation, turkey hunters must rely on their feet. Proper foot care is a major concern for successful turkey hunters, who must keep their feet dry, warm and/or cool, depending on the weather.

I wear a pair of polypropylene sock liners to pull moisture away from my feet and transfer that moisture to the sock. This moisture-absorbing property of polypropylene helps to keep the foot dry, comfortable and feeling good all day long.

Depending on the weather, I either will wear a suit of high-tech long underwear or common cotton underwear. I have discovered that even when hunting in the spring in Texas, long underwear is the preferred underclothing. I like either Browning's lightweight Hunderwear, Haley Hansen's lightweight underwear or some type of polypropylene and cotton underwear. The polypropylene will keep you dry and warm, even if you must hike to your gobbler. When you sit down to call a tom, you will be much warmer because the moisture your body has produced will be wicked away from your skin.

Wearing long underwear often is desirable. Usually in the morning, the weather is quite cool. Even though the day may warm up, if you locate a turkey gobbler before daylight, you may have to take a stand and sit still for some time on the cold ground. If you do not dress warmly enough, you will be very uncomfortable and often will begin to shiver and shake before a bird shows up. If you dress too warm and have to hunt when temperatures are in the 70s and 80s, then you will be too hot and miserable the rest of the day. Lightweight underwear with the ability to wick moisture away from the skin will keep me warm in the morning. If temperatures begin to rise during the day, the wicking effect of the underwear actually will cool me down later in the morning.

A recent discovery for me is that as perspiration is wicked away from the body during hot weather, this wicking phenomenon makes the body much cooler than if you perspire and hunt in lightweight clothing. When hunting in Texas and Mexico, the temperatures may be 40-to 50-degrees in the morning, and 80-to 100-degrees later on in the day during the spring. Long underwear will keep me warm early and cool when the later temperatures in the day soar.

In the late spring and early fall when the morning temperatures may be in the 50s and 60s, I generally wear cotton briefs and a cotton camo tee-shirt. The camo tee-shirt is an essential piece of equipment since it prevents leaves, sticks, brush and bugs from getting next to my skin if these foreign objects succeed in getting past my shirt. Too, a tee-shirt helps ward off the chill associated with early morning hunting.

However, if you wear a white tee-shirt, you are courting because white is one of the colors of a turkey's head. If you are sitting next to a tree and your white tee-shirt is shining, that patch of white is about the same level a normal turkey's head is. Also you are making the same sounds as a gobbler when he calls. If another hunter comes to you, spots that patch of white and hears those sounds of a wild turkey, you may be in harm's way.

The second reason for not wearing a white tee-shirt is that a tee-shirt may crawl up on your neck and become visible when you least expect it. When a gobbler starts coming to your call, he may see that patch of white, pick up on your movement, and be gone.

BOOTS AND SOCKS

Because the turkey hunter lives or dies on his feet, proper footwear is a critical ingredient in successful turkey hunting. Since the sportsman may have to walk, run or wade, he must have footgear that can get him through whatever type of terrain he may encounter in his attempt to get close enough to a turkey to call.

Because Cordura uppers on boots can be camouflaged, this cloth type upper allows the hunter to extend his camouflage all the way to his feet. Boots like those made by Rocky, Browning and Servus feature these lightweight Cordura uppers with either rubber, leather or Cordura bottoms all in camouflage. Make sure the soles of your boots are dark-colored instead of light-colored. A bright yellow sole on a boot will cause a turkey to spot you.

I also hunt with a two boot system. My first pair of boots, my primary pair, are lightweight and made of either Gore-Tex and leather or all Gore-Tex. Boots made of this material are usually lighter and more comfortable than either all leather or rubber boots. I also choose boots that support my ankles and are waterproof to allow me to go through water and mud without leaking.

Selecting the proper sole for turkey hunting is important too. Lug soles will pick up mud, dirt and clay and add weight to your feet. In the spring, flooded areas and mud are commonplace across much of the United States. In most areas I hunt with the exception of the West, I am willing to give up the traction the lug soles offer to prevent the added weight they will pick up. Even when I'm hunting in rocky terrain, I will pick Vibram soles over lug soles. Although Vibram soles may have some ripple to them, they basically are a much flatter, lighter sole.

My turkey hunting boots are to me what good track shoes are to a marathon runner. During turkey hunting season, I often will log from 3-to 10-miles a day in my boots. Wearing well-fitted and comfortable boots that allow my feet to breathe is important to my turkey hunting success.

I carry a second pair of boots with me in a daypack--Red Ball's Flyweight waders and a pair of tennis shoes. Although waders may not seem to be turkey hunting equipment, I usually seem to locate turkeys on the other side of some type of water that is over boot-top high. But I never let water prevent me from going to my gobbler. If a turkey gobbles on the other side of water, I can take off my daypack, remove my boots, unroll these lightweight waders, slip on my tennis shoes and quickly and effectively cross the water, coming out dry on the other side. If you hunt anywhere in the country where a turkey can fly across water, sooner or later you will be faced with the situation of do I get wet to take the turkey, or do I stay dry and let the bird escape. By carrying waders, you can remain dry and still take the turkey.

Under my boots I wear a pair of high-tech socks, either Thermax or a polypropylene in either a wool or a cotton blend. Bulkier socks not only cause my boots to fit better but also provide an added cushion for my feet almost like a second innersole. Since I have on polypropylene sock liners, my feet will be dry. Today most high-tech socks also have the ability to wick moisture and transfer it to the outside of the sock to keep the foot dry and comfortable.

CAMOUFLAGE

The camouflage I choose depends on the terrain I am hunting. Hunters have several different camouflage philosophies.

Silhouette Camo

This type of camo is similar to the World War II and the Vietnam tiger stripe camo-- camouflage patterns that use large, horizontal bands of various types of foliage colors to try and break up the outline of the body. By using wide bands of color, this camo helps the hunter blend into the shadows, shades and foliage of the environment in which he hunts.

Vertical Patterns

The vertical pattern camos like Hide'N Pine, Realtree, Mossy Oak and Trebark are based on the philosophy that most of the color in the woods is vertical like a tree trunk. Original Trebark is composed of large oblongs about two to three inches long consisting of different shades of gray and black to try and match the colors of many of the hardwood trees in the forest. This pattern quickly has replaced many of the WWII patterns and gained acceptance among turkey hunters who usually sit next to trees. A turkey hunter should wear the vertical pattern that most resembles the tree trunks where he is sitting.

Trebark's second pattern, Trebark II, has smaller blocks of color -- reducing the original Trebark pattern by half -- and utilizes two color tones of brown instead of brown and gray. This pattern has sold well and has created a stir in the camo market. I have worn Trebark II in the swamps of Florida and the deserts of New Mexico and have found it to be a universal pattern that fits most terrains.

Three other companies that developed bark-type patterns to capitalize on the demand for this vertical scheme were Realtree, Mossy Oak and Hide 'N Pine. Realtree next appeared on the market after Trebark with a narrow and vertical pattern that includes whites, grays, greens and vertical lines.

A couple years later, Toxey Haas and the folks at Mossy Oak decided brown was beautiful and made a vertical pattern-- Bottom Land -- that was made up primarily of browns and black to match darker woods and more earth tones. Hide 'N Pine came with a bluer pattern with even smaller bars to more closely match pine trees and other trees found in the woods.

All these original, vertical patterns are still selling well today and are applicable for the turkey hunter in most parts of the country.

BlendIn Camo

If you ever watch a hen mallard duck, notice her coloring blends in with the bulrushes and weeds along the edge of the water. Mother Nature has devised a color scheme that matches the feathers of the hen to the surroundings where she lives. This philosophy is what the blendin type patterns duplicate. Blendin patterns often have leaves and bushes on them to appear like the surroundings where the hunter is. The blendin camo, which has introduced horizontal color, shade and form that breaks up the vertical pattern and makes this camo blend in with more varied types of surroundings, has gained tremendous support from both turkey and deer hunters. Realtree is one of the first companies to produce a blendin camo.

A new direction of blendin camo is Mossy Oak's introduction of their Treestand pattern which features tree limbs going across Mossy Oak's basic vertical patchwork. Treestand offers you the vertical pattern many hunters prefer while blending in with the surroundings more due to the limbs crossing the pattern. Mossy Oak has gone one step further and added leaves to their Treestand pattern, to create their Full Foliage pattern.

Most camouflage companies have found that camouflage with a more predominantly brown cast seems to be the wave of the future. Realtree, as well as Bushlan, Hide 'N Pine and many of the other camo companies have followed Mossy Oak's lead into the brown camo.

The makers of the Bushlan pattern decided no pattern on the market blended in well with Texas terrain and the small bushes and shrubs found in more arid regions. They developed a Bushlan green pattern that broke from tradition. Even though most hunters agreed it was well-suited for the Texas hunter, many believed it was strictly a regional pattern as originally was thought of both Realtree and Mossy Oak.

However, sportsmen in all areas have purchased this pattern. Today Bushlan has proven to be a universal camo disguise.

Chameleon's Shadow-Camo, which is made in Oregon, is another pattern that has appeared to be regional in design but has found wide acceptance throughout the nation. Because of the wide variety of colors and shades in this camo, this pattern does what its name implies --blends into almost any terrain where used. Chameleon also has introduced two new color changes --Brown Shadow-Camo, which will be appropriate for dry areas and fall hunting, and Green Shadow-Camo.

All-Purpose Camo

Realtree has a new All-Purpose Camo, which features the brown tones that have been so popular in camouflage in the last few years. Not only is the new Realtree All-Purpose Camo predominantly brown, but this camouflage combines all three camouflage philosophies into one unique pattern.

Although the pattern basically is vertical, it also has leaves and branches on it. The placement and the colors of the leaves and the branches on the pattern allow this camo to break up the silhouette of the hunter much like the large, World War II horizontal patterns do without sacrificing the vertical tree pattern that has gained in popularity. The leaves and branches are placed in such a way the pattern lets you blend in with your surroundings.

All these camouflage patterns will hide the hunter from the turkey. Camo patterns are fashion statements and can be personalized to suit each individual hunter's own belief and philosophy about camouflage. Actually the only wrong camo pattern you can wear is snow camo in the desert or either brown or green camo in the snow. Camouflage patterns are designed to hide the hunter in most areas of the United States during both the spring and the fall turkey hunting seasons. Discuss camo with other turkey hunters in your area and your local sporting goods dealers to determine which kind of camo is the most appropriate for the region you hunt.

Best Picks For Camo

I believe all the camo patterns work. I wear and hunt in just about every camo pattern on the market. However, certain patterns tend to lend themselves better to hunting at different times of the year and under specific hunting conditions. I choose my camo depending on where and when I am hunting. Here are the guidelines I use for determining which camo to wear when and where.

Early Spring

During the early spring before the leaves are thick on the trees and bushes, I usually choose a vertical, all-bark pattern. At this time, tree trunks and the colors of tree trunks will be what the turkey sees since few leaves are on the trees. These patterns fit into the woods' colors more. Not much green is present in the woods because there are few if any leaves out in the early part of the season where I hunt, and blues, browns and grays seem to be more effective patterns for me.

Another consideration in choosing camo for the early spring is air temperature. On cool mornings, you may need insulated camo like Walls' Thinsulate coverall in Realtree's All-Purpose Camo.

Other patterns that also can be used in the early spring, even though typically they are not vertical but do hide the hunter well, include Brigade Quartermaster's ASAT (All-Season, All Terrain), Chameleon's Shadow-Camo, Bushlan's new brown pattern and Predator's brown pattern.

I never have considered the Bushlan pattern as an early season southern hardwood pattern until I played paintball for the first time. Paintball is a recreational game gaining popularity across our nation, as well as overseas, where men dress up in full camo and play Capture the Flag using airguns to shoot paintballs at each other to indicate a kill.

When I played last fall, three times in a row, I sneaked up on the opposing team only to be killed dead with paintballs. I failed to see the enemy who were hiding and wearing Bushlan camo.

Even though this pattern primarily has been promoted as a western pattern, I have found it effective in the Deep South where I live.

Mid-Spring

During the middle of the spring as the leaves begin to come out and more shadow and shade are present in the woods, I often select a leaf pattern type of camo at least for the shirt and either a bark pattern or a silhouette-breaking pattern for the pants. I try to match the ground cover with my pants and the foliage cover with my shirt, as well as wear something with which to break up my silhouette more.

Late Spring

In the late spring, most of the trees will have their leaves. For that reason I generally pick a green leaf-pattern kind of camo or a silhouette-breaking camo because so much shadow and shade are in the woods.

Desert And Rock Camo In Any Season

If you hunt Merriam turkeys in the mountains or Rio Grande gobblers in the desert, gray or bark-type camos seem to work best. I choose a gray camo to match the rocks or a bark-type camo, which also will match rocky and desert terrain. Camos like Bushlan may be a good choice for the Texas desert areas.

Camouflage By Region

Other than the time of year I am hunting for tough turkeys, the area of the country I hunt also determines the type of camo I prefer. If I am hunting the palmetto swamps of Florida for the Osceola turkey, I will select the Realtree Brown-Leaf pattern, Brigade Quartermaster's ASAT pattern, Trebark II or the Hide 'N Pine pattern because of shadow and shade. Mossy Oak's Full Foliage, Realtree's Grey-Leaf, Bushlan Green and Predator Green also will help camouflage me in the predominantly green-colored swampy terrain.

When I am searching for longbeards in the hardwood swamps of the South, Mossy Oak's Bottom Land, Trebark II, Realtree's All-Purpose, Hide 'N Pine, Bushlan Brown, Chameleon or Predator Brown will be my choices. When I go North to hunt in more mountainous terrain with bigger timber that has more gray tones, I often will choose original Trebark, Mossy Oak Treestand, original Realtree, Bushlan Brown, Chameleon or Predator Brown. I also have discovered that where you find numbers of spruce, cedar and pine trees in the North, Hide 'N Pine and Brigade Quartermaster's ASAT also are wise picks in camouflage.

When you travel West to the desert country of Texas, you often will find the turkeys either will be around rocks and bushes or in shade. Although the green or brown Bushlan camo is adaptable to concealing yourself in these areas, I have bagged birds in regions like these in Realtree's Brown-Leaf pattern and Mossy Oak's Full Foliage and Treestand patterns. If you stay in the woodlots where the turkeys roost and feed, patterns like Ranger's Tiger Stripe, Brigade Quartermaster's ASAT and Chameleon also can be effective. All camo companies are correct when they say their camo patterns will work at all times of the year in all terrains in all sections of the country. Choosing camo patterns for turkey hunting is as personal as selecting the type of underwear that suits you best. Each person should pick the pattern that makes him feel the most comfortable and the most hidden.

Pants And Shirts

Features to look for in pants for turkey hunting are drawstrings at the bottom of the pants, double-knee and pants somewhat longer than your usual inseam length. The drawstrings will keep your cuffs from catching on bushes and brush, they will help to hide the socks that may ride above the top of your boots, and they will keep sticks and bugs from coming up your pant legs.

I like double-knee pants, too. An aggressive turkey hunter will do a considerable amount of crawling. Pants with double knees will prevent the pants from wearing out as quickly as those pants that do not have that extra layer of material over the knees. Double bottoms will also keep the seat of the pants from wearing out as quickly, since a turkey hunter must spend much time sitting.

Always choosing pants that are somewhat longer than your usual inseam length will keep you from having a gap between your pants leg and your boots when you are sitting down. If this happens, your leg or sock may be exposed, which can spook a turkey.

I also like the chamois type pants better than the pure cotton pants. These pants are softer, more quiet and much more comfortable than other hunting pants. I prefer a six-pocketed pant because I always have plenty of turkey hunting gear to go in those pockets.

The pants should have buttons and not velcro or zippers. Buttons are more quiet than velcro or zippers and more appropriate to turkey hunting.

The pants also need large belt loops and buttons inside them for suspenders. I have found suspenders are much more comfortable when attempting to keep your pants up than belts are. They prevent a binding at the waist when you sit down. Rarely will you have to pull your pants up when you have to sit quickly, if you use suspenders. You also can wear somewhat bigger pants when you wear suspenders and have a little more room to move around in them than when you use a belt and have to depend on the force of the belt to hold the pants to your waist. Although using either belts or suspenders are personal preferences, I believe a turkey hunter can be much more comfortable when hunting in suspenders than when hunting in a belt. Many pants today have tab adjustments on the sides of the pants. These pull tabs look nice, but they rarely work. I have found them to be non-essential.

One of the most critical factors to look for when choosing a camo shirt is the length of the shirt. Always purchase a shirt with an extra long tail. The turkey hunter may be running, sitting and standing during the day. These activities often will cause the shirt to ride up out of the pants, exposing the back and constantly requiring the hunter to tuck in the shirt. If you have a shirt that is longer than normal, these problems can be eliminated.

Also select a shirt that is somewhat large with sleeves a little long. Having some excess material at your wrist will ensure you will not have skin showing between your gloves and shirt. A problem often happens when a hunter has sleeves the length of the dress shirt he wears. When he brings the gun to his shoulder and bends his arms at the elbows, the sleeves will pull away from the wrists and expose your skin and watchband. These areas may be spotted by turkeys and spook the birds.

I also like a two-pocketed shirt with large pockets. Because these pockets will be where I place diaphragm calls and small, compact binoculars, the bigger they are, the more useful they are. I prefer a shirt constructed of chamois type material, which is more soft and quiet than cotton but a somewhat heavier weight.

Headnets, Gloves and Hats

No camo or hunting aid will prevent a turkey from seeing you if you do not sit still. Generally a turkey spots the hunter not because he is wearing improper camo but because he moves when a turkey is looking at him.

But camouflage is an important key to successful turkey hunting. We can wear camo safely if we hunt defensively. Choose the camo that suits you, the terrain you hunt and the time of year and the location where you chase gobblers in the spring or fall.

There are as many styles of headnets and gloves as camouflage manufacturers, and each turkey hunter can tell you why he prefers the style he chooses. However, I like a soft cotton glove with an extra long wristband that comes 5-or 6-inches up the arm to help cover the gap that usually occurs between my shirt and my gloves. A soft cotton glove not only protects my hand from insects, briars and sticks but also allows me to feel my trigger and safety. Generally I match my gloves with the same camo pattern I am wearing on my shirt.

I prefer a full-face headnet usually made out of cloth rather than netting material, although netting material lets you hear better. A cloth headnet totally hides the head and neck and prevents these areas from being attacked by bugs, which is a concern of mine when I hunt in the South in the springtime. I favor having an elastic or a drawstring system in the headnet. Then I can secure the headnet, and the opening for the eyes will not move around. Since I wear glasses, often I wear one of the wire-frame types of headnets.

I like a camouflage hat with an adjustable headband and prefer a baseball cap style hat. A hat is a very important piece of the total camo suit. When properly worn, the hat helps hide you, and the bill of the cap keeps the sun out of your eyes and helps to hide the whites of your eyeballs from a turkey when you are low on the stock of your gun and aiming down the barrel. An adjustable band in the back of the cap means I can readjust the hat to fit comfortably when I put on a headnet.

THE TURKEY VEST

Another essential piece of equipment for the turkey hunter is a turkey vest with a back large game pocket that is big enough to carry a turkey. A turkey vest has external pockets where you can carry calls, shells, extra gloves and headnets and other equipment you will need. I like a vest that also has internal pockets with zippers or some type of closing other than velcro, which is noisy. These pockets can store binoculars, lunches and other equipment.

A quality turkey vest also should have a camouflaged drop seat that is long enough and wide enough to allow you to lower the seat and sit comfortably on the ground.

Some turkey vests feature a cushion in the back, which adds comfort for the hunter. Often turkey vests come equipped with a blaze orange flag that can be let down over the back of the game bag when a successful hunter comes out of the woods with his bird.

A turkey vest with adjustable straps and some type of fastening in the front allows you to sprint through the woods without your equipment bouncing out the front of your vest as you get into position to call a turkey. A vest's pockets must be big enough to hold box calls and friction calls as well as diaphragm calls.

In my turkey vest, I always carry a camouflaged rainsuit like the ones produced by Rainfair and 10X. Turkey hunters rarely plan to hunt in the rain. But, if you hunt throughout the spring, you will get caught in a shower. Without a rainsuit, you will be forced to make the decision either to get wet in your camouflage or go home and stay dry. However, if you have a camouflaged rainsuit on hand, as soon as the sky clouds up, you can don your rainsuit and continue to hunt even if the rain pours down.

Since a turkey vest is a critical piece of equipment for a turkey hunter, look for one that provides the most comforts and functions regardless of price. Because a turkey vest is a three to six year investment, spend the extra money to purchase a good one.

Blinds

Blinds serve several functions for the turkey hunter and can be constructed in various ways. Portable blinds, which let you move behind the blind, even as the turkey approaches, are particularly effective if you are using a box call, a pushbutton call or a friction call and must move your hands when calling and then put your calls down and pick up the gun when the turkey approaches. Blinds, which are also very helpful for hunters who have trouble sitting still long enough to call a turkey, are essential for novice turkey hunters and youngsters who do not understand how still they must sit to bag a gobbler.

When selecting a blind, choose a lightweight and easy-to-carry blind you can see over that you easily and quickly can put up. Also inspect the blind's stakes, which must be strong yet lightweight and can be put into the ground with little effort. Big wooden stakes are often hard to force into the ground, whereas lightweight, metal stakes may be easier for the hunter to set up.

You may choose to use a natural blind if you are an experienced hunter. Carry pruning shears and you easily can cut small limbs and bushes to set up in front of a tree where you plan to take a stand. When possible, I make some type of natural blind to break up my outline and allow me to move if necessary when a turkey approaches. Three or four small limbs and bushes will do the job. Also you can use pruning shears to trim limbs and bushes in your line of fire that may interfere with your shooting.

Many bow hunters have found blinds make bagging a gobbler with a bow much easier. Because a bow hunter must draw to shoot, most of the time a turkey will spot the archer before he can launch an arrow. A blind that totally covers the hunter yet provides shooting ports can give the bowman a decided advantage and help ensure a more successful hunt.

Binoculars

Binoculars are a critical tool for the turkey hunter. Binoculars allow you to not only see the bird at great distances but more importantly to determine the sex of a turkey before you ever stalk or call the bird. I use two different types of binoculars for two various reasons.

Compact Binoculars

I like small, compact binoculars because I can wear them around my neck or put them in my vest and quickly and easily see and determine the sex of turkeys in the woods while I'm hunting. If I leave this pair of binoculars at home, I will return to get them before I attempt to hunt. Binoculars are very essential for the turkey hunter because they allow you to read the mood of the gobbler before he comes in, which helps determine the type of calls to use to bring him to you.

Compact binoculars are especially popular with turkey hunters since these binoculars add little bulk and weight to the hunting gear. Many companies now make quality binoculars in compact sizes.

Nikon's camouflaged Mountaineer 8X23 waterproof, fogproof binoculars weigh only 15-ounces, are 4-inches X 4-1/2-inches in size and offer a 3-mm exit pupil. The compact Mountaineer with its contoured body and anatomically molded rubber ensure a secure, comfortable grip. Other features of the Mountaineer include precision-aligned lens elements and barrels, a rugged all-metal chassis, diopter adjustment to regulated individual eye strengths, smooth fast focus control and a 25-year limited warranty. In addition, all Nikons utilize only BAK4 high index prisms, for a bright, round, clear image unlike lesser quality binoculars that use cheap, low index prisms. Nikon fully coats all lens elements throughout each and every binocular for superb contrast, vivid colors and crisp detail.

Despite their compact size, all three models of Carl Zeiss' Pocket binoculars, the 6, the 8X20 and the 10X25, offer the same optical and mechanical excellence associated with all Zeiss products. The Zeiss Pocket binoculars which are guaranteed with warranty service available worldwide, offer a variety of features that normally are found only in full-size binoculars with internal focusing and a true, B-type eyepiece that allows full-field viewing for prescription or sunglass wearers. Additionally, the Makrolon housings are tough enough to withstand the most extreme climatic conditions and are rust and corrosive-proof. The Z-type hinge allows the barrels to fold together to form a very compact unit that easily fits into a shirt pocket. The compact size and light weight (the 8X20's are 3-3/4-inches high and weigh only 6-ounces), make this a very popular binocular that is best suited to normal daylight conditions. Like all Zeiss binoculars, the Minis are guaranteed, with warranty service available worldwide.

Pentax Corporation has unveiled a new design for their 7X20 and 9X20 DCF Mini roof prism, center-focusing binoculars. The duo-tone rubber coating of the 7X20 and 9X20 DCF minis gives added protection against moisture, shock and corrosion and provides a surer grip in cold or damp conditions. Their compact, rugged and lightweight construction makes these binoculars ideal for all kinds of outdoor activities, including turkey hunting. The 7X20 measures 3.7-inches X 4-inches X 1.3-inches and weighs only 7.4-ounces, while the 9X20 measures 3.6-inches X 4-inches X 3-inches and also weighs 7.4-ounces. Both models are backed by a limited lifetime warranty and include a carrying case and neck strap.

Jason's Perma Focus 2000 Camouflage binoculars feature camouflaged rubber coating in two compact models for watching turkey at a distance or pinpointing where they are up closer. The Model 191 Perma Focus 2000 7X21 has 393-feet field of view, 13.5-relative brightness, a roof prism and are 3-1/2-inches high and weigh 7-ounces. The Model 205 Perma Focus 2000 7X35 has an extra wide angle 578-feet field of view, 37.5-relative brightness, are 4-3/4-inches high and weigh 23.3-ounces.

Redfield's new waterproof adjust-free binoculars in 7X35 and 10X50 models require no manual focusing and provide an instantly focused picture at all distances from 30-feet and beyond. Minimum focusing distance is approximately 30-feet for the 7X35 model, and approximately 60-feet for the 10X50 model. The roof-prism, straight-barrel design minimizes bulk and helps prevent eye strain. Lenses are coated an precision-ground to enhance image sharpness, clarity and light transmission. Rubber armor coating eliminates glare, and guards against damage and game-startling noise that can occur when binoculars are inadvertently bumped or dropped. Nitrogen-filled barrels prevent leaking or fogging. These binoculars also feature soft, rubber eye cups that permit a full field of view and fold back for eyeglass wearers.

The Bushnell InstaVision compact binoculars have an 8X22mm roof prism model. Amber-coated, high contrast optics ensure a bright, sharp sight picture. A black nylon belt pack case with wide strap and zipper closure keeps the binocular within easy reach for instant use, and is ideal for around-the-waist carrying for turkey hunting. The 8X22 Instavision Folding Roof Prism Compact binocular has a limited lifetime warranty.

Leupold's 7X20mm Armored Pocket Binocular with an angular field of view of 6.8, a twilight factor of 11.8 and a 2.9mm-exit pupil weighs only 9.5-ounces and is available in black leather grain finish, or in olive green rubber armor. Both powers, 7X and 9X, feature retractable eyepieces, which accommodate glasses and come in a durable Cordura nylon case.

Simmons' Realtree Camo Folding Compact Binoculars are offered in 8X21mm and 10X25mm sizes. These binoculars are roof-prism design and have fully-coated optics. Field of view at 1000-yards is 372-feet and 220-feet, respectively. Also offered in black and other camouflage patterns, the lightweight binoculars are rubber armored for a quiet, non-reflective finish. They are furnished with a zippered case with a belt loop for easy carrying.

Full-Size Binoculars

The second set of binoculars I choose for turkey hunting are the bigger, heavier types all companies make. I like the larger binoculars for field checking and roosting turkeys. Bigger binoculars are usually brighter binoculars. They are too heavy to carry in the woods when you are hunting, but they do allow you to see under lower light conditions.

In the middle of the day, when I am riding in a vehicle and looking for turkeys in a field, these binoculars allow me to see the turkeys brighter and clearer than the compact binoculars do. Later in the evening when I go into the woods to try and see turkeys flying up to the roost, the larger binoculars let me distinguish gobblers from hens. Then I will know where to set up the next morning to try and call a gobbler to me.

RANGEFINDERS

Employing a rangefinder like those made by Browning or Ranging will aid you in judging the distance you are from the bird. Then you know when you squeeze the trigger that the pattern you have seen on the shooting range will be the pattern that covers the turkey's head and neck.

MISCELLANEOUS EQUIPMENT

Several other items I consider as essential turkey gear include ...

- a compass to show the hunter the direction he should take to a turkey and how to walk out of the woods.

- a small Maglite to help the hunter navigating before daylight and after dark.

- a fanny pack to store gear and calls.

- several different types of calls -- especially a box call, a slate, a pushbutton and various sizes and kinds of mouth diaphragms -- because some birds only want to hear certain types of sounds. If you do not have the calls that produce those sounds, you will fail to get your bird.

- three candy bars for when you are in the woods longer than you plan.

Turkey hunting is an exciting sport and can be very enjoyable for the hunter who has the proper equipment. Although other equipment including guns, shells and scopes will be discussed later, these basic essentials are what you need to begin the sport of turkey hunting. Comfort, fit and function are the three key words a turkey hunter must consider when choosing equipment for hunting. The more comfortable you are in the woods, the longer you can sit still, the easier you can move through the woods, and the more enjoyable your hunt for a wily gobbler will be.

CHAPTER 3 - CHOOSING GUNS, SHELLS, LOADS AND GUN ACCESSORIES

The way you play the game for turkey hunting determines the type of shotgun you choose. Some turkey hunters believe, "If I can see the gobbler, I want to be able to take him." These hunters will opt for a 3-1/2-inch Magnum 12-gauge shotgun or a 10 gauge that may reach-out as far as 40-50 yards. Other hunters think, "If I can't call the bird to within 30 yards, then I haven't earned the right to take him." Still others are convinced that, "I want the lightest, easiest-to-handle turkey shotgun that I can carry." Throughout my turkey-hunting career, I've walked down all these roads that have led to my selecting the right turkey gun for me.

Yet another consideration in choosing a turkey gun is the marriage that takes place between a hunter and his gun. Some hunters believe that, "I know how this gun shoots, I know how it patterns, and I'm convinced that if I get a tom within the range where I want to take the shot, my ole shotgun will deliver the coup de grace. So, why should I buy a new gun when my old gun is the most-dependable gun I've ever had?" Too, some turkey hunters prefer to shoot an all-purpose shotgun they can use for hunting turkeys but also waterfowl and upland game.

And, finally there's the turkey hunter who always wants to date the newest girl who comes to school. Every year gun manufacturers produce newer and better turkey shotguns. The hunters who purchase these new guns live by the philosophy,"I want to hunt with the newest and best shotgun on the market." Like other people have reasons they pick their shotguns, these hunters have a just case for the guns they select.

When you consider all the different reasons that turkey hunters use to pick the shotguns with which they hunt, you'll realize that the turkey hunter's shotgun is as personal as the type of underwear he or she chooses. For this reason, I've listed in this book some of the guns I've used to take turkeys over the years. At this time in my life, I have three favorite turkey guns: my Remington 1100 3-inch Magnum mounted with a scope and no choke; my Thompson Center 3-inch Magnum 20 gauge with a Hunter's Specialties' Widow Maker Choke; and my Benelli 3-inch Magnum 12 gauge Vinci.

My ole Remington is my reliable gun. Ever since I've had this gun, I've been able to depend on it and take turkeys with it. Yes, I've also missed turkeys with this gun, but the misses have been my fault, not the gun's. In more-recent years, I've been required by my job as an outdoor writer to try the Thompson Center single-shot 3-inch Magnum 20 gauge with a Widow Maker Choke. I've been totally surprised at how accurately and lethal this small "pop-gun" is. Although this 20 gauge is a single shot, it delivers a deadly load out to 40 yards and even further. Because it's lightweight, easy to carry and handle, fits my face and has a very-low recoil, I've fallen in love with this gun. I believe it to be the perfect gun to start-out a young or beginning hunter. And, as we get older and don't want to carry a big, heavy turkey shotgun, this Thompson Center 20 gauge is perfect for an older hunter to take afield.

However, I'll be amiss if I don't mention the Benelli Vinci. To have a shotgun that you can take on many-different kinds of hunts, including ducks, geese, upland game and turkeys, this gun is my favorite for go-anywhere, do-any type of shotgunning. The Vinci will reach-out and touch a gobbler, and it's comfortable to carry and also fits my face when I marry my cheek to the stock to aim accurately.

Because of the evolution of the turkey shotgun, I believe we'll continue to see changes and improvements on the shotguns we can choose with which to go into turkey woods. However, one thing is for certain. The way you choose to hunt turkeys and the relationship you have with the gun you take to the woods will be the most-deciding factor on which turkey gun is the best for you and how successful you'll be.In the days of the mountainmen, a turkey shoot was an event where men clad in buckskins carried flintlocks and percussion cap rifles and attempted to shoot a live, tied-at-the-foot turkey in the head as the bird ducked and dodged behind some type of cover. Rifles were used instead of the shotguns shot today.

The early marksmen had to be able to shoot straight and accurately, and they also had to foretell the unpredictable moves of a wily turkey. Today with binoculars to spot and observe turkeys and 3-inch magnums, 3-1/2-inch magnums and 10-gauge shotguns shooting either No. 4 or No. 6 shot, taking a turkey should not be very difficult.

However, as most turkey hunting experts say, "If you hunt turkeys long enough, you will miss some."

What causes us to miss turkeys? Can we reduce the number of misses we experience? Today we can increase our shooting accuracy by being aware of the different types of guns available, choosing the best one for each of us and using hunting aids and new sighting devices that will enable us to shoot not only more accurately but more quickly.

WHY YOU MUST BE ABLE TO JUDGE DISTANCE

No matter which gun or scope you shoot, if you cannot judge accurately the distance you are from a bird, you will not be able to determine the effectiveness of your shot once you squeeze the trigger. Even if you know the effective range of the gun, you will be unsure whether the pattern will put enough pellets in the gobbler to bring him down. Misjudging distance is easy. If you are a new hunter, you will be unaccustomed to seeing a turkey in the woods. When a turkey stands erect, he may look much bigger than most people expect. Judgment of distance is the first step in understanding the patterning of your gun.

When you are in the woods, try to determine where a certain distance is from your stand, say 10-yards. That will let you know where 20-yards, 30-yards, etc. is. Pick out a landmark at each as a reference point. Then when a turkey appears, you will know about how far he is and whether or not he is within range.

One of the best techniques for determining distances is to use a rangefinder. Often when a hunter utilizes a rangefinder while hunting turkeys, he believes he is doing so to determine the distance to an animal. He brings the rangefinder to his eye, focuses it on the target, reads the distance, puts it back in his pocket, picks up his gun and prepares for the shot. But this much movement spooks the turkey and is not the most effective way to use a rangefinder.

A better way to utilize the rangefinder is when game is not in sight. Guess the distances of landmarks in the woods, and then use the rangefinder to find out how far away something actually is. You will train your eyes to be more precise in judging distances and also game. The more you practice, the better you will be at pinpointing distances, and the more prepared you will be when a turkey appears.

Another method of estimating distances is to check the distance from your calling position to different objects in your field of view. Do this while you are sitting down and calling the gobbler. Determine the distances of these objects, and then make a mental decision not to take a shot unless the gobbler walks into the effective area, usually within 35-yards of you.

Most importantly, never force a shot. Do not shoot no matter what, and never let the desire to bag a gobbler get in the way of what you have learned about distances and your ability to down a bird. Making this kind of choice requires mental and physical discipline, because allowing a turkey to walk away is difficult. But by doing so and then moving to a new position and calling again, you will increase your chances of actually bagging the bird later.

Many turkey hunters spends hours practicing their calling but very little time practicing judging distances. If a hunter calls a turkey in but does not know how far the turkey is from him when he takes the shot, chances are he will miss the bird. Before you pattern your shotgun or decide on which shells to use, practice being the best judge of distance you can be.

HOW TO PATTERN YOUR SHOTGUN

Many hunters believe the phrase, patterning a shotgun, means standing 30-yards from a target, squeezing the trigger and determining how many pellets have put tiny holes in the paper. If this method is yours, you may be missing more turkeys than you are bagging. One shot does not yield enough information.

To effectively pattern your shotgun, put targets at 10-, 20-, 30-, 40-and 50-yards. Then you can see what your gun will do at several different distances. If a hunter slightly misses his aim when a turkey is in close, the hunter will not hit the turkey because all the pellets in the shell may miss the bird. However, if the turkey is farther away, the pattern opens up, and the pellets distribute over a larger portion.

When patterning your shotgun, try to shoot at the targets from the same position you expect to be shooting at a gobbler in the woods. For most, this is sitting with your back against a tree and the gun up on one knee.

WHAT SHOT SIZE?

Every hunter has his own opinion about this question, and most have valid answers. There is even a philosophy that the gun, not the hunter, dictates what size shot should be used.

Your shotgun will pattern every shot size differently. A shotgun that may throw No. 6 shot all over the paper and only place one or two pellets in the kill zone may hold a tight pattern with No. 4s, putting six to ten pellets in the kill zone. Some shotguns hold a tight, close pattern when shooting duplex shells, and some do not. Duplex shells are a combination of No. 2s and No. 4s, while others combine No. 4s and No. 6s. The best way to learn which is best in your gun is to shoot a variety of shot at various distances, no matter what works best for your hunting buddy.

Another factor that plays a major role in the effectiveness of a shell is the brand name. Remember, various brands pattern differently in the same gun. The best way to determine which shell and shot produces the best pattern in your gun is to buy several brands of shotgun shells in the same shot size and test each at varying distances. If you do not like what you see, move on to another shot size, and repeat the test.

WHEN IS THE SHELL AT FAULT?

The big Merriam turkey I had seen coming from 50-yards away now was in full strut - reflecting all the hues of his bronze feathers. The bird's head seemed to glow. His white crown, his red wattles and the blue around his eyes and throat lit up like neon lights against the dark background of the hues of green, black and bronze.

When I clucked, the tom dropped his strut, raised his noble head and prepared to die. I squeezed the trigger and was ready to make the quick, 20-yard trot required to recover the flopping bird. But this turkey did not flop. Instantly he changed his mindset from that of a proud bird attempting to show off his manhood to a red hot hen into the mode gobblers are best at -- running and flying.

I was dumbfounded. Although the tom should have been dead, he was race car running, feathers in the wind. I was so amazed I failed to take a second shot. In my mind, there was no way I could have missed that bird. The only reasonable answer was that somebody must have poured the shot out of my shell, which proved not to be true.

Some of the excuses an outdoorsman usually offers when a turkey fails to go down after he squeezes the trigger include...

- ..."Those sorry shells. I knew I should have bought the better brand."

- ..."Maybe I should have been shooting No. 4s instead of No. 6s."

- ..."If I'd had one of those 3-1/2-inch guns, I bet that turkey wouldn't have gotten away."

Shotshells are to the turkey hunter what fishing line is to the bass angler -- the link between the hunter and the gobbler. If the shells fail or do not produce as they have been designed, then the hunter misses, and the turkey escapes. The shells you shoot will determine the turkeys you take.

According to Dick Dietz, public relations manager for Remington Arms Company, "Because turkey hunters generally do not shoot large numbers of shells, I advise them to pay a little more money and buy the best shells they can get. If they plan to shoot cases of shells like dove hunters do, then price is a consideration. However, most turkey hunters rarely will shoot more than five to ten shotshells per season. If the best shells cost a nickel or a dime more, the wisest thing he can do is pay the extra money to ensure a successful hunt."

A critical factor in purchasing the best shells for turkey hunting is to buy shells that cause the pellets to fly straight.

As Dietz explains, "To shoot a tight pattern, the shot needs to stay as perfectly round as possible. If the shot becomes bent or uneven, the shot will have an uneven surface and fly erratically."

Naturally the next question hunters are interested in learning the answer to is what causes shot to fly straight? Dietz says several factors are involved, including buffering, the amount of antimony in the shot and the shot cup itself.

"Buffering is a polyethylene material that is put into the shotshell with the shot and fills in the spaces between the pellets," Dietz continues. "The proper buffering is more important as the pellet size gets bigger. The initial impact of the firing can cause the pellets to be scrunched down and deformed. But by filling in the empty spaces between the pellets, then when a shell is fired, the buffering keeps the pellets from being pushed against one another as much and reduces the deformity of the shot. I suggest a turkey hunter considers a buffered shell if he's using a larger shot. The buffering works best when you're shooting the larger shot like No. 4s or more.

"The amount of antimony shot in it determines the hardness of the shot, because antimony is a substance added to the lead to harden it. A harder shot seems to deform less and fly straighter. However, you can't add more than a certain amount of antimony to the shot or else the shot will lose the weight and the density of the lead that give the shot good ballistics. A high antimony shot is about 6-percent antimony and makes for a good turkey shot.

"Also, the shot cup inside the shell is critical to the shell's performance. This plastic cup acts as an overpowder ceiling wad and seals the powders' gases behind the shot column. Too, the shot cup encases the pellets and keeps them from getting deformed by touching the inside of the barrel. The cushioning at the bottom of the shot cup reduces the impact of the shot when the shell is fired and thereby pellet deformation."

I prefer a copper-plated shot, because I believe this copper plating tends to make the pellets harder and makes the pellets fly straighter. But Dietz chuckles and says that, "Copper plating does make the shot look prettier besides making the outer surface of the pellets a little harder and reducing deformation. However, since the copper is a very, very thin coating around the lead, we really don't know how much harder the copper-coated shells are."

When I load my gun to go turkey hunting, I usually place No. 6 shot in the barrel of my automatic and have two No. 4s behind it. My thinking is that I want the densest shot pattern possible at close range. Then if I miss, the heavier No. 4 shot can inflict more damage even with fewer pellets at a greater distance.

Some of my hunting buddies have just the opposite philosophy. They choose the heavier No. 4s as their first shots believing they have more knock-down power and use the smaller No. 6s as back-ups for taking a second shot at a running turkey.

When I asked Dietz what shot size was best for the turkey hunter, he told me about a survey he had conducted.

"I asked thirty of the nation's best turkey hunters and guides what shot size they preferred," Dietz recalls. "At that time, No. 6s were favored by the majority of top flight turkey hunters with No. 4s coming in second. They told me they wanted pellets that were hard enough and big enough to get penetration into the turkey's head, yet they wanted enough pellets to produce a very dense pattern. They seemed to think No. 6s gave the best combination of pellet size and pellet density."

A few years ago Remington introduced a duplex shell which combined two different shot sizes in the same shell. The idea was an attempt to make the ultimate turkey load and to solve the age-old problem of which should the hunter shoot -- No. 4s or No. 6s? With the duplex load, the hunter could shoot both shots in the same shell.

"The duplex shells were an attempt to provide a range of pellet size at a given distance from the bird you'd be shooting," Dietz explained. "In the beginning, our company had hoped to come up with an alternative shell. The duplex shells on the average patterned better than the single pellet loads since the hunter got a denser and a more evenly distributed pattern with the duplex shells.

"I recommend the 4X6 duplex shell for turkey hunting. This shell gives the turkey hunter the six shot he seems to prefer, but also has some 4s in the pattern to produce better penetration than the 6s alone will provide. The 4s also will add a little more penetration when a hunter is taking a shot at a turkey on the outer fringes of acceptable turkey shooting range. These duplex shells pattern so well that usually you will have about as many shots in the killing diameter of the pattern as you do with No. 5s."

The best way to know whether you prefer duplex or single shot size shells is to take both types of shells to a patterning board and test them yourself.

When the 3-inch magnum shotguns first came on the market, turkey hunters adopted this bigger shotgun like a long-lost brother and assumed it would increase the range at which they could take a turkey. Some hunters even moved up to a 10-gauge gun and shell so that they would be able to reach out and touch a turkey at greater distances.

Although I always had believed the bigger shells would cause pellets to shoot further, Dietz mentions that, "In terms of pellet energy, you don't get any more range with a 2-3/4-inch shell than you do with a 10-gauge shell. Pellet energy is determined by the size of the pellet and the speed at which it starts. Even though you move up in size or shotshell, you don't really get any more range.

"However, at any range when you go up in shell casing size, you add more capacity for the shot, which means you add more shot. For instance, more shot is present in a 3-inch shell than in a 2-3/4-inch shell. As you go up in shotshell size and increase the number of pellets the shell will hold, you can produce a denser pattern at a greater distance. A 10-gauge shell will hold more pellets than either a 3-inch shell or a 2-3/4-inch shell. Therefore, the larger shell will produce a denser pattern even at a further range."

Just like the bass fisherman has learned all he can about better lines to catch and hold more and bigger fish, we as turkey hunters need to understand more about the shells we shoot and how to select the best shells with which to harvest turkeys.

Rather than choosing one particular brand over another, I suggest you buy five or six kinds of shells in different shot sizes and see which shell and which shot patterns best in the gun you plan to use to hunt turkeys. Then you will know for sure when that gobbler is standing at 30-yards or less craning his neck and looking for you that if you miss when you touch the trigger, the shell is not at fault.

WHAT LATEST SHELLS ARE AVAILABLE

Winchester Group of Olin Corporation

According to John R. Falk, public relations manager for the Winchester Group, "Winchester suggests using our copper-plated shot pellets for bagging turkeys. These shot pellets are built to strict specifications which, when combined with Super Grex buffering and special wad and Mark 5 protective collar, reduce shot deformation to deliver uniform, dense patterns at longer ranges."

The Winchester Group has designed a new 10-gauge turkey load, a 3-1/2-inch Double X magnum that delivers 2-1/4-ounces of copper-plated No. 6 shot. This load creates an impressive, dense pattern with over 500 No. 6 pellets for clean kills. The new load comes in 10-gauge Trebark camo packs.

Also, Winchester produces 2-3/4-inch, 12-gauge turkey loads, the Double X Magnum load. This 12-gauge turkey load has a 1-5/8-ounce charge of No. 4, 5 or 6 size copper-plated shot. This load, which has made a number of impressive, one shot kills in field tests, will be packed in 10-round Trebark camo packs, also.

Federal Cartridge Company

A new Premium 12-gauge turkey load from Federal Cartridge Company features No. 6 lead shot in a 3-1/2-inch shell. With the heaviest 12-gauge charge available --1-1/4-ounces --this Premium Magnum produces dense, even patterns at long ranges. The 3-1/2-inch load provides 10-gauge performance in a 12-gauge gun. The copper-plated, extra-hard shot is cushioned by a plastic buffer that prevents pellets from deforming.

Remington

Remington has new turkey hunting ammunition also, including Nitro Mag shells and Duplex shells. The Nitro Mags are buffered magnums with extra-hard shot for dense, turkey hunting patterns and are available in 10-gauge magnum, 12-gauge 3-inch and 2-3/4-inch magnums and 20-gauge 2-3/4-inch and 3-inch magnum loads in either No. 4 or No. 6 shot sizes. Also, the 20-gauge 3-inch magnums come in No. 7-1/2-shot.

Duplex shells are Remington's exclusive, patented shells with two different shot sizes for maximum combination of penetration and pattern density. Available in 12-gauge 2-3/4-inch and 3-inch magnums, 2X6 and 4X6 dual shot combinations, these shells are known for their exceptionally dense and even patterns.

HOW TO DETERMINE WHICH TURKEY GUNS ARE BEST

The shotgun you choose to hunt wily gobblers with is as personal as your signature, fits you as comfortably as a new suit of underwear, is as dependable as a best friend and demonstrates your style of hunting.

For instance, Allen Jenkins of Liberty, Mississippi, president of M.L. Lynch Calls, uses a distinctive turkey hunting strategy that suits him. Although no one can mistake Jenkins for an offensive end for the Chicago Bears, he does resemble a bantamweight boxer. The gun Jenkins prefers to shoot never can be confused with a cannon but rather is more like a fly swatter. The double barreled, 20-gauge Browning Citori with the modified and full barrels seems more appropriate for quail hunting than turkey hunting -- unless you know Jenkins, who is a master turkey caller.

"For me, the sport of turkey hunting is to be able to master the bird with my knowledge and calling skills," Jenkins says. "To take a shot, I first have to outsmart the turkey. If I can call a gobbler in to less than 30-yards of where I'm sitting, then I've defeated the bird and have the right to decide whether I want to take him or let him go. If I can't get the bird closer than 30-yards, he wins the game, outsmarts me and leaves with his life.

"I'm not saying this type of hunting is how every turkey hunter should hunt, but it is my style. If I'll be taking shots at less than 30-yards, then why would I carry a cannonlike gun into the woods? The Browning Citori is lightweight, comfortable to carry, tightly patterns No. 4 shot and tumbles the toms I defeat. In other words, that gun does all I ask it to do."

Allen Jenkins' shotgun is his trademark not only as a hunter but also as a master caller. Jenkins wants a tom in close enough to bag it with his 20-gauge, or he prefers not to take the turkey. If calling a gobbler in close is more important to you than actually bagging a bird, then a smaller gauge gun is appropriate. However, others who want more range opt for larger gauge guns.

Eddie Salter of Brewton, Alabama, has won the World Turkey Calling Contest twice and has been hunting turkeys all of his life in the heart of some of the best turkey hunting in the nation. Salter, who is built like a middle linebacker, reads a situation and then sets his course to seek and destroy. Like the linebacker, the response Salter chooses must be accurate, powerful and deadly. Salter is also a traditionalist who believes that if his shotgun has proven deadly accurate under all hunting situations, then why should he change?

"The longer sighting plane you have, the more accurately you will be able to sight and shoot turkeys," Salter explains. "That's why I shoot a Remington 1100 12-gauge with a 30-inch barrel. I've always used a long-barreled gun and have bagged my fair share of turkeys with this longer barrel."

Although Salter's gun is long and weighs a few ounces more than other turkey guns may, Salter mentions that, "I really don't hunt in cover that thick. The ability to move the gun to shoot between trees is not that big a problem for me. Since I'm accustomed to the weight of the gun, I don't believe the few ounces more that the extended barrel weighs is a handicap. I'm willing to walk or run a long way to a turkey. I use all my knowledge and skill to get that bird into a place where I can take him. Then to compromise two or three inches on the length of the barrel or an ounce or two in the weight of the gun to give up the accuracy of the longer sighting plane just doesn't seem to make much sense to me.

"One of the problems I've encountered with turkey hunting is convincing someone to continue to use what's working for him. If you are accustomed to shooting a long-barreled gun and consistently bag turkeys with it, then there's no reason for you to give up that weapon."

Paul Butski, of Niagara Falls, New York, is one of the new wave of turkey hunters who hunt very aggressively and spend much time hunting in several states. Butski has won the Grand National Turkey Calling Championship three times, the U.S. Open Championship six times, the Levi Garrett All-American Open twice and the Masters Open Invitational once.

"I like the Remington 1100 with a 24-inch barrel," Butski comments. "Many times when I have to make a final move with my gun, there may be a small sapling or a twig in front of me. With the shorter barrel, I can make that move and not hit the twig. I've always liked shooting an automatic, and the Remington 1100 has been a dependable weapon for many years. As long as a gun is functioning properly, I'll continue to hunt with it. "Because I think the primary consideration for choosing a turkey gun should be how reliable a gun is, I advise everyone to use a gun for turkey hunting he has learned to depend on and has shot for several years.

"I agree with Salter that I do give up the longer sighting plane a longer-barreled gun will provide by using the 24-inch barrel. However, usually when you're turkey hunting, you have plenty of time to get down on your gun and aim at the turkey before you must shoot. That's why I don't believe the shorter barrel is much of a handicap. I also like this gun because it comes with a dull wood finish and a Parkerized barrel. Although some people put tape on their guns and barrels to camouflage them, I prefer to have a dull finish from the beginning."

Butski is also a strong advocate of utilizing a sling on a turkey gun, because he has found a sling offers him more freedom of movement and a more even distribution of weight, thereby making his carrying a gun less fatiguing. Besides being an advocate of having slings on shotguns, I also know first hand the effectiveness of both the short barrel as well as the long barrel on a 12-gauge since I hunt with a Browning five shot automatic and a Remington 1100 SP. These guns are 3-inch magnums, which I believe is essential for better knock-down power and increased range on a turkey.

A gun I have begun hunting with is the Winchester pump 3-inch magnum turkey gun. With the pump gun, I usually hold my shot until I am absolutely certain of the kill before squeezing off. When I am shooting an automatic, I often find myself unconsciously taking a lesser shot --knowing that instantly I have a follow-up shot.

I have found the Winchester pump to be very accurate and comfortable to carry as well as deadly on toms. In one recent season, I bagged an eastern, a Merriam and a Rio Grande turkey using this Winchester. The good looks of the laminated wood stock and grip also make it a point of pride in a hunting camp.

My friend, Thurmond Gillintyne, had a style of turkey hunting that bordered on insanity, because Gillintyne had something to prove. Through years of hunting, Gillintyne had developed an intense hatred for the eastern wild turkey. Since Gillintyne was not a great turkey caller, nor had he spent enough time in the woods mastering the sport to become a proficient woodsman, consequently the old longbeards consistently outsmarted him. Grown men scorned by their sweethearts would not be nearly as upset as Gillintyne was when a big, boss gobbler stopped at 45-yards, strutted and drummed but never came in any closer. Afterwards Gillintyne would be so angry he would leave the woods with his stomach tied up in knots.

Then one day Gillintyne came into turkey camp all smiles and told us as he pulled out a new Browning 10-gauge that, "I've got a gun now that will reach out and touch those toms that have been making a fool of me. Just let one of those gobblers stop out there at 45-yards now, strut, drum and think I can't get him."

Sure enough that morning, just as the woodducks flew into a nearby beaver pond to feed, we heard Gillintyne's cannon report. By breakfast, Gillintyne was back in camp with a fat longbeard.

A 10-gauge is dramatically effective on turkeys, especially for the hunter who wants to extend his range and take birds at a greater distance. Although many may say that utilizing a 10-gauge is over-gunning a turkey, those same critics may feel that westerners should not take gobblers with rifles.

The ethics associated with hunting wild turkeys are varied, according to the part of the country and the terrain where you are hunting. Your pleasure may be another's sin. In many areas of the West, bagging a longbeard with a rifle, which many easterners consider a mortal sin, is as acceptable as cheering for your team at a football game. Many who hunt the West with rifles will take a longbeard with whatever rifle they happen to have handy at the time. However, most prefer the .222 or the .243 for hunting turkeys.

When you start hunting turkeys, your primary concern as a beginner is to bag a gobbler -- whether it is a longbeard, has a short beard or almost no beard at all. Next you usually begin looking only for longbeard gobblers and give up hunting jakes, because the sport involved in hunting them is not as challenging. Then as you mature and have the opportunity to bag more turkeys, you may concentrate on spur length. For instance, Allen Jenkins constantly looks at a gobbler's foot as the bird comes in to where Jenkins is calling. If the turkey does not have spurs longer than one inch, Jenkins will not shoot.

The final step of maturity as a turkey hunter is to search for a more challenging way to bag a tom. You may decide to try and take a turkey with a bow or a muzzleloader. In my first muzzleloading season, I shot a Connecticut Valley Arms (CVA) turkey special, which is a single shot, black powder, 12-gauge with screw-in chokes.

Black powder shotguns do not pattern like conventional shotguns do. They require more time on the pattern board, more patience and much more shooting than conventional guns to be able to understand what will happen to your shot pattern when you squeeze the trigger, the cap pops, the gun goes off, and the smoke begins to rise. I have discovered that to consistently put enough shot in a turkey head silhouette with my blackpowder gun, I need the bird to be at less than 20-steps, which means I will have a very challenging hunt.

WHAT ARE SOME FAVORITE TURKEY GUNS

These guns are available for the turkey hunter. Once you decide which style of hunting you prefer, you can pick the gun that suits you best.

U.S. Repeating Arms

Winchester Turkey Gun

Winchester Model 1300 Shotgun.

The National Wild Turkey Federation has selected the Winchester Model 1300 12-gauge turkey gun by U.S. Repeating Arms Co., Inc. as gun of the year. This turkey gun weighs only 7-pounds and features a checkered, camouflaged stock and forearm, a non-reflective matte finish and an engraved receiver. This pump action shotgun has Winchester's Armor-Lock Rotary Belt system and comes with a sling, swivels and a recoil pad. The 22-inch barrel has Winchester's famous floating vent rib and Winchoke tubes in extra full, full and modified.

Browning

CitoriLightning and PBS Pump

Double barreled, 20-gauge Browning Citori.

Browning's new Citori Lightning 3-1/2-inch 12-gauge over-and-under and BPS 3-1/2-inch 12-gauge pump give 12-gauge users a versatile shotgun chambered in the newest 12-gauge cartridge. New Invector Plus Choke Tubes feature back bored barrels (.754 bore) and come standard with Browning's new Invector Plus threaded choke tubes that are designed to handle the extra demands of 3-1/2-inch magnum loads.

Browning's Citori Lightning 3-1/2-inch magnum 12-gauge will be available with 30-inch or 28-inch barrel lengths in Grade I only. The stock and forearm are of select walnut with a high gloss finish, a classic rounded pistol grip and a trim forearm. The average weight of the 30-inch model is 8-pounds, 9-ounces, and the 28-inch model weighs 8-pounds, 5-ounces.

The Browning BPS Pump 3-1/2-inch magnum 12-gauge, weighing in at 8-pounds, 12-ounces, is offered in standard Hunting or Stalker models in 30-inch or 28-inch barrel lengths. The Stalker version's stock and forearm will feature a new graphite-fiberglass composite. The metal finish is a matte blue on the barrel and receiver. The Hunting models have stocks and forearms of select walnut in high gloss finish and cut checkering. The metal surfaces are polished blue.

Remington

SP-10 Magnum

BPS Game Gun with 20½-inch barrels.

In designing the new SP-10 Magnum, a 10-gauge autoloading shotgun, Remington has drawn heavily on its past experience for strength, durability, functional reliability and esthetic appearance in guns. A new trigger group and a redesigned gas system with two gas vent ports to reduce powder residue build-up on critical moving surfaces are some of the features of the SP-10 Magnum. Further improvements to the shotgun's overall design include a new feeding and extraction system and the addition of an elastomer buffer to the slide extension for shock resistance. All critical cam, pivot and retaining pins have been designed for maximum strength and durability. Gas system components, bolt, carrier, operating handle and shell stop latch are all constructed of stainless steel.

11-87 SP Magnum Autoloader & SP Magnum Pump Action These two guns from Remington, the 11-87 SP Magnum Autoloader with a 26-inch Rem Choke barrel and the 870 SP Magnum Pump Action with a 26-inch Rem Choke barrel, work exceptionally well with regular full Rem Chokes for turkeys. However, they will provide even denser, tighter patterns with the new Remington Extra Full optional turkey chokes that produce 80-percent plus patterns with most popular turkey loads -- No. 4s, No. 6s and Duplex 4x6s. The relatively short 26-inch barrels, dull wood and metal finishes, carrying slings, 3-inch chambers and established reliability of the two shotguns make them ideal for turkey hunting.

12-Gauge 870 Special Field

Remington 12-Gauge 870 Special Field.

This pump action gun from Remington with three-inch chambers, interchangeable Rem Choke system, straight English stock and 21-inch barrel is a handy gun to carry into the woods for gobblers.

Savage

Model 24

Savage Model 24-F-12T.

Savage's turkey gun, model 24-F-12T, comes with a .222 or a .223 Rem rifle barrel and a 12-gauge, 3-inch magnum bottom tube. The camo Rynite stock, interchangeable chokes (extra full tube supplied) and factory swivel studs add up to features any turkey hunter appreciates.

Mossberg

Model 500 Camo

When sportsmen expressed a need for a camo shotgun, Mossberg responded with a 12-gauge Model 500 Camo that is geared specifically to the requirements of turkey hunters and features a drilled and tapped receiver for scope bases, quick detachable swivels, camo slings and tough, synthetic stocks and forearms. The Speedfeed models give you quick access to as many as four extra rounds spring-loaded in the buttstock.

Model 500 Turkey/Deer Camo Combo

This 12-gauge pump gun combo, which has a choice of two interchangeable barrels and features a 20-inch Accu-Choke barrel as well as a 24-inch slugster barrel, a synthetic forearm and a Speedfeed buttstock, already is drilled and tapped for scope mounting and includes swivels and a camo web sling.

Classic Doubles

Classic Model 101 Waterfowler

This over-and-under shotgun, originally made for Winchester, now is offered exclusively by Classic Doubles. With a 30-inch barrel, non-glare finish on buttstock and forearm along with a matte finish on both barrel and frame, this Waterfowler is the perfect shotgun for ducks and geese as well as turkey when extra concealment is mandatory. The stock and forearm are made of the highest grade, semi-fancy American walnut.

Precision Sports

Parker Hale Model 645E-XXV S x S

A field gun, 16-gauge, manufactured in Spain by Ignacio Ugartechea, S.A., to the specification of Parker Hale, Ltd., of Birmingham, England, and imported into the U.S. by Precision Sports, the Model 645-E-XXV is an ideal upland gun. Weighing 6-pounds, 6-ounces and measuring only 42-3/16-inches overall, it is a typical Churchill variety, except for being 16-gauge. The barrels actually measure 25-3/16-inches long, complete with tapered center rib. This well-constructed gun handles well and produces some excellent patterns.

Weatherby

Over-And-Under Shotguns

Weatherby Orion Grade 1 Shotgun.

Weatherby has added three new grades to their existing line of over-and-under shotguns. The Athena Grade V has a much more detailed, intricate engraving pattern than the existing model which has been renamed the Athena Grade IV. The same attention to detail is applied from the precision mating of barrels to the highly figured stock with fineline hand checkering.

Two new grades have been added to the existing Orion. The Orion Grade III has game bird scenes engraved on a silver grey nitride finished receiver which, complements the beautiful Claro walnut stock. The existing Orion shotgun is now identified as the Grade II. Added to this series is the Orion Grade I, which is a richly blued receiver with no engraving and a lesser grade of stock wood. The buttstock is fitted with a plastic butt plate rather than a recoil pad. The Athena and the Orion come in 12-gauge field models.

Stoeger

IGA Single Barrel Shotgun

Stoeger/IGA Reuna-Single Barrel with choke tube.

This rugged top-break shotgun features a unique locking system. Pulling rearward on the trigger guard releases the underlug engagement, thus opening the action. Simple mechanical extraction allows for convenient removal of spent shells. A half-cocked setting on the hammer provides the safety mode. The stock and semi-beavertail forend are of durable Brazilian hardwood in this rugged gun that shoots where it points.

IGA Side-By-Side Uplander Shotgun

Stoeger/IGA Uplander-Side by Side with choke tubes.

This gun will provide years of trouble-free, dependable performance. A vice-tight, super-safe locking system is provided by two massive underlugs. The safety is automatic. The solid sighting rib is matte finished for glare-free sighting. Barrels are of Moly-Chrome steel with micropolished bores to give dense, consistent patterns and are formulated specifically for use with steel shot. The stock and forend are hand-checkered in durable hardwood.

Heckler & Koch, Inc.

Benelli Montefeltro Super 90-Turkey Shotgun

Benelli Montefeltro Super 90 Uplander.

This 7-pound, 1-ounce 12-gauge with 3-inch chamber has an inertia recoil, Montefeltro rotating bolt operating system with a five magazine capacity. The barrel length is 24-inches with an overall length of 43-inches. The screw-in chokes for this satin walnut stock gun with matte black finish include full, improved and modified.

Connecticut Valley Arms

CVA's Trapper Shotgun

Connecticut Valley Arms PS219 Trapper Shotgun.

This 46-inch long 12-gauge muzzleloader comes with three easy to change chokes: improved, modified and full. The single barrel is mounted on a select hardwood stock, which features an English style straight grip, and is fired by an authentic v-type mainspring lock with color case hardened lockplate and hammer. The 28-inch barrel has a brass bead front sight, hooked breech and a snail type bolster with convenient cleanout screw. Lightweight (5-1/2-pounds), this gun swings quickly and is smooth to follow a turkey.

Nu-Line Guns, Inc.

2.5-Inch Turkey Hunter Tubes

These tubes have been produced for turkey hunting using No. 2, No. 4 or No. 6 lead shot. The tubes have an extra long conical lead and a specifically designed choke for tighter, more dense patterns, resulting in clean, one shot kills.

WHICH SCOPES TO USE

A turkey hunter can improve his marksmanship skills and his chances of making a successful shot by adding a high-quality scope to his shotgun.

Simmons

Simmons now offers two scopes designed especially for shotguns. Simmons' shotgun scopes are adjusted parallax-free at 50-yards to facilitate accurate shots at shorter distances. They also have long eye relief, a feature that enhances safe and accurate shotgun shooting.

For turkey hunters, the Simmons' line features is the #7790 ProHunter 4x32mm shotgun scope. Like other scopes in the ProHunter series, this shotgun scope has a special light-enhancing lens coating for improved target definition and accuracy -- a real plus when turkey hunting. It has an eye relief of 5.5-inches.

The quick-sighting #21005 2.5x20mm shotgun scope with a 5-inch eye relief is in Simmons' popular, affordable, Deerfield line. The compact size of this scope is a benefit to turkey hunters who may want to keep added weight and bulk to a minimum.

Both Simmons' shotgun scopes have one inch tubes and 1/4-minute adjustments for windage and elevation. They are fogproof, waterproof and shockproof and are covered by the Simmons' warranty.

Redfield

Also consider the Redfield 1X-4X, 114006-variable scope, which is painstakingly tooled from a single, one piece tube and then carefully hand-fitted with multicoated lenses. Each lens fits so securely in place that it shrugs off magnum recoils with ease.

Positive, 1/4-minute click adjustments in windage and elevation let you make quick, in-the-field adjustments and always return to your exact original zero. This Redfield scope with its written lifetime warranty is guaranteed waterproof, shockproof, fogproof and has an optional AccuTrac range finding system, as well as an anodized, scratch-resistant finish, which also is totally impervious to rust.

Nikon

Nikon's 1.5-4.5X20 scope is a good balance between magnification and field of view for turkey hunting. Also this scope's minimal weight and size make it ideal for shotguns. This Nikon variable scope has accuracy that does not vary with a tight group at each and every power setting yielding unsurpassed repeatability. This scope features ultra-fine, super-high resolution lenses which yield complete clarity and precise detection of camouflaged turkeys. The multicoating of every lens element and proper blackening of all internal metal parts reduces flare and image ghost-out.

The 1.5-4.5 also has long eye relief, which means no eye-jamming, even with magnum calibers. These scopes have been purged of air and water molecules, filled with nitrogen gas and sealed absolutely tight with O-rings to keep the scope from fogging or filling with water when caught in a downpour or dropped in a lake. This Nikon scope also features a lifetime warranty for optical and mechanical integrity including waterproof, fogproof, shockproof performance.

Zeiss

The Zeiss Diavari-C 1.5-4.5X18T riflescope has center tube mounting, inch graduation, a short scope with a rubberized objective bell, a small objective diameter, a particularly large eye relief and constant reticle size during power change so as to hide as little as possible of the target. This compact, lightweight scope permits very low mounting, which is ideal for shotguns.

Bausch & Lomb

The Bausch and Lomb 2X model 64-0228 offers the same outstanding features and fine performance of full-size Bausch and Lomb riflescopes in a compact, lightweight design. This scope offers full fogproof, waterproof integrity and hard surface multicoated optics for maximum brightness. Accuracy and precision sighting are provided by reseatable 1/4-MOA click adjustments. The one piece body tube with integral adjustments ensures superior sealing and perfect optical alignment.

Leupold

The Leupold 2.5X Compact shotgun scope is parallax-adjusted to deliver precise focusing at 75-yards, as opposed to the 15-yards which often is typical of riflescopes. This scope features a special heavy duplex reticle that shows up better against heavy, brushy background and makes finding a turkey in a hurry easier. This scope also is waterproof and rugged and is backed by the Leupold full lifetime guarantee.

Aimpoint

The Aimpoint 2 Power has a fixed, low power electronic sight with a floating red dot. The 2 Power is the only unit with built-in magnification. The shooter now has the speed and accuracy of a red dot sight, combined with the range of a low power scope. Because the magnification is in the objective lens instead of the ocular lens (as with previous screw-in attachments), the dot covers only 1.5-inches at 200-yards. This allows the hunter or shooter to see the target at longer ranges than before. The 2 Power can be used on all types of firearms and is complete with one inch rings and all accessories.

Burris

The Burris 1 1/2X Fullfield scopes for receiver mounting on shotguns feature a huge field of view and light gathering ability. Rugged recoil-proof and fogproof construction allows shotgun slug hunters to dramatically improve their accuracy. Running shots during low-light conditions are now possible with this scope, which has a 65-foot field of view, exclusive Hi-Lume multicoated lenses, full field wide angle field-of-view sight picture, steel-on-steel precision click adjustments and a super-hard anodized outer tube and is fogproof, nitrogen-filled and "O" ring sealed with a lifetime warranty. The Fullfield is 100-percent made in the USA.

CHAPTER 4 - FINDING OUT HOW TO HUNT

Learning to turkey hunt is much like learning the game of chess. You can read all the books about the sport, watch the masters play and attempt to play with novices, but the best way to become proficient at the game of chess or turkey hunting is to enter a contest with the masters themselves.

Turkey hunting is a situation, decision-making process that is much like using the English language because once you learn a rule of turkey hunting, you soon will realize at least five exceptions exist to that rule. For instance, turkeys do not cross water, except sometimes when they live in swampy terrain, when the birds are very aggressive, or when you get a gobbler so excited he will wade across water. Toms will not fly across a river to come to you, except when you sound like three or four excited hens ready to breed and simulate another gobbler coming to those hens. Master turkey hunters know when and how to use these exceptions. If you can hunt with a knowledgeable and seasoned turkey hunter, you will learn how to hunt turkeys better, quicker and more effectively.

However, a problem associated with hunting with a master turkey hunter is many masters of the sport enjoy hunting turkeys more than they like to train newcomers. Usually novice turkey hunters talk too much, walk too much, move too much and are not patient enough to kill a gobbler.

WHY TURKEY HUNT WITH A GUIDE

The easiest, least expensive, quickest way to learn the sport of turkey hunting from a master hunter is to employ the services of a turkey hunting guide at a hunting lodge on lands that have plenty of turkeys. Often novice hunters make the mistake of going to areas where few or no turkeys are available to hunt. To learn the sport, you must test your skills against the turkeys themselves. The more toms you encounter in a day of turkey hunting, the more opportunities you will have to test the things you have learned. Also when you hunt private lands, you will not experience as much interference from other hunters as you will on public lands.

But to learn the most about how to hunt turkeys, you must change the philosophy of many guides at most hunting lodges. The general philosophy at hunting lodges is that the guide will find the turkey for you and call the bird in to allow you to take the shot. Instead, talk to your guide before the hunt. Tell him you are not nearly as interested in killing and bagging a turkey as you are in learning how to turkey hunt. Have the guide ...

- explain to you why you are going into the area where you will be hunting, where the turkeys should be and why they are supposed to be in the area.

- tell you why you are moving to the turkey from the direction you are, why you stop and set up where you do, how he knows which way the turkey is facing, why he thinks the turkey will come from a certain direction, why he is using specific calls, and why he asks you to make particular calls.

- describe what the turkey is probably doing on the way to you.

- guess where the turkey should appear and why he should be there.

- explain why a turkey does not come to you, if that happens.

- tell you why you move in closer to the turkey or decide to call the turkey from a different place.

- call for the shot when you see the turkey.

- walk you back to the spot from which the turkey gobbled and try to show you the direction from which the turkey came, after the bird is down.

- be your teacher. Then you will learn more in three days of hunting with a guide than you can in a year or more of hunting on your own.

WHAT YOU LEARN FROM OTHERS

If you are not fortunate enough to hunt with a guide on private lands, you still can learn to hunt on public lands. Use this book as a resource guide.

However, any time you can hunt with another, more experienced hunter, whether or not he is a guide, you drastically increase your knowledge of the sport.

In 20-to 40-days of hunting turkeys each season, I try and spend at least two thirds of the mornings I hunt in the woods with other hunters. Although I have hunted the turkeys for more than 20-years, every time I hunt with another hunter I learn a new tactic, a different calling technique or a better way of moving through the woods. For me, turkey hunting is a continuing education. If you have the chance to hunt with someone with more experience than you, always seize that opportunity, and learn from these other hunters. I do enjoy the solitude and the thrill of going one-on-one with gobblers, but I also have found the sport of turkey hunting is far more fun for me when I share it with a friend.

WHAT YOU CAN LEARN FROM BEING A MEMBER OF THE NWTF

Another way to learn how to turkey hunt is to join your local chapter of the National Wild Turkey Federation (NWTF), an organization of men who hunt the beards and spurs. At these meetings, the members share their hunting knowledge, make friends with each other and learn of opportunities to hunt with other sportsmen of like interests. Often you will meet the conservation officers of areas you want to hunt, and they will know where to find land and turkeys to hunt as well as direct you to a knowledgeable turkey hunter who may help teach you the sport.

HOW TO LEARN FROM A TURKEY HUNTING VIDEO

Another productive way to learn the sport is to study turkey hunting videos. One of the advantages present in many of the new videos on the market today is they show the elapsed time from when the hunter first hears the turkey gobble until he actually sees the bird or takes the shot.

Most sportsmen who view turkey hunting videos watch them primarily for entertainment. However, if you will study the video with a pencil in hand and make notes, especially about the elapsed time of each hunt, you soon will learn about how long is required to call in a gobbler.

On the video, you will see the hunter call and the turkey respond. Then often a note will appear on the screen saying, "45 minutes later." Then you will hear the turkey gobble again, the hunter start to call, and you will see the bird off in the distance. Another break in the video will note the next scene is 20-minutes later. The gobbler will be at about 100-yards out coming to the caller. After another break, you will see a note that states that 20-minutes has passed. Then you will watch the bird being shot or missed. Although the video only has run from three to five minutes, the elapsed time from when the bird first has gobbled to when the bird is actually taken has been 1-hour and 25-minutes.

After viewing the video, you understand the tom did not come in within the five minutes shown on the video and that 85-minutes passed from the time the hunters heard the bird until the turkey was actually harvested. You will get a better picture of what an actual hunt is like and the amount of time required to call a bird to within shooting range by taking notes and studying the video rather than simply viewing it.

To be successful, you must be able to apply this knowledge. Use the timetables you have set up from watching the video as a rule of thumb when you hunt turkeys.

When you are in the woods and you call to a turkey, look at your watch. When you take a stand and begin to call to the bird, remember that on the video the turkey does not appear for 20-minutes or so. Realize the bird you are calling may take that long to come to you. Although the tom may respond quicker, give him at least the 20-or 30-minutes required on the video to get the bird to within 100-yards.

Turkey videos usually are made by master turkey hunters who realize the importance of patience. Make note when you watch a turkey video of ...

- Who is the hunter?

- What type of call is he using?

- How often is he calling?

- What type of turkey is he calling to - an eastern, an Osceola, a Rio Grande, or a Merriam?

- What type of terrain is he hunting?

- Where and how is he taking a stand?

- How much is he calling?

- Why is he using certain calls?

- How far is he from the turkey when he takes the shot?

- Why does he take the shot when he does?

- Why does he miss the turkey, if he does miss?

- What does he do immediately after the shot?

- How does he carry the bird out of the woods?

- Why has he hunted the way he has in that specific area? If you cannot learn the answers to these questions as you watch each of the hunting sequences on a turkey hunting video, write the producer of the video, and ask him to answer the questions for you.

WHY TAKE A TAPE RECORDER IN THE WOODS WITH YOU

Most of us are not blessed with the great memories we think we possess. But we all realize the best way to utilize any information you learn is to be able to remember what you have learned. Statistics have shown we retain only 10-to 15-percent of what we learn for the first time. However, by repeated listening, we can increase that percentage to 50-to 75-percent. Use this knowledge, and apply it to turkey hunting. Then you can develop a system of learning more from each hunt you attend.

Purchase an inexpensive, microcassette tape recorder and a 60-minute microcassette. Use the slowest speed option on the recorder. Put the recorder in a zip-loc plastic bag in your front pocket. As you hunt, record everything you learn on that tape recorder. Keep up with ...

- What time of morning you hear the first turkey gobble. This information will help you determine at about what time of morning the turkeys in the area you hunt will begin to gobble each morning.

- Where you are when you hear the turkey gobble and which compass direction the turkey is from where you are.

- Which direction the road or path you are on travels. For instance if you are standing, on the side of a woods road, look at your compass, and note if the road is North and South. Put that information on your tape recorder. When you next hear the turkey gobble, tell the direction to your recorder. Then you will know where that turkey should gobble the next time you hunt him in the morning and how to get to and from the turkey.

- Whether the turkey is gobbling aggressively or very little. Then you will have a better idea about calling to the gobbler once you get close to him.

- What the various terrain breaks are that you cross as you go to the turkey. Did you cross planted pines, hardwood timber and/or a mountain? Was there thick cover between you and the turkey? This information will be most important if you ever return to hunt that same turkey.

- What type of area you set up in to call the turkey.

- How quickly the turkey calls back to you.

- How much time has been required from when you first have sat down to call the turkey to when you first see him.

- Whether the turkey comes in quickly or slowly.

- Why the turkey hangs up and why the tom does not come to you.

- What time you take the shot.

- Which direction the bird flies after you have missed him.

This information is important to the success of your next hunt. Turkeys have a very definite pecking order. When one tom is bagged out of an area, many times you can return to that same spot later in the season and call in another gobbler. This second gobbler has moved up the pecking order from being a subordinate tom to being a dominant one. Often this bird will travel the same route, roost in a tree in the same region and meet his hens in the same spot where the first gobbler has met his hens. By recording your hunt, you prepare for another hunt in the same area. You also will be able to capture everything you have learned and then relisten to it when you return home.

HOW TO USE A HOME COMPUTER IN TURKEY HUNTING

If you have a home computer, you can feed in data from each of your turkey hunts and have a good time learning about turkeys and turkey hunting. By keeping statistics on your personal computer, you can learn ...

- What time of morning you have heard most of the turkeys gobble during the season,

- What is the average time a gobbler takes to come to you,

- What mistakes you have made and what successes you have had,

- What time of day you are most likely to take a turkey and many more statistics not only about turkeys and turkey hunting but also about yourself as a hunter. Using the computer helps you to see a trend in the turkey hunting mistakes you make and prevent making those same mistakes in the future.

For me, finding out how to turkey hunt is much more enjoyable than squeezing the trigger on a tom. Determining better ways to find turkeys, call turkeys, hide from turkeys and outsmart turkeys is the ultimate challenge of the sport of turkey hunting There are many different ways to learn the sport. To become a master turkey hunter, you must accept the fact that you have begun an educational process that never ends. I only will stop learning about how to hunt wild turkeys when I am six feet under the ground and looking at the bottom of the gobbler's feet that is reading my tombstone.

CHAPTER 5 - SCOUTING FOR TURKEYS

The hunters who successfully bag their birds each season are the men who spend more time scouting and less time hunting. Generally turkeys will stay in the same area more or less -- rarely wandering more than a mile to 1-1/2-miles from where they roost. If you can pinpoint where turkeys are roosting or where they are feeding, strutting, dusting, bugging or loafing, you usually can find these same birds in the same regions at the same time of day each day. But to locate specific turkeys, you first must find land to turkey hunt.

HOW TO LOCATE PUBLIC LANDS

Many states home national forests, which have been set aside by the federal government to ensure wild places for Americans to hunt, fish, camp, hike and enjoy the outdoor experience. Often national forest lands will have huntable populations of wild turkeys.

Begin your search for wild turkeys by calling the U.S. Forest Service which should be listed in your phone book. If you cannot find the number for the U.S. Forest Service, call your state's Department of Conservation or your local game warden/ conservation officer and ask him for the phone number. Then contact the U.S. Forest Service, and ask them which area of the national forest in your section of the country should provide the best turkey hunting. Get the phone number of the area ranger, and call him to set up an appointment. Ask him to bring a map of the close-by national forests that have turkeys.

When you meet with the ranger, study the map. Have him recommend where to hunt for turkeys. The forest ranger should know more about the national forest than anyone else since usually he is in the forest daily.

Your next choice will be state game lands, often called wildlife management areas. Most states usually have an area manager for each of their gamelands who patrol their areas daily and will be able to tell you where and how to hunt turkeys on their lands. Ask the area manager to mark a map of the region to pinpoint where you most likely will discover turkeys.

Next talk to large landowners in your state -- timber companies, utility companies, coal companies and large corporations which own vast tracts of woodlands. By contacting these corporations and determining if they have lands for the public to hunt either through a fee or a paid permit system, you often will locate good turkey hunting lands close to your home.

Another quick yet reliable way to find both public and private lands for hunting turkeys is to contact the conservation officer or game warden in the area you want to hunt, because these men usually patrol one to three counties per day. They know which companies own the best turkey land, and whether or not the land is open to public or private hunting. Because they are defenders of wildlife, they will also know the hunting policies of the landowners whose property they patrol.

HOW TO FIND PRIVATE LANDS

If I had to go into a new state where I never had hunted before and did not know anybody, I would use a systematic approach to finding turkey lands for hunting. To locate quality hunting lands, first determine who knows the landowners in the counties where you hope to hunt, who will be the best source of information and who, if you befriend them, will help you find a place to turkey hunt.

When I attended college at Livingston University in Livingston, Alabama, which was situated in a very rural county, initially, I did not know anyone in the area. Although there was an abundance of woodlots and turkeys to hunt with probably more birds in Sumter County than almost any place else in the world, I did not have permission to hunt on any of those lands. I began my research at the center of all information in any community, the barber shop. If only a few barber shops are in a county, the barber will be acquainted with every male. Not only does each man who climbs up into the chair tell the barber his life history, but the barber's chair is the center focal point for male gossip in any community. Hunting often will be the topic of conversation during the spring. The barber will know the man who has turkey hunting land, how much land the property owner has, where the land is located, what the turkey hunting potential is on that land and what the possibilities are for hunting that land.

Also the priest or the pastor of the largest church in a community will be aware of which of his parishioners turkey hunt and/or has turkey lands.

Another source for locating turkey hunting lands is the banker. At times large landowners and farmers must borrow money or seek the services of a banker. Because the banker is responsible for the financial life of a community, he is a man most landowners will befriend. Most bankers I have met in rural communities hunt.

Also contact the county sheriff since the sheriff's department in any county must compile vast information on everyone in the county. At one time or another, he probably has come to the aid of everyone in the county. He will know who owns what property and what your chances are for obtaining permission to hunt private land in his area. He even may help you get permission to hunt private lands. that you cannot hunt. Remember too your rural letter carrier who knows everybody in an area.

HOW TO BEGIN TO SCOUT

Once you have found a place to turkey hunt, then you need to pinpoint where the turkeys are on the land you want to hunt. One quick, simple, easy method will locate turkeys on any property -- ask the landowner. He will know the spots and the time of day he generally sees the birds. If you are hunting public lands, the person responsible for the protection of that land always will know where the turkeys are located because he travels the land daily and sees much of the game on the land. Forest rangers, wildlife management area directors and game wardens will be aware of where turkeys are. This strategy will save you hundreds of hours of scouting time and help you go to where you can see or hear turkeys.

HOW TO SCOUT

Most articles on turkey hunting preach the value of scouting but do not tell you how to scout, what signs to look for and how to try and find birds. The most obvious way to scout is to go into the woods and look for turkeys. Note where you find the birds. Then return to that same spot at about the same time another day, and you reasonably can expect the turkeys to be there. But this information alone is not enough to consistently bag a gobbler.

Scout Without A Gun Or Hen Calls

The best way to scout for turkeys is to hunt them without a gun. Go into the woods before daylight, and listen for turkeys to gobble. A mistake novice turkey hunters often make when they are scouting is to take turkey calls with them and call to a tom when a turkey gobbles. This type of scouting ...

- gives the hunter a thrill because he can communicate with the turkey before the season and possibly call the bird up,

- proves this particular turkey can be called to and that he will answer and come to a call and

- educates the gobbler to calling, making him much more difficult to call when the season arrives.

Instead, I recommend all turkey hunters leave their turkey calls at home when they go into the woods to scout for birds before the beginning of the season. When you are scouting for birds, you only want to know where the turkey is, where he is going and what he is doing. You do not want to call a tom to you. The more times you call a turkey to you, the more he will understand about hunters and their calling and the less likely he will be to respond to calling when the season opens. When you go into the woods before the season, only carry a crow call, an owl call or a hawk call with you. These calls will make a turkey gobble, however, they will not cause the tom to come to you.

Mark Maps

When scouting before the season, take a topographical map and an aerial photo of the land you plan to hunt with you. In most regions, a topographical map can be purchased from the U.S. Geological Survey. Contact your county farm agent if you have difficulty in obtaining maps. Once you discover a turkey, mark that bird's location on your map, and assign him a number or a name. Then you will know where to find that gobbler during hunting season.

The quickest, easiest way to scout for turkeys in the morning is to drive woods roads, firebreaks or any other type of road in an area and stop every 200-to 300-yards and call. Each time you get a response from a different turkey, note that turkey's location on your aerial photo or topographical map.

If no roads go through the property you hunt, use some form of identifiable landmark to move across the land. If you are hunting mountainous terrain, walk the ridges of each mountain you hunt, call from the tops of the ridges, and try to pinpoint the locations of the turkeys you hear gobble. If you are hunting farm land, walk the edges of fields, and record where the turkeys are. If you are hunting in flatlands, utilize creeks that flow through the woodlots to locate gobblers.

If turkeys do not gobble on their own in the mornings, use your owl call to force them to gobble. After the sun rises, blow crow calls or hawk calls to entice the toms to talk. Once you find a roost site when scouting, realize that probably that same turkey will use that same roost site during turkey season.

Once I locate a gobbling turkey, I also mark the compass course I must take to reach that particular gobbler's roost site. Then if I return to the spot where I have heard the turkey before daylight, I will know which direction to travel to get to the tom.

Learn A Turkey's Schedule

Most turkey hunters only scout to help them take gobblers during the first two hours of light in the spring. However, to be a good turkey hunter and to more than double your odds for bagging a bird, you need to know where the turkey goes and what he does all day long. For me, understanding a turkey's daily plan is what hunting is all about and captures the essence of hunting.

When you hear a turkey gobble in the morning from the roost, get within 100-to 150-yards of that gobbling bird and listen for him to fly down. If that particular tom is a bird that gobbles often, he usually will gobble in the places where he is feeding and where he meets his hens.

Make very attempt to stay with the bird all day to learn where he goes when he flies down, where he feeds, where he struts, where he dusts and which field he eats bugs in as well as dusts and mates. Watch the turkey in the field, notice about what time he leaves the field and where he enters the woods when he leaves the field, information that can be invaluable later in the season. In states that permit all-day hunting of turkeys, you need to know where the turkey loafs in the middle of the day to dodge the heat, the course he takes back to his roost tree and about what time he flies up into the tree. Besides listening to gobbling turkeys to determine their daily routine, you can use binoculars to watch the turkeys. By observing turkeys, you soon will learn which of the gobblers is the dominant turkey, which ones are the subordinate birds, which hen is the dominant hen and which hens are the subordinate hens. Understanding this information will aid your success during the season.

Another way to determine where turkeys go and when they go there is to study the land itself. If you hear a turkey gobbling in a particular section after he flies down from the roost, more than likely this will be a strut zone. Wait until the tom leaves that place before going to where the turkey has been gobbling -- usually a clearing, a road or a firebreak. You may be able to see scratch marks on the ground where the turkey has dragged his wings as well as turkey tracks, turkey droppings and turkey feathers.

Pinpointing where a turkey struts is important. If during hunting season you fail to call up a gobbler when he flies down off the roost, you may be able to move immediately to the strut zone and call the turkey into that site, because that is the place he is going even if you do not call him. When a turkey leaves his strut zone, often he will move to a field or an open spot to feed. Since turkeys are creatures of habit, locating the route the turkey takes from his strut zone to the field, open area or acorn flat where he feeds will mean you can relocate and set up a stand near the trail he takes to his feed and call the bird to you from that spot -- if you miss the turkey at his strut zone.

The easiest way to bag a turkey is to call him to you along a route he normally travels each day. If you do not encounter the gobbler along the route he takes from his strut zone, learn where he enters the field or woodlot where he feeds in the middle of the day. Most of the time, turkeys will enter and leave a field or a feeding region in approximately the same location -- usually a very open place where the turkeys can see for some distance -- if they have not encountered danger at these spots. Taking a stand in these regions will increase your chances of bagging a bird.

When a turkey is feeding, dusting, bugging and mating in an open area like a field, a clearcut, a pasture or a meadow, sometime between 11:00 A.M. and 1:00 P.M. the sun will begin to heat up the gobbler's feathers, forcing the turkey to leave the open areas and move back into the woods to cool off in the shade, feed and breed until the afternoon sun starts to go down, cooling the open spots. Then turkeys may move out into the openings once more and feed before they fly up to roost.

Generally turkeys like to roost either on high points where they can see a long way, over water so no predator can get to them or in very big trees where they can see in all directions. Often the turkeys will walk within 100-yards or less of the tree where they want to roost before they fly up. If you hunt in a state that permits all-day hunting, and if you know the route the turkey takes back to his roost tree, you often can call him to you just before fly-up time.

If you will scout for turkeys prior to the season without a gun or a call, you not only will learn more about how, where and when to take toms, you will enjoy the sport more. But be cautious not to spend all your time learning the whereabouts of only one gobbler. If someone else bags that bird on opening morning, all of your scouting will be useless.

Try and learn all you can about at least five to six turkeys prior to the season. Find turkeys well away from roads and easy access places. Then if other hunters have located the turkeys closest to the road, you still will have turkeys to hunt deep in the forest.

Especially if you are hunting public lands, learn to give up the easy turkeys. If you locate a gobbler roosting less than 200-yards from a public road, more than likely every other turkey hunter in that region also has found that same gobbler. Assume that someone else will get that turkey on opening day. Pinpoint a turkey's location further in the woods that is not as easy to hear or get to that most other turkey hunters will not locate.

To be a successful scouter, always assume other people are scouting for these same turkeys. Attempt to find gobblers you feel no one else will discover. Only by outhunting the other turkey hunters will you consistently have gobblers to bag.

WHAT TO LOOK FOR WHEN SCOUTING

The dropping of a hen turkey usually will be round and puddle-shaped, whereas the dropping of a male turkey will be in the shape of a question mark.

A gobbler's track will have a longer middle toe than a hen track. A hen's toes each will be about the same length. These turkey tracks are easiest to find where the ground is clean like fields, roads or firebreaks. The best time to see turkey tracks and to learn how and where turkeys move on your property is immediately after a rain. After an all-night downpour, turkeys will walk in open places to let the wind and the sun dry their feathers. If you drive or walk down a road or the edge of a field, you can locate a turkey by seeing his tracks after a rain.

The wing feathers of the gobbler often will be broomed or broken off on the ends, because the bird has been strutting. The friction created from dragging his wing tips across the ground or leaves will cause his wing feathers to be squared off or broken on the ends. A hen's wing feathers almost always will be rounded.

A strut zone often will be in an open area and sometimes will be denoted by a clear spot in the leaves or on the road with scratches where the turkey's wings have dug small trenches in the ground.

A dusting site, which is a bald spot on the ground with loose dirt in it, will be found on a road or the edge of a field. Turkeys dust to clean their feathers and rid themselves of parasites.

You can find a feeding area in the woods noting where leaves are pushed back and piled up. Turkeys use their feet to pull leaves back to find worms and nuts on which to feed. Generally a roost site will be a large tree with numbers of turkey droppings around it.

WHICH CALLS TO USE FOR SCOUTING

When scouting, only use calls to make a tom shock-gobble or gobble as a reaction to a sound rather than using his gobble to communicate to other turkeys. A turkey shock-gobbles for the same reason you may scream when somebody jumps out from behind a door and says, "Boo." Calls that will encourage a tom to talk without coming to where you are include the owl call, the crow call, the hawk call, the coyote howler and the pileated woodpecker call.

Early in the morning, before the sun comes up, owls will begin to hoot. Turkeys often will gobble to the hooting of the owls. When you owl hoot, give one or two hoots. Then be quiet, listen, and see if a gobbler will answer you. Only give one or two hoots, because if a turkey is very vocal in the morning, he may gobble as soon as you hoot. If you give a long series of hoots, you may not be able to hear him gobble because you are calling while he is gobbling. If one or two hoots does not make the turkey gobble, then make a series of hoots that sound like who-cooks, who-cooks, who-cooks-for-you-all. This rhythm and sound will produce the most natural rhythm of hooting that turkeys will answer.

Begin your hooting softly. A turkey may be close by, and you do not want to blow him out of the tree with loud calling. If you do not get a response after you hoot, hoot louder. If you still do not hear a turkey gobble, hoot very loudly. If a turkey still fails to respond, move to another spot, and repeat the same process.

If you are in the woods later in the morning, notice that turkeys will gobble when a crow gives its high-pitched scream. If you fail to get a gobble from a turkey utilizing an owl call, try a crow call later on in the morning. Both the crow call and the owl call have the ability to produce a gobble at almost any time of the day.

To make a lock-lipped longbeard give away his location, use a hawk call or a pileated woodpecker call which have high-pitched shrieks many turkeys will answer with a gobble. A hawk call and a woodpecker call are especially effective later in the day. Other sounds will cause turkeys to gobble including jet planes flying overhead, whistles or horns sounding on a highway or at a factory, or loud tugboats moving on a nearby river. Any loud, unusual sound can make a turkey gobble and give away his location. Some turkeys will gobble to car doors slamming, chain saws cranking up, school buses hitting potholes which rattles the windows and sirens of passing ambulances on a highway. When scouting for turkeys, listen for loud, high-pitched and unusual sounds. You may hear a turkey gobble right after that sound.

By spending the time to scout for turkeys, you will understand the birds far more than the occasional hunter does. Scouting and learning the ways of the wild turkey are what true hunting is. Squeezing the trigger is just target practice.

CHAPTER 6 - LEARNING TO CALL

Kee-kee

I talk dirty to turkeys. Using my box call, my slate call and my diaphragm calls, I promise the birds the most exciting sexual encounters they possibly can imagine. When the tom shows up close to me for a date, instead of sex, he gets lead in his head.

Turkey hunting is one of the fastest growing sports in America today, because more and more hunters have learned how to call turkeys. Through calling, the hunter actually communicates with a tom and can ...

- pinpoint the gobbler's location,

- determine the turkey's mood,

- engage in conversation with the tom,

- change the gobbler's mood,

- create an imaginary hen that lures in the tom and/or

- position the turkey for a shot.

When you go one-on-one with a gobbler, you have to enter his world, think like he thinks and talk like he talks. In the movie, "Patton," George C. Scott, who plays Patton, stands on a hill and screams at the famous German general, Rommel, as Rommel's tank corps retreat, "I've read your book."

Because Patton had read the book Rommel had written on military strategy, he was able to defeat Rommel during World War II in the deserts of Africa. To beat the smartest military strategist in the woods, the wild turkey, you not only have to know what he is thinking and understand where he wants to go, you must carry on a deceptive conversation to attempt to bring him to you.

The first Native Americans realized this when they tried to chase a turkey down and kill him with either a rock, a spear or a bow and arrow. They must have said to themselves, "There's got to be a better way to hunt turkeys."

Early hunters noticed during the spring of the year when a hen turkey started to call, often a gobbler would come to her. Hunters determined if they could produce the sounds of wild turkey hens, then instead of chasing the gobblers, they could lure the birds to them.

The first turkey caller more than likely used his natural voice. As the sport of turkey calling evolved, woodsmen soon learned they could scratch on wood, blow on leaves of bushes and trees and rub sticks and rocks together to make a sound to which gobblers would respond. You not only must learn to make the calls of the wild turkey to lure in a gobbler, you also must know when to say what and how to say it to a gobbler. You never will take your girlfriend to a quiet restaurant where the lights are low, the music is soft, and the atmosphere is romantic, look into her eyes and then scream at the top of your lungs, "I want to marry you!" You will not walk up to your next-door neighbor in his backyard, peer over his shoulder as you spot large billows of smoke pouring from his upstairs window and whisper in a low, calm voice, "James, your house is on fire."

A mistake newcomers to the sport of turkey hunting make in their calling is they forget the most critical ingredients for effective communication are emotion and feeling. Even when they have learned to make the calls turkeys want to hear, they do not consider these foundations of communications. But emotion and feeling can change the meaning of the turkey's language.

WILD TURKEY SOUNDS

The Cluck

If you ever have watched chickens in a barnyard, you know they seem to cluck for no reason at all. When they are feeding or just like some people whistle or hum, turkeys often will cluck, a call hen turkeys use to also say, "I'm over here."

When a hen gets more excited, either because of danger approaching or seeing movement she cannot identify, she will give excited clucks. If she hears a gobbler sound off from the rooftops, and she is very excited and ready to breed, she will give an impassioned series of clucks called cutting. If the hen is frightened, she will give an alarm cluck. Even though only one, short, crisp sound is made, that sound can communicate many different moods and feelings.

The gobbler also clucks. His clucks often will be more raspy than the hen's. Sometimes he will cluck to let other turkeys know where he is or when he sees something he does not understand. Immediately before a tom runs off, he will cluck differently and make a sound called a putt. The emotion and the rhythm of the call determine what the bird is trying to say more than the sound itself.

The Purr

The purr is a low, guttural sound hens usually make when they are feeding. This very contented sound is one hunters use to calm down a turkey hunting situation when a gobbler gets too excited. When a hen begins to purr, she is like a woman who hums. She does not have anything on her mind, but she feels good about herself and what she is doing and is very content with her situation in the world.

However, when this same sound is made by gobblers with emotion and feeling added in, the purr is one of the most aggressive sounds a gobbler can make. This type purr is known as the fighting purr. Although the sounds are similar in name and tone, often the volume and speed with which the sounds are made and the emotion they attempt to communicate carry different messages to the birds.

The Yelp

The yelp, one of the most common sounds made by turkeys, carries many messages. The yelp can be compared to someone's talking to himself -- a very contented call with plenty of noise but little or no communication to another individual. The yelp can be utilized in the fall as a distress call by an older hen to call a scattered flock back together. This form of yelping, which is then known as the assembly call, is packed with excitement, concern and pleading.

The yelp also can be an excited mating call, sometimes called cackling that the hen uses to tell the gobbler she is in the mood to breed and is on the way to meet him. The hen can make this same call to say, "Hey, big boy, I'm over here at my house. If you want to have a romantic encounter with me, you've got to come to where I am."

Another form of yelping hens and gobblers employ is to tell each other where they are in the woods and to say, "I've found some good groceries over here. If you want to eat, come over to where I am."

In the morning when hen turkeys first wake up, they will give a series of low, light yelps, much like a yawn. This tree calling, as it is known, says, "I'm up in this tree, and I'm awake. I haven't really decided to fly down yet. But when I do, I'll let you know where I am."

Young gobblers have a difficult time first trying to yelp. Because their voice boxes are not fully developed and they are not sure about how to make the sound they are attempting to give, their voices pop and crack much like a teenager's whose voice goes through a change. In an attempt to yelp, young gobblers will make a kee-kee sound before beginning to yelp. This form of yelping is called the kee-kee run or the young gobbler's squealing call by hunters.

Many times turkeys will combine these sounds and a combination of sounds to communicate even more information. The way these sounds are combined and the emotion that is used to combine these sounds make up the language of the wild turkey.

The Gobble

The gobble is the sound made by the male turkey and is used in several ways. The turkey gobbles primarily to tell hens where he is so they can come to him to be bred. An older turkey gobbles to demonstrate his dominance and to let younger male birds know he is the supreme turkey and claims the right to breed all the hens in the area. When an older, dominant bird gobbles, he generally will cause the subordinate male birds to cease their gobbling.

A turkey also gobbles in reaction to different sounds in the woods. Often these sounds are as low-pitched as the call of a pileated woodpecker. Turkeys will gobble to the sound of jet airplanes passing overhead or car doors slamming a type of gobbling called shock gobbling. Some believe this kind of gobble is the result of a turkey's being surprised by the sound he hears.

Drumming

Turkeys make other sounds too you must understand to hunt them. A gobbler makes a drumming sound, which is much like the noise you hear when an eighteen wheeler truck starts up a steep grade and revs his engine to pull the load. Then as the truck begins to slow, he shifts gears to make the pull easier. The sound is similar to "p-t-t-t-vroom," which also is a very excited mating call a gobbler will use. Many older gobblers who have learned that gobbling lures in hunters just as quickly as it pulls in a hen ready to mate, may cease their gobbling and use only this drumming sound to call their hens in to breed. The drumming sound is a very important one for you to know and possibly learn to use.

The Scratch

Another sound turkeys make is scratching in the leaves as they search for food. Other turkeys often will come when they hear this sound, much like a farmhand who has learned to identify the sound of the dinner bell and knows lunch is being served when he hears that sound.

Wings Brushing

Another very subtle sound turkeys make is the sound of their wings brushing against the sides of trees and bushes as they walk through the woods. You can use this sound to mask your movement through the woods.

Flying Noises

Turkeys also make noise when they fly. When a turkey flies up or down from the roost, the other turkeys in the area know what that sound means. Too this sound may trigger the same action by other individuals in the flock. Turkeys also fly and beat their wings in the air as a way to escape danger. Understanding these sounds will help to make you a more effective turkey hunter and help you to better communicate with turkeys.

CALLS TO USE

The Box Call

In the early 1900s, hunters discovered they could whittle a box out of wood and attach a paddle to the end of the box to produce the sound of the wild turkey. During this time, several enterprising sportsmen began to make turkey calls to sell, and they taught hunters how to use them. For instance, M.L. Lynch of Homewood, Alabama, the founder of Lynch Game Calls, traveled the South like a revival preacher, stood on street corners in front of drugstores and hardware stores, used his box calls to draw in crowds and sell his products and taught thousands of people how to call turkeys.

A thin-walled wooden box with a paddle lid attached to one end, the box call produces a sound when you slide the lid across the side of the box. The side and the lid of the box are chalked, and the friction created from these two chalked surfaces coming into contact with each other will make all the calls of the wild turkey.

Some boxes use a series of rubberbands, which allow you to hold the box and shake it back and forth to imitate a gobble. To produce a yelp, slide the lid across the side of the box with one sweeping stroke. To make a cluck on a box call, strike the lid against the side of the box with one quick, popping stroke. A cutting sound consists of making several fast clucks in quick succession. Pull the lid across the side of the box lightly and slowly to give a purr.

To produce the maximum amount of sound from a box, hold the lid of the box perpendicular to the ground, and strike the lid sharply with the side of the box, which will increase the volume and make the call seem to pop. Until the last 20-years, the box call was the most frequently used device to call in gobblers.

The Pushbutton Box Call

This simplest of all calls for you to use requires only that you push a peg with your finger to produce a hen call. With this call, you can cluck by simply tapping the end of the peg with the palm of your hand. Produce yelps by pushing the peg three or four times in succession. You can cut by utilizing the palm of your hand to pat the peg in rapid succession. Push the peg slowly and gently with your finger to make a purr.

The pushbutton call also can be taped to the forearm of your shotgun. Then you can operate the call and hold your gun at the same time. This call is deadly on toms and currently is being used by many of the nation's leading turkey hunters.

Friction Call

The original friction call was a slate call. The hunter held in his hand a piece of slate and formed a sound chamber by cupping his hand around the slate. By roughing up the top side of the slate with a fine piece of sandpaper, the hunter then scratched a wooden peg across the top of the slate and produced the sound of a wild turkey hen.

However, forming the proper sound chamber to get a true turkey sound often was difficult. In later years, the slate was encased in a box that created the sound chamber, and the box had a hole in the bottom. The sportsman held the peg and scratched the upper surface of the slate as he had before. The sound was produced in the box, came through the hole in the box and out the opening into the hunter's hand.

But today many new products are being used to make friction calls beside slate. Plexiglass surfaces and plastic boxes and even aluminum are fast replacing slate rock and wood boxes.

Most friction calls work on the principle that to produce the sound, you move a striker across the surface of the call. To cluck, you simply make one, short, sharp strike on the surface of the friction call. Produce the cut by making several fast clucks. Hold the striker like a pencil pointing back toward you, and make small, circular motions to produce a yelp. For a purr, make a light cluck on the call with the striker, and then continue to draw the striker across the surface of the friction call.

The Mouth Diaphragm Call

In the late 1920s, a rabid dog was the catalyst used to produce today's most popular call -- the mouth diaphragm. Jim Radcliff, Jr., of Andalusia, Alabama, was in New Orleans, Louisiana, being treated for rabies when he met a street entertainer who made bird calls with his mouth. Radcliff worked with the street entertainer to modify and change the entertainer's diaphragm call made of a small, hinged, horseshoe-shaped piece of lead and a thin piece of latex rubber to sound like the call of the wild turkey. This call was one of the first diaphragm turkey calls ever made.

Today the lead horseshoe of the diaphragm turkey call has been replaced with lightweight aluminum, thinner pieces of latex are being used, and the body of the call is covered with fabric or plastic used, and the body of the call is covered with fabric or plastic tape. To use the diaphragm call, place it in the roof of your mouth, and utilize your tongue to meter air over the latex rubber to produce wild turkey sounds. The amount of air and the frequency with which the air is blown over the rubber reed determines the kind of call the diaphragm call will make.

Put your lips together. Blow out a short, sharp burst of air, and smack your lips at the same time to make a cluck on the diaphragm call. To cut on a diaphragm call, make a rapid series of clucks. By metering air over the diaphragm and dropping the jaw as the air passes over the rubber reed, you can make a yelp. To purr, which is the most difficult call to create on a diaphragm, make sure your lips are moist. Then blow out while vibrating your tongue and lips up and down.

The pitch and the tone of the diaphragm call are determined not only by the amount of air passed over the reed and the force with which the call is blown but also by the number of latex reeds used to make the call and whether or not the reeds are split. Some diaphragm calls feature two calls taped together to make one diaphragm call, which produces a different sound. The more reeds a call contains, often the deeper and more coarse or raspy the call sounds. The split reed also makes the call more raspy.

The diaphragm is the most difficult call to learn to use. You must seat the call properly in the roof of your mouth, position the tip of your tongue in the proper place on the reed and learn just how much air produces the different sounds of the wild turkey. The best way to learn to use the diaphragm call is to listen to an audio cassette. Put the call in the roof of your mouth, and then try to say the word "shoot" while blowing air over your tongue and vibrating the reed.

Not only does the diaphragm mouth call realistically produce the sound of both hens and gobblers, it also gives you the advantage of hands-free operation and little or no movement when you are attempting to bring a gobbler to within gun range. If a gobbler veers to the right or to the left when he is just out of gun range, you can call softly to the bird using the diaphragm and cause him to turn and come to you. If you need to give a call to make a tom quit strutting and stick his neck up to enable you to get a shot, you do not have to move with a diaphragm call to give a cluck or a yelp. If a hen calls to a gobbler in front of you and tries to pull the tom away from you, without moving, you can call that gobbler back utilizing a diaphragm call.

A problem associated with any kind of turkey call is that particular types of calls -- whether diaphragm or friction like a box or a slate -- all speak with the same voice. To change the voice of those calls, you must change your calls. Although carrying a backpack full of box calls or slate calls through the woods is cumbersome, by utilizing diaphragm calls, you can take five to twenty calls with you in a small pouch in your shirt pocket. Then you can change calls and voices quickly and easily without being burdened by the weight of the calls or moving very much.

The Gobbling Call

Although hunters utilize boxes to gobble, the Red Wolf Gobbling Tube also is very effective to use to make turkeys shock gobble. However, when a hunter uses a gobbling call, he makes the sounds other hunters are hunting. This call can be dangerous to use. This call is not recommended to be given on public hunting lands and only should be utilized on private hunting lands with extreme caution.

Other Calls

The tube call or snuff can call was first invented when hunters of yesteryear cut a hole in the bottom of a small snuff can, cut one half of the lid away and stretched latex rubber over the hole in the lid leaving a small opening between the rubber and the remaining lid through which air could pass. Blowing air over the rubber made a louder call and often a more raspy call.

The wingbone call originally was made from two bones in the turkey's wing. The bones were glued together to form a small pipe around 6-to 7-inches in length and about 1/4-inch in diameter. To produce clucks and yelps, hunters sucked on the wingbone rather than blowing air through it. Sucking small puffs of air through the wingbone call produced a cluck, while longer, faster puffs of air sucked through the call made the yelping sound of a hen turkey.

Other calls utilized to cause turkeys to gobble that are not turkey calls include owl hooters, pileated woodpecker calls, hawk calls, coyote howlers and crow calls.

Today turkey calls are made out of many different materials and come in a wide variety of shapes and descriptions. Most turkey hunters agree that to effectively hunt and call the wild turkey, you must be able to use several types of calls. On any given day, a gobbler will come to one call when he will not respond to another kind of call.

Remember though, a little calling goes a long way when you are talking turkey to a tom. You do not have to be a master of all the calls to enjoy the sport of turkey hunting and be successful. If you can produce a cluck and a yelp on any one of the calls, you can call in a gobbler.

WAYS TO IMPROVE YOUR CALLING

Practicing with a turkey call will improve your skill in calling a turkey. But practicing the calls incorrectly will not help your turkey calling ability and even may decrease your effectiveness.

I believe the most essential piece of equipment for becoming a good turkey caller is a tape recorder. Go to a turkey calling contest, and record the calls of the best contestants. Listen to the way they make the calls and especially the rhythm they use in giving the calls. Then imitate the same calls utilizing the same rhythm. Next, use another tape recorder to tape record yourself calling. Play both tapes back. Notice how closely you imitated the calls being made by the masters.

Also carry your tape recorder with you into the woods, and record the calls the wild turkey makes in the spring. There is no better teacher anywhere than the wild turkey. Attempt to combine the sounds you hear from turkeys in the wild and the sounds the contest caller gives. When I have recorded master turkey callers and then played my recorded tape back, often I have realized I have called too fast or too loud or have not used the rhythm or the cadence the masters have. From listening to them on a tape recorder, I have learned to imitate the calls they make.

A method to improve your calling that I recommend highly is to take your recorder to an area in the woods where you have spotted turkeys before, set it up in a tree, move away 100-yards and start your calls. The calls of the turkeys walking by the tape player will be recorded as well as your calls to the turkeys. You may learn when you replay the tape from the woods that you are calling much too loud with a diaphragm caller. You may not have realized this from practicing indoors.

Also to improve your calling, find a tame turkey. Few turkeys or turkey hunters can distinguish between the calls of a tame turkey and a wild turkey. Listen to tame turkeys, and attempt to imitate their conversations.

Be sure the call you are using fits you. Just because a diaphragm call is built a certain way and has a specified amount of tape on it does not mean the call will fit your mouth. You may need to trim quite a bit of tape off your mouth call to get it to fit better in your mouth. You may not be able to make the sound you want to because you have not been matched with the best call for you.

This idea applies not only to diaphragm calls but also to slate calls. The design of many slate calls requires you to move the peg in circles to produce the right sound. On other calls, a half circle will do. On some calls, a back-and-forth motion is needed to yield the best call. The lids on a box call are meant to slide across the side of the box without being forced or having any pressure applied to them. The lid of a quality box caller then should slide back across the box without making any sound. Be certain you know what to do with the call you have and that the call fits you.

STRATEGIES FOR CALLING

Everything you needed to learn about calling gobblers you learned in high school. High school girls were very effective in teaching you how to call wild turkeys. If you had paid attention to not only what high school girls said, how they said it, why they said it and what effects their conversation or lack of conversation had on high school boys you would know exactly how to motivate gobbles with their calling.

Think about what high school girls do to high school guys to lure them in for dates, and you will understand what calling strategies to use for toms.

- This gobbler has been asleep all night and has had wild dreams about beautiful women and exciting times. His testosterone level is extremely high. As soon as he wakes up, he not only is ready to breed but wants to breed. The first thing he does is begin to call a list of his girlfriends. Although most may answer him, not all are ready for an early morning encounter. However, this gobbler is very selective about the girls he takes out on a date at sunrise. He has his own personality and prefers a specific type of girl. To call this gobbler to you, you must know what kind of girl the tom wants to have a date with on this particular morning.

  Remember from your high school days that girls fell into several categories. Some were beautiful, quiet and shy girls, did not talk much and were not very sexy. But often they had a more romantic lure than other girls. Other girls would go out with any boy who called them on the phone. Usually these girls talked too much, but they could be very exciting dates. Another group of girls were very flirty but wanted to be romanced, courted and taken to the best place in town before they even would give you a kiss. During your high school dating career, you probably went out with more than one of these kinds of girls, depending on the mood you were in and how you felt on the day you asked them out. Your emotional level and hormone level determined what type of girl you wanted to go out with on that particular day.

- The wild turkey gobbler has many of the same emotions during the spring when he is courting hens. When he wakes up in the morning, he tries to locate a hen in the same mood as him. For instance, if you hear a turkey gobble in the morning, answer him back quickly with a series of yelps. If even before you finish giving three or four yelps he gobbles the second time, then you know that turkey is very excited and eager to meet his hen immediately. You can call back to him with some cackles that say, "Okay, big boy, I know you're over there. Come on over here, and we will have a romantic interlude."

If the turkey gobbles back again, you know he is very excited and more than likely coming to you in a hurry. You may want to continue to call to him with excited calls until he flies out of the tree and hits the ground. Then you better have your gun up and be ready to take the shot.

- This same turkey may respond differently on another morning after he gobbles. When you answer him with hen calls, he may wait from one to five minutes before he gobbles again, which indicates this turkey is not very excited about mating. He is not looking for one of those sexy girls who talks a lot. On this morning, he prefers a calm, quiet date. He may choose to go out, but he is not in any hurry.

Call to this bird calmly and infrequently with light yelps and purrs. Do not talk to the tom any more than he talks to you. By matching the emotional level of your calling to the emotional level he demonstrates with his gobbling, you are more likely to pull that turkey in than if you try and change his mood. The most productive way to call a turkey to you is to duplicate the mood or emotional level of the tom you are attempting to call. If that action fails to produce a gobbler, then try to change the mood of the turkey you are calling.

- An offended gobbler may not be too hard to call. Have you ever noticed high school football players in the summer on the beach? They will strut -- showing off their muscles and their manhood, especially if a good-looking high school girl is sunbathing in a bikini nearby. Usually this girl gets her guy not by initiating the conversation or letting him know in any way she is interested in him but rather by casually looking at him every now and then. One of the lures high school girls utilize to bring in muscular, proud, young athletes is to ignore them and act disinterested. Often this action on the part of the female offends the young man's ego and forces him to prove he is much more desirable than she thinks.

The same tactic high school girls have used for many generations to lure in young men also will work when you are trying to pull a gobbler into gun range. Oftentimes when a turkey gobbles, struts and drums, he believes the lure of his beautiful feathers and the sound of his masculine voice are all that are needed to make a coquettish hen come on the run to him for some romance. All the rules of nature dictate that the hen goes to the gobbler when she hears him or when she sees him. When the hen does not come, the turkey's manhood is offended. In his mind, he is thinking, "She does not see how big, strong and proud I am. I need to get closer to her. Then she can see what she is missing."

As the gobbler moves closer, he begins to strut and gobble more, thinking he is sure to impress the hen. But instead of matching his mood by giving exciting calls, you will be wise to calm the situation down by acting like a disinterested girl on the beach who is more concerned with making sandcastles than talking love to a football player. Give soft clucks and yelps or soft purring like a contented hen, or simply scratch in the leaves to calm the situation down. Pretend as though you are a hen not interested in mating. When the gobbler hears these contented, disinterested sounds of a hen, often he will calm down and decide that to have a date with this particular hen, he must relax his muscles, drop his feathers, quit talking so much and walk closer to her where he can whisper in her ear.

When he makes that decision and starts coming to you, he usually will be within shotgun range, and you can take him. Wild turkey gobblers, just like high school football players, often lose their heads because of the romantic talking of young girls. You have changed the mood of this turkey from very aggressive and active to being calm. You have reduced his emotional level and his excitement level to get him to come to you.

• Some gobblers do not want to expend any energy to mate a hen. That bird may think, "I'm the best thing that ever has happened to that hen. She can't find anybody better, prouder, stronger or possessing a higher quality of genes for future generations than me. If she wants to breed with the best tom in the woods, she can come find me. I'm certainly not going out of my way to meet her. I don't have to because I'm the best."

This bird demonstrates many of the same emotions and feelings the first string quarterback on a high school state championship team has. All the girls are in love with him. He does not have to call a girl up and ask her for a date. If she wants to go out with him, she can call him or come over to his house. When you find a gobbler with that attitude, often the only way to take him is to change his emotional level and his mood and promise him more fun and excitement than he ever has thought he may find.

You may locate a gobbler like this when you are hunting. situation. This gobbler already may be with hens, or he may be across some type of natural barrier like a river, a creek, a slough, a ditch or a valley. Generally, turkeys do not like to cross a barrier. This gobbler probably may take the emotional position of, "If that hen wants to breed with me, she can expend the energy to fly the creek because I'm not going to go to her." You will know this is the turkey's mindset and mood when you call to him, and he gobbles back but will not come to you.

The best tactic is to try and get to him. But if you are not willing to swim a river, cross a deep gorge or wade a swamp, you must change the emotional mood of that turkey to get him so excited he is willing to do anything to reach you.

You must build the emotional level of your calling. After giving a few yelps and determining the turkey is not going to come to you, give some excited cuts and cackles. Let the turkey know you are very excited about seeing him and will like for him to come to you. If a sequence of calls fails to produce a bird, use two or three different types of calls like the diaphragm, the box and the slate to speak with different voices. Then you can sound like three or four different hens that are all excited, ready

to breed and telling the gobbler to come to them, which will be more pressure than most gobblers can stand. His ego will be inflated, his sexual mood will be raised, and his desire will be intensified.

However, if cutting and cackling with several different calls fails to make the tom move, the final step is to challenge his manhood. After a series of loud, excited cuts and cackles with various calls, then gobble after making sure you can see in all directions and are not gobbling in front of another hunter. Then that tom may think a bunch of excited hens that he considers his hens, the ones he's supposed to breed, are across the river. Because they have been calling so much and has not gone to them, another gobbler has moved in on his harem. Often by painting this type of picture in the mind of a gobbler, you will force him to commit the unnatural act of flying across a terrain break to come to you and will change his emotional mood from passive to active and then to aggressive.

- A tom with a very high emotional level quickly will gobble back to your calling and may need to be calmed down by your giving light yelps and purrs and perhaps even just scratching in the leaves. When the gobbler thinks you are disinterested in him and will not come join his harem, then he may bring his harem to you. Once again, you have changed the emotional mood of the turkey with your calling to get him to perform an unnatural act and come to you.

REASONS FOR NOT CALLING

The most important ingredient in effective calling is knowing when not to call. Many hunters overcall turkeys. The most productive calling is the least amount of calling you can do to make a turkey respond to you. The purpose of all calling is to get a bird to come to you. Once you have a bird moving toward you, usually you do not need to continue to call except in isolated instances.

A true turkey hunter wants to make the turkey hunt him. At a certain point in a successful turkey hunt, you change your strategy from being the hunter to becoming the hunted. To bring a tom in close enough to take a shot, you must give that turkey reason to and come find you. Once you have called the gobbler, have determined his emotional level and either matched that level of emotion or changed that level of emotion, have the tom's attention and have caused him to become interested in you, now talk to him as little as possible, and let him find you.

If you ever have watched turkeys in the woods, notice they walk very slowly most of the time. A turkey's stride is most often less than 12-inches. If you call to a turkey 100-yards away and that bird is walking naturally to you, 30-to 45-minutes or as much time as an hour may be required for him to reach you. If that gobbler is not very excited, he may take even longer.

However, if you continue to call, the gobbler may think, "If that hen's so excited, I'll just stop right here and let her come to me instead of going to look for her." The turkey will hang-up or stop coming and expect you to move toward him.

When you determine the turkey is coming to you, quit calling. If you do call, make your calls infrequent, very soft and short. Often if I believe I have a gobbler coming to me, and I think he may not know exactly where I am, I very carefully and slowly slide my hand down to the ground and scratch in the leaves to let the turkey know where I am but not excite him so much he stops coming to me.

Patience, more than a lot of calling, will give you a shot at a turkey. Most novice turkey hunters call too much and sit still too little. Effective turkey hunters call very little and sit in one place for a long time. Although our society teaches the faster you go, the more you get, in turkey hunting, the reverse is true. The slower you go, and the less you move, the greater your odds are for bagging a bird in most situations. However, as Thoreau once said, "A fool can make a rule all other fools will follow, and there are exceptions to this rule."

When you are hunting ...

...public lands,

...older, smarter turkeys,

...turkeys on the other side of terrain breaks or

...turkeys that hang-up you may have to hunt more aggressively. But even when you are hunting aggressively by plenty of moving and calling, patience will be more responsible for your bagging more gobblers than calling will, when you do sit down to call a turkey to you.

CHAPTER 7 - HUNTING SPRING TURKEYS

During the spring of the year, a young man's and a young gobbler's fancies both turn to love. Mother Nature in her infinite wisdom has chosen the most beautiful time of the year for the courtship of both man and birds.

I believe a wild turkey must look forward to spring all year long. Unlike humans, he only has about six weeks to court, breed and reproduce. At this time of the year, he becomes very aggressive and chases hens with a vengeance. Young birds let their sex drives supersede their survival instincts. But older birds are often much more cautious and let Mother Nature encourage the hens to play the roles they have been designed to play.

The hen turkey understands the philosophy of male chauvinism. When a gobbler talks, not only are the hens supposed to listen but they also are to come on the run to get bred. In the natural order of things, hens go to a tom when he gobbles. When a hunter calls in an attempt to bring a gobbler to him, he asks that gobbler to perform an unnatural act.

Young and inexperienced toms will violate the laws of nature to go to a receptive hen. Older gobblers that have had more hunter encounters will require a hen to follow Mother Nature's advice and come to them. The male turkey has learned he then can stay out of harm's way.

SCOUTING FOR SPRING GOBBLERS

The most critical key to taking a gobbler in the spring is to know where a gobbler will not go. Probably every wild critter at some time will break one of the rules they are not suppose to break. However, there are certain rules most gobblers rarely violate.

1. Turkeys do not like to cross water to come to you. Although I have seen turkeys wade sloughs, fly across creeks and even fly across rivers, generally, a gobbler will not cross water if he can help it. If you know

where the creeks, rivers, streams and gulleys are, you have a decided advantage when you begin to call a turkey. If a tom gobbles across water on the other side from you, your best chance of bagging that bird is for you to cross the water and call from the same side of the water where the turkey is.

2. A turkey most of the time will not move across a ditch, a hill or a valley to come to you. Pinpoint the ditches, gulleys, hills and valleys in the region where you are hunting. If you can call the turkey from the same hill he is on, he is more likely to respond to you than if you try and call him across a valley or a ditch. Or, you can begin your calling from the top of a hill and call from the ridges rather than the valleys. Turkeys prefer to walk uphill rather than downhill. Also your calls will carry further from the hilltops than they will from the valleys.

3. Turkeys prefer to walk in open woods because they understand that predators usually lurk in thickets. If you know where the thickets are and you hear a turkey call on one side of the thicket and you are on the other side, you immediately will realize your best opportunity for bagging that bird is to get around the thicket. Then it will not be a barrier between you and the turkey.

4. A turkey can duck under a fence or fly over the fence, but usually, he will not. Once again, if you hear a turkey gobble, your best chance to get that bird to come to you is to be on the same side of the fence he is.

The more you understand about the land you plan to hunt, the more successful you will be during turkey season. If you know turkeys like to walk in open woods where they can see 50-to 60-yards in front of them, then you quickly and easily can determine not only where you need to hunt but also where you must take a stand to try and call a gobbler to you.

SETTING UP ON SPRING TURKEYS

The term setting up means choosing the spot where you will sit to call the turkey to you. Picking the best place from which to call is another important factor for your success in turkey hunting. If you select a site the turkey will not come to, then all your calling will be fruitless.

When considering a place to set up on a gobbler, walk through the woods, and continue to look behind yourself for a big tree in a clearing that you can sit down next to if you hear a turkey gobble. Then, you will understand what the gobbler will see when he comes to you and pick out a much better place to take a stand than if you select a stand site in front of you.

Generally, look for a tree wider than your shoulders but not necessarily the biggest tree in an area. Because the largest tree will stand out like a red light, a turkey usually will look at that tree first as he comes into where you are. Make sure no thick cover is around the tree, and pick a place where you can see at least 30-yards or more in all directions. But if possible, choose a spot where your vision is limited to about 40-yards. As soon as you do spot a turkey, you only will have a few seconds before you can shoot.

81

The longer you can see a turkey, the more time he has to spot you. I prefer to set up where a clearing of about 30-yards is in front of me and on either side. Then, as soon as I see a gobbler, I can take a shot.

If you get too close to a turkey and have to spend time looking for a spot to set up, then you may have to make a decision as to whether or not to look for a good location and a big tree or to sit down immediately.

One of the worse places I ever took a stand for a turkey was in the middle of a dirt road. A hunting companion of mine, Bo Pitman, and I had hunted turkeys all morning long. At 10:00 A. M., we were walking a woods line owling a gobbler and trying to make it talk. When Pitman hooted, a gobbler sounded less than 30-yards away. If we moved at all, the bird would see us. We quickly sat down in the middle of the road with no cover and called the tom. Luckily a small, rolling hill was in front of us. Speedily the gobbler came in but he spotted us just as he topped the hill. Before he could putt and run, my shotgun reported. The bird tumbled. Seldom would you be successful taking a bird from a bad position like this.

Given the option, I will choose a tree wider than my shoulders to set up beside because then I have back cover. Also the turkey cannot see my body move nearly as easily. I generally carry a small pair of pruning shears with me. Then I quickly can cut any bushes and branches sticking up in front of me. I do not try to build a big blind. I just want to put six or eight bushes in front of me to break up my silhouette and hide my movement.

If I plan to use a box call for a long time, if I am taking a novice hunter with me, or if I believe I will have to wait some time for a turkey to come in, I may carry a portable blind with me. A portable blind allows you to move more and is particularly effective when you take youngsters or inexperienced hunters who are not able to sit still to turkey hunt.

USING WOODSMANSHIP

A proficient turkey hunter who knows the land and understands the turkeys on that property can pick the best spot to set up and never have to call to the turkey to take him. Experienced turkey hunters use the term woodsmanship quite frequently. Often you will hear the phrase, "Woodsmanship will be responsible for bagging more turkeys than calling will." But what does the term woodsmanship really mean when applied to turkey hunting? A good woodsman ...

- knows everything about the land -- the areas where the turkeys feed, water, roost, loaf, strut, cross roads and enter and leave fields.

- passes through the woods without spooking animals or birds. He puts his heel down first, rocks forward, feels the limbs, sticks and branches under his feet, moves his foot to keep from breaking those limbs and then shifts his weight from his back foot to his front foot before repeating the process.

- moves slowly through the woods. He understands the faster he moves, the more game he will spook and the less likely he is to get a shot at a turkey.

- knows when to run through the woods. If he must run 1/2-mile down a dirt road to get a gobbler, he will make this move quickly.

- studies all he can about turkeys and knows where a turkey will not go, when to call and when to be quiet. He understands the importance of patience in turkey hunting success.

- is a student of nature. He learns how to blend in and become a part of the woods rather than being an alien in the environment.

The better woodsman you become, the more you will enjoy the sport of turkey hunting and the better turkey hunter you will be.

BEGINNING THE HUNT

A turkey hunt begins when a tom gobbles. On most warm, bluebird days, a turkey will start to gobble on his own before daylight. Many hunters will go into the woods and owl call immediately to try and make a turkey gobble. However, I prefer to wait until sunrise. If a turkey gobbles on his own, then he usually is a more excited turkey and will be easier to call to than if you have to force the turkey to gobble by owl hooting. Probably some owls in the area will be hooting anyway.

If the bird does not gobble on his own just before first light, I will owl hoot to convince the tom to talk. Once the turkey gobbles, then you must determine from which direction the turkey is calling and about how far you are from the turkey -- which are very difficult skills to learn. Usually I will let a turkey gobble two or three times before I go to him. Then I am sure which way the bird is facing when he gobbles.

Knowing which direction the turkey is looking when he gobbles is critical to determining distance. If the turkey is looking away from you when he gobbles, he will sound much further away than he is. If you do not know the turkey is looking away from you when he gobbles, you run the risk of getting too close to him and possibly running him off the roost. If you know the turkey is facing you when he gobbles, then you can take a stand, set up further away from him and be less likely to spook him.

Once you pinpoint where the bird is and what direction he is facing, then shorten the distance between you and him. If you can get between 100-to 150-yards from a turkey and take a stand next to a big tree in fairly open woods, you will be ready to begin calling.

However, before you start to call, clear all the sticks and leaves that make noise away from the base of the tree. Be careful not to leave bare ground when clearing the sticks away. Only clear away enough brush to give yourself the ability to move around the tree without breaking limbs or making a lot of noise. If possible, cut a few small bushes to set in front of you to break up your silhouette, or use a portable blind. If the turkey already is on the ground or you hear him fly down before you get your blind built, sit next to the tree quickly, and forget about the blind.

SITTING ON A TURKEY STAND

How you sit on a turkey stand determines how long you will be able to sit without moving. I never sit on my leg because my leg will go to sleep and tingle. Then I will have to move. Even if I am lucky enough to get off a shot from this position, sometimes a much worse fate awaits me.

In the early years of my turkey hunting, I took a stand one morning and folded my leg up under myself. Although this position was comfortable for awhile, as the bird began to come in, I felt my leg going to sleep. Because I wanted to take the bird, I would not move but instead concentrated all my attention on the turkey. My patience finally paid off in success. When the bird was at 22-yards, I fired, and he tumbled.

Immediately I jumped up to go to the bird, but my now-numb leg would not support my weight. I fell flat on my face. Falling down was bad enough but not being able to get up because my leg had gone to sleep was much worse. To get to the bird in a hurry, I had to crawl through flooded timber, acquiring plenty of mud along the way. I learned a great lesson -- do not sit on your leg when you are turkey hunting.

The proper position is to sit square on your seat, knees bent in front of you and shotgun resting on your knee facing the direction from which the turkey sound has come. You can sit in this position comfortably for some time. If you do have to make minor adjustments as the turkey comes in, you can move easily from this position.

CALLING

Turkeys on the Roost

Once you are in position, and the turkey is gobbling, begin giving some soft tree calls, which are very soft, light yelps the hen turkey makes while in the tree before she flies down to let the gobbler know where she is. Then the tom can come in this direction when he flies down. If the gobbler answers the hen's calling by gobbling back immediately, you may not have to make any more calls. If you hear the turkey fly down, he may fly directly to your stand without your doing any other. However, if he does not come straight to you when he flies down, give a few yelps. Listen for the turkey to respond. If he gobbles back and you hear him moving toward you, do not call again.

The purpose of calling is to make the turkey come to you. Once he starts moving to you, then ready for the shot. Point your gun in the direction you expect the turkey to come from, and wait on the shot. Predetermine what 30-yards are from you. I usually do this by picking several trees in front of me I believe to be about 30-yards away. Before I take the shot, I require the turkey to pass by those trees and come in to where I am. If the turkey does not come into my killing ground, I do not take the shot. Many old-timers when they set up, simply cluck three times and throw their turkey calls away to make sure they do not overcall to the bird. One of the mistakes many turkey hunters make is calling too much to a turkey.

This tactic often will produce best on private lands with turkeys that have not been hunted or have been hunted very little. The more turkeys are hunted, the more calling you may have to do.

If you are hunting later in the season or on public lands, you may want to use more sneaky techniques and more sophisticated calling. On public lands, the quicker you can get a tom to come to you, the better your chances are for bagging him.

A more aggressive form of calling is to take a stand and give a tree call. Once the turkey answers back, wait about five minutes, and give a fly-down cackle, a series of fast, excited clucks followed by excited yelps. As soon as you make the fly-down cackle, pat the side of your leg with your gloved hand to simulate the beating of the wings of the hen as she flies down. Wait about two minutes. Then begin to cut, a series of fast clucks that denote excitement and the willingness of the hen to breed. Often this series of calling will seem to snatch a gobbler off the limb. Because he may run to you, be ready for the shot. If the gobbler is slow in coming to you, you can continue to cut until the bird is close enough to see you. Then stop your calling, and prepare for the shot. One of the problems associated with being this aggressive is this form of calling often will cause a gobbler to come in and stop 50-to 60-yards from you and hang up. When a turkey hangs-up, he stops coming to you and then struts and drums -- expecting the hen to come to him. Three strategies may work if a turkey hangs up:

- Quit calling altogether. The turkey either will stop strutting and drumming and come to you, or he will walk off away from you thinking the hen has left the area.

- Begin to scratch in the leaves, and purr like a disinterested hen. This technique often will hurt the turkey's ego, let him know a hen is in the area and make him think if he comes in closer, maybe the hen can see him and come in to him to breed.

- Give soft yelps when the turkey drops his strut to let him know you still are in the area. However, as long as a tom is gobbling and coming to you, do not call. Remember, a turkey walks very slowly through the woods. More than likely, the bird will require more time to get to you than you think he will. Be patient. These methods will pay off.

Turkeys on the Ground

However, if you do not find a gobbler until after the birds have flown down, take a stand about 100-yards from the turkey. Remember when a turkey is on the ground, the woods absorb most of his gobbles. When you hear him, he will sound much further away than he does when he gobbles from a tree. Do not set up as close to the turkey as you will if you hear that same bird gobbling from a tree. Most of the time when you hear a turkey gobble on the ground clearly and distinctly, he is close enough for you to call immediately.

Call to the turkey the same way he calls to you. If the turkey gobbles as soon as he hears you call, then call frequently to the bird, possibly as much as once every two to three minutes until you know he is coming to you. If the turkey waits from 15-seconds to 1-minute before gobbling back to you after you call, then call very little to the turkey. Answer the turkey with the same amount of calling he answers you. If the turkey gobbles back excitedly and double or triple gobbles, give him excited calls like cuts and cackles. If the turkey gobbles back disinterestedly by barely gobbling or waiting a long time before he gobbles, give him calm calls like a few light yelps or clucking. Match the gobbler's mood with your calling.

MOVING AND STAYING

Most turkey hunters either stay too long in a calling position or leave a calling spot too quickly. Knowing when to go and when to stay is a critical key to successful turkey hunting. As long as a turkey is coming to you or answering your calling, stay in the spot where you are calling. When the tom starts moving away from you and is out of sight, then move, try and get ahead of the turkey, change calls, and call the bird again.

In the past when a turkey has quit gobbling, I have assumed he has left the country and is not coming to me. However, generally the opposite is true. When a tom stops gobbling, especially an older bird, most of the time he is coming to you. He may move in silently and suddenly appear with you hearing nothing but his footsteps. Today when a turkey stops gobbling, and I believe he is gone, I look at my watch and wait a full 45-minutes before I leave my calling position. This tactic has enabled me to bag from

25-percent to 40-percent more turkeys than I once took when I left my calling site too quickly. Before you learn when to stay and when to go, you probably will spook several turkeys because you leave too quickly.

On different days, each turkey will demonstrate various moods. No clear-cut rules always apply. The more gobblers you attempt to call, the more you will learn about turkey hunting. The very successful turkey hunters I hunt with usually operate on a sixth sense based on years of experience and hundreds of gobblers hunted. After you have had several turkey encounters, you will learn more about when to call, when not to call, when to move and when not to move.

TAKING THE SHOT

If you shoot too quickly, you will miss the gobbler. If you wait too long, the bird will see you, and you will not get a shot. Understanding when to take a shot on turkeys often is the difference in having a successful or an unsuccessful hunt. I decide when to shoot by applying these rules.

- Do not take a shot at more than 30-yards. Once I set up my killing ground, I have earned the right to take a shot, if I can call the turkey into that area. If the turkey does not come into that 30-yard range, he wins this round of the contest, even if I am shooting a 2-3/4-inch 12-gauge, a 3-inch magnum 12-gauge or even a 10-gauge, which can reach out to 40-to 45-yards. I still choose to play the game at 30-yards. If I am shooting a 20-gauge or a blackpowder shotgun, I want the bird at 25-yards or less. Although I have made shots at 8-and 10-steps from the tree, these shots are not good because the shot pattern will not have an opportunity to open up and cover the target as well as it does at 20-yards or more. Most veteran turkey hunters will tell you the closer a turkey is to you when you take the shot, the greater your chances are for missing the bird.

- Never take a shot when you do not have a clear path to the turkey's head and neck. If a blade of grass, a tree or a bush is between me and the turkey's head and neck, I will not take the shot. The spinal column and skull of the turkey are very small. Any obstruction between you and that spinal may collect the lead intended for the turkey's head. You may miss the bird.

- Do not shoot a turkey in the strut. When a turkey is in the strut, his head and neck are coiled back into his feathers, making the target smaller and allowing the feathers to turn the lead. All you have to do to break a tom out of the strut is cluck. The bird usually will drop his strut, stick his head up and give you a clean shot.

- Do not take a running shot at a turkey, unless you are convinced you can make it. The chances of bagging the bird usually are reduced, and the chances of injuring the bird are greatly increased.

- Take the first good shot the tom presents when he walks into your killing ground. If you wait for a better shot, often the gobbler will see you before you get off that better shot.

- Do not rush the shot. Often a turkey hunter tells himself the lie that, "If I don't take this shot, I'm not going to get a shot." More than likely, if you take an iffy shot, you do not have a shot. Wait when you hear yourself make a statement like that. If a turkey does not present a good shot, do not take it. Let him walk off. Then either try to call the tom back, set up on him in another place, or hunt him another day. If you shoot and miss, you have educated that gobbler which will make him much more difficult to hunt.

UNDERSTANDING SPRING TURKEYS

A young spring gobbler like a jake or a 2-year old bird can be relatively easy to take. But an older gobbler that has several hunter encounters can drive you nuts. Since turkeys in the spring want to breed, sex is your ally.

Although some turkeys are easy to call and bag, the more hunting pressure turkeys experience, the more difficult they will be to take. Being patient, scouting carefully, listening to the birds, learning to talk to them and making the turkey hunt you will pay off in turkey dividends for you.

Do not be discouraged when a tom beats you. Turkeys always win more times than hunters do. Even the greatest turkey hunters in the nation will be defeated by more gobblers than they will be successful in bagging. Spring turkey hunting is exciting because every morning, the turkey hunter has an opportunity to test his hunting skills and knowledge against one of the smartest creatures ever created -- the bronze turkey baron of the spring woods.

CHAPTER 8 - HUNTING FALL TURKEYS

The birds of fall are both the easiest and the hardest to take, depending on their lengths of their beards and spurs. The longbeards of the fall are the most difficult turkeys to bag at any time of the year. But the jakes, which are less than a year old, are easy to take.

The hunter's strategy for taking the turkeys of fall is completely different from techniques used in the spring. Sex is no longer important to the gobblers. The birds already have passed through their mating cycles, and the hens have made their nests, laid their eggs and reared their young. Fall calling and hunting tactics are based primarily on the social order of turkeys more than on the sex drive of the birds.

The woods also have changed. No longer does the sportsman have the lush green foliage of spring to hide in and around because now the woods are barren. Food is hard to find, and in many areas of the country, snow covers the ground. Fall hunters often wear different camo patterns than spring hunters do. Too, the food sources of the turkeys change in the fall. Here is a look at the world of the turkey to help us learn how that world differs in the fall and the spring.

During the fall of the year, the turkey's primary diet will be nuts and seeds they can forage on the forest floor. Many times the birds may have to scratch through snow to find food. One of the best areas in which to locate turkeys in the fall is around livestock, because livestock face the same problem as turkeys do -- finding food.

In the far North when snow covers the ground during turkey season, often you will see turkeys on the white carpet of snow in the pastures of a dairy farm. When dairy farmers clean out their heated barns and spread the manure on their pastures, this manure is warmer than the snow where it is placed. The manure has undigested grain in it that is easy for the turkeys to find and eat. Contact a dairy farmer when you are scouting for fall turkeys.

Ranchers who produce beef cattle also will put hay and grain out for their animals during the fall. These food sources for the livestock also contain small seeds and grain on which the turkeys can feed.

In the South where turkey hunting is permitted during the fall, squirrels are often the animals to look for when you are hunting turkeys. Squirrels feed on many of the same seeds, acorns, dogwood berries and other mast crops that wild turkeys eat. Once you pinpoint a hardwood area with a heavy squirrel concentration, you usually will find a productive place to hunt turkeys.

Many turkey hunters squirrel hunt in the fall to scout for turkeys before fall turkey season opens. While walking drainage systems and bagging bushytails, they look for turkey feathers, droppings and turkey scratchings and hope to see turkeys as they squirrel hunt. Once the squirrel hunters determine where the turkeys are ranging, then they know where to begin their search for the longbeards of fall when the season arrives.

Because turkeys travel some distances in the fall, flocks can leave numbers of tracks. A skilled woodsman can determine the direction of the turkey's movement, how much time has elapsed since the turkey has passed by, and whether males and/or females are in the flock by examining the tracks. Tracks also can aid you in making an educated guess about the number of turkeys in a flock.

When the woods are changing colors, fall hunting can be a wonderful experience. The challenge of taking a tough tom is probably greater in the fall than at any other time of the year. However, some states do not have a fall season.

WHY HAVE A FALL SEASON

Although you may think some states do not have a fall season because of too small a turkey population, the reasons behind having or not having a fall turkey season are usually not that simple. Certain states use the no fall season method as a tool to control their flocks, whereas other states let tradition decide whether or not they have a fall season.

For example, Alabama, my home state, has one of the largest turkey flocks in the nation. However, only twelve of its sixty-seven counties have a fall turkey season, but why? Oftentimes, the strongest motivation for doing anything is tradition. In Alabama, the twelve counties with a fall turkey season always have had a fall season. About thirty-three states now have fall turkey hunting seasons, compared to forty-nine states that have spring seasons for turkeys.

We all know the Pilgrims and the Indians celebrated Thanksgiving in the fall with a turkey dinner. Besides tradition, an additional reason for having a fall season is the turkeys are not breeding during this time, and hunting is less likely to impact the breeding time and affect the new turkey population.

Usually when a case is made against a fall turkey season, this philosophy is voiced by purist turkey hunters who believe young toms should not be harvested and that shooting a male bird less than a year old is not sporting. Some sportsmen prefer not to bag a gobbler unless his spurs are a certain length, such as one inch. Sometimes when hunters want to impose their own hunting codes on others, they petition their state departments of conservation to not have a fall turkey season. Opinions of the state's hunters and the conditions of the turkey population dictate what wildlife management in states and counties decide about fall turkey hunting.

WHICH CAMOUFLAGE TO WEAR

Usually the best camouflage for fall will be either predominantly gray or brown patterns. Because the woods are changing colors or the leaves all are gone by fall turkey season, the tree trunk-type patterns may prove to be the most appropriate.

I am convinced that turkeys can see the hunter much better in the fall than they can in the spring. The floor of the forest is cleaner, and the hunter's silhouette stands out better. The fall turkey hunter must pay close attention to his camo and even may prefer to hunt with a blind. Because the woods are so open in the fall, where the hunter sets up is far more critical to his success in the fall than in the spring.

HOW TO SET UP ON FALL GOBBLERS

Since the fall woods are open and a turkey's eyesight is so keen, if you set up in clean woods where the a gobbler wants to walk, the chances of his seeing you before he gets close enough for you to take a shot are very good. But a terrain break can be beneficial to the fall turkey hunter. A slightly rolling hill, a mountaintop, a small ridge or any type of hump in the ground you can put between you and the turkey will increase your odds of bagging that bird. That hump or hill will act as your blind. Then when the turkey walks into view, you can see him. If he's within gun range, you will have an opportunity to bag him.

However, if you are forced to take a stand in an open area where a tom can watch from 100-to 200-yards as he comes in, your chances for success are reduced greatly. But never set up in a thicket or any kind of thick cover. Turkeys in the fall, like turkeys in the spring, will avoid thickets. If you must set up in the open, sit still, and pray the turkey does not see you before he gets close enough for you to take a shot.

One strategy some turkey hunters have used successfully to bag fall gobblers is to hunt from treestands. Deer hunters know turkeys will walk under their stands and never look up to see them. This tactic is especially effective if you know where turkeys are feeding every day. However, turkey hunting in the fall may mean covering a vast expanse of ground. Often when you locate a flock of turkeys, you will not have time to put up a treestand. But hunting from treestands can be effective if you scatter a flock of longbeards and plan to sit in one spot for some time.

HOW TO HUNT THE YOUNG BIRDS OF FALL

The male turkeys, which are born in the spring, are called jakes in the fall. These birds are just learning how to become gobblers. They have not had any hunter encounters, are not nearly as wary as their longbeard seniors, have not learned how to gobble and have only two things on their minds -- finding something to eat and staying with their mother and the other birds from their flock. The flocking instinct is very strong in both young gobblers and young hens, and the old hen's primary consideration is to keep her flock together and to warn them of danger. Most fall turkey hunters find a flock of turkeys feeding together and scatter the flock to have a chance to bag young gobblers.

Two words that sound similar but carry entirely different meanings when you are considering disrupting a flock are scatter and scare. When you scatter a flock of turkeys, you get as close as possible to the flock before surprising them and causing the individual birds to come off the ground and fly to all points of the compass. When you scare a flock of turkeys, you do not get close enough to them to create a scatter, but instead, force most of the birds to run or fly off in the same direction. If you scare a flock of turkeys, you greatly reduce the likelihood of being able to call the birds back to you. When you scatter the flock, you do have a chance of calling the birds in and bagging a young tom.

How to Scatter a Flock of Turkeys

Once you see a flock of turkeys, do not immediately run at them and try to scatter them. Wait patiently, and determine in which direction the turkeys are feeding. Once you know the birds' line of travel, attempt to circle to get in front of them, take a stand, and wait for the birds to approach. Let the turkeys come to you.

Notice the makeup of the flock. Are any longbeards in the flock? Is the group of turkeys primarily a young flock consisting of hens and young jakes? Or, have you lucked into a bachelor band of gobblers comprised of male birds two years old or older? Understanding the age structure of the flock allows you to decide how and where to hunt the birds. If the flock you are watching is comprised mostly of young birds -- jakes and hens -- then you know your hunt will be over quickly. If older gobblers are in the flock, realize your hunt may last until the end of the day or for the next three days.

How to Take Young Gobblers

Let a flock of young turkeys come as close to you as they possibly will. Then jump up, run at the birds, scream, and holler. Run toward the center of the flock to scatter birds in all directions. Watch to see in which direction most of the turkeys fly off.

Once the turkeys have taken to the air, find a stand site, usually a large tree you can sit next to with some type of hill in front of you. Listen for the turkeys to begin to call, which often will happen within 5-to 30-minutes after they have been scattered.

Two basic calls bring in young gobblers in the fall -- the kee-kee run (the young gobbler's squealing call) and the old hen's assembly call. Young gobblers that have not learned to gobble yet will give a high-pitched, kee-kee sound before they give a coarse yelp. These toms are trying to learn to talk like turkeys but have not learned yet how to gobble. By giving the kee-kee run, you will sound like a lost jake calling other jakes back to you. Because young gobblers want to band back together as soon as possible after they are scattered, this call effectively brings in young gobblers to where you are.

The old hen assembly call consists of a series of loud, pleading yelps that start out slowly and then become louder and faster. The old hen assembly call, which is the call the dominant hen utilizes to bring the flock back together after it has been scattered, often will cause young jakes to come to you on the run.

What Problems Are Associated With Hunting Young Jakes Often after you scatter a flock in the fall and begin to call, a dominant hen may come in first and begin to try and call the flock back together away from you. If she is successful, you may not get a shot. Your best tactic is to get up and run the old hen off by putting her in the air. Then she will not have a chance to assemble the flock. After she has left the area, sit back down, and begin to call again.

Often young gobblers will come in quickly in groups of two or three as soon as you begin to call if you have scattered the flock effectively. As soon as you start to call to a scattered flock, have your gun at the ready, and be prepared to take the shot, since the hunt for young birds in the fall may be over within 10-to 30-minutes after you scatter the flock and start to call. However, wait until you can isolate one young tom from the group, if they come in together, before you squeeze the trigger.

HOW TO HUNT LONGBEARDS IN THE FALL

The fall longbeard is the most difficult bird to bag, especially if he is a lone longbeard. A bachelor gobbler more than two years old that stays to himself will test the mettle of any turkey hunter. Even the best turkey hunters in the nation often may walk off when this knight of the sharp spurs throws down his gauntlet. In the fall, bachelor birds are very unpredictable, often antisocial and difficult to hunt.

Woodsmanship, more than any other factor, is the key to taking a fall longbeard. To deliberately hunt a turkey like this, you have to know him intimately -- where he lives, where he feeds, where he roosts, and where he goes during the day. Generally you have to learn all this information without hearing the bird talk. Or, if the fall longbeard does make sounds, they will be very few. Patience will be your strongest ally as you sit still for a long time and make very few calls. You must realize when the bird does come in that the only sound you will hear may be his footsteps.

Longbeards in the fall have personalities and styles all their own. No general rules exist about how to best hunt these birds. But if you will study a turkey and watch him without his seeing you, he will teach you how to take him.

Bachelor Flocks of Longbeards

Your best chance for bagging a longbeard is to find a bachelor flock of birds, sometimes called amigos, that are two and three year old birds that seem to prefer the company of each other rather than a flock of hens. This bachelor band may consist of three to thirty gobblers, depending on the turkey population where you hunt.

Turkeys are very social in nature. Often a bachelor flock will remain together throughout much of the fall because they prefer one another's company. However, the lure of running with the boys is in no way stronger than their will to survive. Getting back together after they have been scattered is not nearly as important to longbeards as it is to young gobblers. To bag a longbeard in a bachelor band, you must scatter the flock in the same way you do the young turkeys. However, after the scatter, walk about 50-to 100-yards in the direction where you have seen several of the longbeards fly. Take a stand,

and get comfortable. Wait 30-to 45-minutes before giving one to three coarse gobbler yelps, which are much more drawn out and more raspy than a hen's yelp. Once you have made that call, wait 45-minutes to an hour before you call again.

Longbeards will be slow to group back together. Great patience and skill are required to call an amigo back to within gun range. At least 50-percent of the time, none of the amigos will return. These birds have survived for at least two years because they are woods-wise and hunter-shy.

Fall longbeards in a flock can be called. However, you may have to sit in the same spot and call for a half day or three consecutive days to get a shot. Generally if you are an experienced turkey hunter, have put in hours scouting and are a very confident caller, you should be able to bag a spring gobbler within three days. If you are an inexperienced hunter, have spent the time required to scout the area and already are a good caller, plan on five days to two weeks to bag a fall gobbler.

One tactic a fall hunter will use is to try and locate a flock of longbeards in the morning, scatter that flock and then go somewhere else to hunt until late afternoon. About 2:00 or 3:00 P.M., return to the site where you have scattered the flocks, sit down, and then begin to call to the longbeards. If the birds fail to come in by dark, leave the area, go home, get a good night's sleep, and return to that same spot at daylight the next morning with your lunch packed. Then you can sit and call all day long.

Boredom is your biggest enemy when hunting the birds of fall. Patience is your best ally. Determination most likely will prove to be your winning strategy.

If you take a fall amigo without ambushing him but by calling him, you deserve a trophy. Then you can pull your chair up to the table beside any of the nation's top turkey hunters. You have earned the right to be there.

How to Hunt the Lone Wolves of Fall

The lone wolf of the fall is the ultimate prize in all of turkey hunting because he is the most difficult gobbler to bag at any time of the year. Even though the lone wolf tom's sex drive may cause his demise in the spring, in the fall he is the wisest, most elusive, most difficult to call and the most highly prized creature in the woods.

A lone wolf may be the only gobbler that has survived from his entire year class of gobblers. In most areas of the country, a lone wolf will be at least four years old. In the fall, he shuns the company of not only hens and jakes but also amigos. He much prefers his own company to that of any other bird, rarely is social and usually is moody. Because of his age, the lone wolf has learned just about every trick any hunter can try to play on him.

To bag a lone wolf gobbler, you must learn all you can about where he lives, roosts, feeds and travels and when he goes where he goes before you ever attempt to call him. One of the best ways to obtain this information besides scouting may be by talking to deer hunters during deer season. Ask them if they spot a lone wolf in the woods to make mental notes about when and where he shows up and to share this information with you. Then you may have a chance to take him.

Once you pinpoint the area the lone wolf frequents, go there. Call very little, just to let the tom know another turkey in his region. Then the next move is the lone wolf's.

When he decides he wants the company of another bird, he will come to your calling. If he does not want your company, he will not respond. Your most productive strategy is playing a waiting game.

More than likely when the lone wolf comes in, he will not announce his presence. He may spot you from 50-yards away, and you never will take him in that area. When a lone wolf does come in, he is keenly aware of danger and realizes he should see a hen. When he does not spot another turkey, he may leave the region. Then you must find another place and utilize another call to try and take him.

A lone wolf may respond to gobbler yelps, hen calls or young gobbler squealing calls. Since this tom is an individual, no set rules can be laid down to bag him. Only by trial and error, the process of elimination, and spending many hours in the woods can you learn how to most effectively hunt this turkey.

The lone wolf gobbler ...

> ...has helped to put turkey hunters in insane asylums,

> ...has the power to twist your mind as well as change your character and your personality as you become consumed with bagging him,

> ...is one a turkey hunter with a wealth of knowledge, who consistently has bagged turkeys each spring and has been successful with amigos and jakes in the fall, must hunt to prove himself as a master hunter,

> ...will test every bit of turkey hunting wisdom you have if you hunt him fairly.

> ...will educate you in how to hunt tough turkeys -- more than you can learn from any book, video, magazine article, or tape, and

> ...will teach you patience is your greatest ally.

If you decide to go after a lone wolf, understand your chances of failing are at least 75-percent or more during the fall season with your odds for success far less than 25-percent. Your reputation as a turkey hunter will be in jeopardy, and many who know you may think you are crazy to spend so much time trying to take a turkey that fools you on every outing. But with every agonizing defeat, you have an opportunity to learn one more strategy that may aid you in your eventual success.

If you do bag one of the lone wolves of the fall woods, you deserve the highest accolades in all of turkeydom, because you have achieved the pinnacle of success that few even strive for and even fewer obtain. You will be head and shoulders above all others who go into the woods to hunt the gobblers of fall.

CHAPTER 9 - HUNTING THE EASTERN WILD GOBBLER

When the Pilgrims stepped off the "Mayflower," they were just about out of food. They had eaten all the salted meat and dried vegetables they had packed for the trip and now wanted fresh meat cooked on an open fire.

When one of the first Pilgrims saw what he thought to be a huge chicken that was bigger and fatter than any of the chickens he had had in his barnyard in the Old Country, he ran to catch it. But he found that not only could the chicken outrun him, it could fly too.

Ever since that day when the first colonists landed on the shores of the New World, Americans have been chasing those giant chickens we call turkeys today.

Native Americans had been hunting turkeys for years. Some Indian tribes ate turkey, while other tribes used the parts of the turkey such as feathers for ceremonial robes, fletchings for arrows and brooms to sweep out their lodges, spurs for sharp points for arrows and other body parts for ceremonies and in everyday life.

The eastern wild turkey, Meleagris gallopavo silvestris, which was the first wild turkey most Europeans encountered, soon became a staple food for the early frontiersmen with an estimated 10-million eastern wild turkeys living in the Continental United States. Then during the 1800s, market hunters reduced their numbers drastically. Beginning in 1912, many states started restocking turkeys in the United States. In 1989, an estimated 3.5-million eastern wild turkeys were in the United States, and each of the more than thirty states that originally homed eastern wild turkeys today has huntable populations in them.

The eastern gobbler is distinguished from the Osceola, the Merriam and the Rio Grande mostly by color. The eastern wild turkey is the darkest of all the subspecies of the wild turkey with the darkest feather tips and feather colors ranging from chestnut browns to very dark browns. The size of a turkey mostly depends on the region in which the bird lives rather than the subspecies to which it belongs.

Because the eastern wild turkey is found in most of the eastern half of the United States - from Florida to Maine and as far west as Iowa, the eastern bird has the widest diversity of habitat of all kinds of turkeys and is the building block on which most hunters learn the sport of gobbler chasing. Hunting eastern wild turkeys can be divided into the habitat types in which they are found, since where the eastern wild turkey lives dictates the tactics required to hunt them. Understanding the lay of the land through pre-season scouting or information provided by topographic maps is an integral element to success. Knowing the locations of streams, fences or other obstacles also will help the hunter avoid them when he sets up to call. Also many of these same eastern bird strategies are applicable when hunting Rio Grande, Merriam and Osceola turkeys.

MOUNTAIN TURKEYS

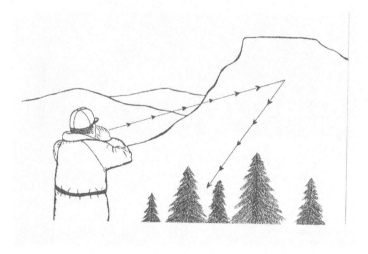

Mountain turkeys usually are much easier to locate than turkeys in flatlands and swamps because you can climb a high ridge, begin to call and hear turkeys on both sides of the mountains and those far from you on other mountains. The higher a turkey is off the ground, and the less foliage his gobble must pass through, the further his gobbling will travel.

Another tactic to use for locating gobblers is to travel the roads through the mountains. Stop your car often, get out, and listen for turkeys to gobble on either mountain the road goes between -- using locator calls like the owl call or the crow call to try and get toms on either mountain to gobble. Utilizing these techniques you can cover more ground and locate more turkeys than the hunters who hunt on heavily forested flat land.

To take mountain gobblers, remember that turkeys prefer to walk uphill rather than downhill, perhaps because most of their weight is forward of their legs. When you discover a tom in the mountains, your best chances for calling to him and getting him to come to you are either to be on the same level as the gobbler when you call or to take a calling position slightly above the turkey.

If the gobbler is on one mountain and you are on another, your best chances for calling that turkey to you are to go to the mountain where the turkey is and call the bird. If the tom is on top of the ridge, climb to the top of the ridge, and try and call the gobbler to you, a tactic that puts you on the same level as the gobbler. Then he can walk straight to you without having to move up or down. If the turkey is on the side of the ridge, take a calling position just above the bird, and attempt to call him up to you.

Another problem associated with hunting mountain turkeys is you may have a tendency to misjudge distance if you are accustomed to hunting turkeys on flatlands and in heavily foliaged forests. A bird gobbling from a tall tree on a high ridge may sound as though he is only a few yards away when actually he may be a 1/2-mile away.

Also if a gobbler on the side of a mountain is facing another mountain in front of him, then when he gobbles, the sound of his gobbling will hit the mountain across from him and bounce back. If you are on the same side of the mountain as the turkey, the bird may sound as though he is on the mountain in front of you or across from you instead of on the mountain and the same side of the mountain where you are.

This effect is much like your looking into a mirror. When you stand in front of a mirror, your image goes from where you are to the mirror and then bounces back. Sound travels in much the same way and can bounce off a mountain like your image bounces off a mirror. When you hear a tom gobble, you assume the bird is where you have heard the sound coming from like someone who has seen you in the mirror thinks you are where they have seen your image, when you are not there at all. Often I have crossed a mountain only to arrive at the other side and realize the turkey has been gobbling within 100-yards of where I have been standing. The sound of the bird's gobbling simply has bounced off the mountain and caused me to go to where I have heard the sound rather than remaining on the same mountain as the turkey.

Generally, turkeys like to strut and mate either on tops of ridges, on benches on the sides of mountains or in the valleys at the base of mountains. Turkeys prefer to roost in trees either on top of or just off to one side of a mountain. When a tom flies down from his roost, he usually will meet his hens either on the top of the mountain or at the bottom of the mountain. Although turkeys will feed on top of a mountain, more than likely they will feed at the bottom of a mountain. Mountainous regions may encompass many acres, but most of the time, the two most productive places to hunt for turkeys are on a mountaintop or at the base of the mountain.

In most areas, where the turkeys are positioned on a mountain is determined by three factors: sex, food and temperature. During the spring, turkeys most likely will roost on the tops of the mountains and either breed on ridgetops or in bottoms. Although usually turkeys will feed in the bottoms, if an abundance of acorns or other foods is present on the ridges, the turkeys may remain in that high country all day.

As the temperatures warm up later in the spring, if fields and food lots are at the base of a mountain, the turkeys may feed at the base of the mountains in the morning but move up the mountains to find the cooler temperatures in the middle of the day. Then they possibly may come down the mountains when the temperature has cooled in the afternoons and sometimes fly to the ridgetops to roost at night. Many turkeys normally follow these general rules however, certain birds always break the rules. Assume none of these rules are absolute.

My strategy for hunting mountain gobblers is to either walk the ridges or drive the roads between the mountains early in the morning to try and locate a gobbler. I hunt the bottoms of the mountains, the fields and the acorn flats after 9:00 A.M. In the middle of the day, I return to the ridges, call, remain there until I locate a turkey in the bottoms or hear a turkey start to move toward the base of the mountains to fly up in the afternoons. I have learned you can locate more turkeys and reach them quicker by spending your time on the tops of the mountains rather than at the bottoms. Mountain gobblers will test your mettle as a turkey hunter because often you will have to cross several mountains to get into position to finally call a gobbler.

SWAMP LAND TOMS

When you hunt turkeys along a flood plain or in swampy terrain, the first decision you must make every morning when you get up is that you will get partially wet or totally wet before the day is over. Swamp turkeys always seem to be on the other side of water from where you are. However, turkeys will cross water at times.

Turkeys like to roost over water because they realize predators will have a more difficult time finding them and getting to them. Turkeys also soon learn from which direction hunters come. If they roost over water and hear danger on one bank, they can fly to the other bank. If turkeys are accustomed to being pressured from one particular direction in swampy terrain, then when they fly down from the roost, they will move away from that hunting pressure to a region where they do not think they will encounter a hunter. Older gobblers also realize most turkey hunters will not cross water to try and get to them.

You must make a choice of three options when you go into swampy terrain to hunt turkeys. You can ...

- wear hip waders and assume the turkey will not be across any water higher than your hips.

- carry a backpack with chest-high waders in it. I prefer Redball's Flyweight waders, which are lightweight and easy to carry, can be slipped on and off quickly when I need them and have an inflatable air bladder at the top of the waders. Then if I do step in a stump hole, I will not sink, or if I trip and fall, the waders will not fill completely with water. I also pack a pair of lightweight tennis shoes to put on over my stocking feet waders, and the backpack serves too as a carrying device for my hunting vest and my boots to keep them dry as I traverse the swamp.

- get wet. I usually carry a heavy-duty garbage bag and a roll of duct tape in the back of my hunting vest. If I have to swim a creek or wade water over armpit-deep to reach a turkey, I can put my boots, clothes and hunting vest in the garbage sack, tape the top of the garbage bag shut with duct tape and carry the sack and gun over my head when I slide into that cold, spring water.

If I do not get wet, I feel I have won a small victory. If I am forced to get wet to go to a gobbler, I already have made the decision about what I will do before I have left camp. However, I do carry equipment to try and get the least wet possible and/or to get dry quickly. I also put my box calls and my slate calls in ziploc bags, expecting a dunking.

I spray all my clothing, including my gloves, hat, mask and shirt with insect repellent. Because water will wash off insect repellent as will my perspiration, I carry a can of insect repellent with me. Then I can increase my protection from the biting bugs whenever necessary.

Occasionally when you are hunting in a swamp, you will encounter a snake. But do not let your fear of snakes hinder you from hunting turkeys in a swamp. Probably more turkey hunters who hunt in swamps are injured or killed in car accidents each year on the way to hunting than they are injured or killed by snakes. Although I am not foolhardy, I do look where I am going. Statistics indicate that death from snakebite is one of the most rare causes of death in the United States. Do not let fear inhibit you from hunting turkeys in a swamp just because snakes are there.

To consistently take turkeys in swampy terrain, your biggest ally will be knowledge of the land and the water rather than your calling ability. If you know where the dry and wet spots are, then you will understand where the turkeys must be to keep their feet out of the water. You also will know how and where to cross the water and how to get to turkeys without having to swim.

Remember when you are hunting swamp turkeys in thick and rich swamp foliage, sound does not carry as far as in other terrain. A bird you barely can hear gobble only may be 150-yards or less away. If that same tom gobbles on top of a mountain, you probably will be able to hear him 1/2-mile or more away. Use this information to take a stand in a swamp at what seems to be much further away from the turkey than you will in open country. If you hear a turkey gobbling loud in the swamps, you may be only 30-or 40-yards from him. The best thing you can do is sit down quickly, call very little and prepare for the shot.

Swamp turkeys often do not cover as much territory as turkeys do mountain gobblers do. Swamps usually have an abundance of food, and the birds do not have to go far to feed, roost, meet their hens, strut and drum. Often a swamp turkey will use the same tree to roost in for several nights. Once you locate a swamp gobbler, he may stay in that same general vicinity -- often less than 300-acres -- throughout the entire day. Because the woods are often very thick in swamps, you rarely will see the gobbler before he is within shooting distance, which is an advantage to the hunter.

FIELD GOBBLERS

Turkeys that live on the edge of a field or around agricultural crops can be difficult to bag. Older, smarter birds have learned they can fly down into the middles of fields, feed, dust, strut, mate and see danger coming from all different directions. I have met some longbeards that will fly from the roost to the middle of a field, remain there all day and then fly up to their roost at dark. A nightmare to hunt, some of these toms will be almost impossible to take.

Generally turkeys will roost in nearby woods, fly down into the woods, walk to the fields to feed, dust and mate, spend most of the morning there, move out of the fields as the sun gets hot and their dark feathers absorb that heat, loaf in the edge of the wood line in the shade until the temperature in the field begins to cool down in the afternoon, return to the field in the late afternoon to feed, dust and mate again, walk out of the field before dark back through the woods close to their roost and then fly up to their roost before dark. Although most field turkeys follow this schedule, some birds break these rules.

Several tactics will help you take a field gobbler.

* Set up on the edge of a field, and try and call the gobbler to that edge. This tactic is often effective when more than one gobbler is in a field. Most of the time, the dominant gobbler will stay with his harem of hens. But when a subordinate gobbler hears a hen calling just off the edge of a field, he may come running to you because he thinks he may have the opportunity to breed a hen before she goes to the older gobbler.

* Challenge the dominant hen. A flock of turkeys in a field made up of hens and gobblers usually will have a dominant hen that determines which way the flock feeds. If you consistently call to the gobbler utilizing hen calls and that dominant hen thinks you are a rival for her position in the flock, she may come to the edge of the woods looking for you and bring the rest of the flock with her, including the old gobbler.

* Wait until all the hens leave the gobbler in the middle of the field. When he is in the field and lonesome, you may be able to call him to you.

To locate field gobblers, drive roads through clearcuts and agricultural lands, and use binoculars or spotting scopes to look for gobblers. The best time of day to do this scouting is around 9:00 or 10:00 A.M. after most gobblers are off the roost and probably in the field.

Notice which way a gobbler goes into and out of a field. More than likely, he will utilize that same path each morning and afternoon. He has developed that route because he never has encountered danger on it and has learned he can see danger approach if he walks that course. Usually the route a gobbler takes to and from a field will be through open woods or big timber where he can see a great distance. If the turkey is walking to and from the field, you can take a stand along the route he is taking and call him to you. Often, very little calling will be necessary to bag a gobbler like this because you will be sitting near the path he normally travels.

BIG WOODS TURKEYS

The eastern wild turkey tends to like older age timber and especially hardwoods. Hardwoods provide nuts the turkeys can feed on, shade where the turkeys can hide from the sun and roosts where the turkeys can sleep at night. In many areas, turkeys spend most of their lives in big woods. When hunting open woodlots of mature timber, you will be able to hear the turkeys gobble further than you can hear them in the swamps but not as far as you can hear the birds when they are in the mountains.

Turkeys in the big woods often will be found in the same areas where deer and squirrels live because all three animals feed off the same forage. The more open the woods, the more likely you are to see turkeys. Because a turkey's number one mechanism for defense is his eyesight, he prefers to stay in open places under the canopy of the forest where seeing you will be easy for him.

When I am hunting in big woods, I do more listening than I do walking. The turkey can hear you walking through the woods as you can hear him walking, which can be both an advantage and a disadvantage. If you walk like a hunter, the turkey probably will be spooked. However, if you walk like a turkey, the turkey's hearing you is an advantage.

When I'm walking through the woods, I try and change the noises I make from human sounds to turkey-like noises. I want to sound like a hen walking through the woods as she goes through her daily routine in the woods. Turkeys walk differently from humans without a regular, cadenced step that a hunter has. I take erratic steps like a turkey -- perhaps three steps before waiting, then one step and wait again before making four steps.

However, turkeys do make noise in a regular rhythm with their clucks, purrs and scratching in the leaves. I cluck and purr and scratch in the leaves with my foot. The cadence I use to scratch. Turkeys scratch with a definite rhythm -- scratch; scratch scratch; scratch. Clucks and purrs are the contented sounds hens make as they feed. With my walking and with the sounds I make, I want to sound as much like a hen turkey as possible as I go through the woods.

But remember, you are imitating the sounds of turkeys -- the same sounds other hunters are expecting to hear when they are looking for turkeys. If you hear anything else walking in the woods or any gobbler or hen sounds, stop where you are. Identify the sound and what's making it before you continue. If you see another hunter, give up the hunt, and use your natural voice to say in a very loud, distinctive tone, "Hey, buddy, I'm not a turkey, I'm a hunter." When you walk like a turkey, you must be extremely careful to hunt defensively because the turkey you are fooling may be wearing camouflage instead of feathers.

NORTHERN BIRDS

The main difference between northern birds and southern birds is the places you have to hunt. Generally the vast majority of turkeys harvested in the North are harvested on public lands, whereas in the South and the West, most turkeys will be taken on private lands. Because of the North's large populations, not as many large, private landowners are in the area as in the South. Because large northern landowners often have their lands leased to hunting clubs, most northern hunters hunt public game lands and national forests.

In the South and Midwest, the land is mostly agricultural with large timber companies, large private landowners and ranchers who own and lease the land, which usually contains more private hunting than public hunting. The big ranches in the West also will be privately held and only can be hunted by permission or by buying a lease.

By knowing that northern turkeys primarily will be found on public hunting lands, the tactics to hunt them will be somewhat different than the techniques of southern and western hunters. When you hunt public lands and a turkey gobbles, you must get close to him and call him to you quickly before another hunter hears him gobble and goes to him. When hunting on public lands in the northern United States, you must outcompete the other hunters to bag the birds. However, if you do not take a tom in the first two hours after daylight, your chances of bagging a northern bird drastically increase after 9:30 A.M.

Turkey hunters often are two hour hunters, whether you find them in the North, South or West. The highest concentration of hunters usually occurs for a hour before daylight to two hours after daybreak, and the birds soon adapt to this hunting pressure. If you are hunting turkeys in the North on public lands, your hunting from 9:00 A.M. until noon in states that only permit half-day hunting or hunting all day long in the states that permit all-day hunting will be productive times.

Although the eastern wild turkeys of the North do not exhibit any different traits than the easterns living in the South, the hunting pressure, the terrain and the method of hunting are different.

SOUTHERN TURKEYS

Some southern states always have had viable turkey populations. Also many large landowners in the South traditionally have protected wild turkeys with some states never having had a year without a turkey hunting season. Numbers of the turkeys that have been stocked throughout the nation have come from the South. Some hunters believe that the southern eastern wild gobbler is the toughest turkey to take.

Ben Rodgers Lee of Coffeeville, Alabama, who was the grandfather of modern day turkey hunting, once explained that, "Never have the wild turkeys in Alabama not been hunted in the spring. The turkeys that gobble the most get shot the quickest. The turkeys that gobble the least survive the longest. Through the process of natural selection, I believe Alabama hunters and those in other southern states one day will produce a turkey that will not gobble. All the good-gobbling birds die young. The hushed-mouth gobblers survive the longest and do the most breeding. Although I have hunted turkeys all over the country, I still am convinced the southern turkeys are the hardest ones to hunt."

Even though Lee's logic sounds credible, when we check his thinking with biologists, we learn some errors exist in his assumptions. Most turkeys gobble because that characteristic is part of their nature and is how they call in their hens to breed. However, because turkeys in the South have been hunted so much, they may have become more call- and hunter-shy.

Southern turkey hunting also has two characteristics that set it apart from northern turkey hunting because the majority of birds are found on private lands. Southern turkey hunters tend to be more patient when calling gobblers. If an hour or two hours is required to call up a turkey, then the southern hunter will remain in his calling position and wait on a turkey to arrive. Because not too many other hunters are around to compete with, the southern hunter will let a turkey gobble repeatedly and come from a long distance to get to reach him. In the North, if a hunter waits an hour or two for a tom to come to him, more than likely someone else will bag that same bird.

Southern hunters have a slower, more patient style of hunting than northerners, even though the birds are the same.

MIDWESTERN GOBBLERS

The turkeys living in the Midwest Corn Belt generally are larger and tend to gobble more than either southern or northern turkeys. Perhaps these birds have more food available and experience less hunting pressure. Missouri seems to be the mecca to which all hunters of eastern wild turkeys bow where 22-pound gobblers are common, and hearing thirty to forty eastern wild turkeys gobble in one morning is not unusual.

Because of the sheer numbers of turkeys available to hunt, the turkeys of the Midwest tend to be hunted differently than either the turkeys of the North or the South. If you are hunting an eastern gobbler on either side of the Mason-Dixon Line, you may hunt that same gobbler all day long. But in the Midwest -- especially Missouri -- if you do not call in one gobbler, you may have three or more toms to work before your hunting day is over. Recently one morning in Missouri, Brad Harris, the public relations director for Lohman's Manufacturing, and I called six different gobblers to within gun range from daylight until 11:00 A.M.

Midwest turkeys are closely tied to agricultural fields, especially grain fields, unlike the turkeys in the North or the South because of the vast amounts of grain grown and harvested in the Midwest. Another interesting aspect of hunting the birds of the Midwest is these turkeys seem to like much more calling than the birds in the East. A hunter can have a very good time calling often to these turkeys. In most instances, you will find more gobblers traveling together in the Midwest in the spring than you do in the North or the South. When you call, you may call up two, three or even four gobblers at one time.

The eastern wild turkey is the same subspecies bird whether he lives in the North, the South or the Midwest. The primary differences in these turkeys are the amount of hunting pressure they experience, the type of terrain where they live and the availability of food from which they have to choose. The hunting methods you employ in any one of these regions will produce gobblers in other areas of the country where you find the eastern wild turkey after factoring in the terrain and the hunting pressure.

The eastern wild gobbler has received historically the most hunting pressure of all wild turkeys. Many hunters have said the grand slam of turkey hunting actually is bagging four eastern wild turkeys rather than bagging an eastern, an Osceola, a Rio Grande and a Merriam.

CHAPTER 10 - TAKING THE OSCEOLA

Of the five races of wild turkey in the United States, the Osceola gobbler, which sometimes is called the Florida turkey, is probably the most difficult bird to take. The Osceola is no more elusive to hunt than the eastern, the Merriam or the Rio Grande turkey, and no more skill is required to successfully hunt Osceolas than turkeys in other regions. However, because of the Osceola's limited range, gaining access to hunt the birds creates a problem for sportsmen.

OSCEOLA HUNTING IN FLORIDA

The Osceola gobbler sets up his home in Central and southern Florida where the real estate cost is high, the sun is hot, and the demand for land is ever increasing. Most of the range of the Osceola is on private ranches. Although some public hunting lands are in this region of the Sunshine State, the hunting pressure is high for these birds.

Florida is unique in the South because the state does not have and has not had the plantation system of agriculture most areas South of the Mason Dixon Line have. Florida's agriculture always has been a ranch type system like that of the West rather than the antebellum style of agriculture. Most private lands in Florida are held by large landowners with very limited private hunting for Osceolas available.

Two private hunting camps have Osceola populations on their lands that can be hunted for a fee. Fisheating Creek Hunting Camp in Palmdale, Florida, features 20,000-acres located in Glades County on Highway 27 on the western side of Lake Okeechobee, 60-miles South of Ft. Myers and 100-miles east of West Palm Beach. Outdoor Adventures, a camp of 7,000-acres, is located near Orlando in Polk, Osceola, Lake and Sumter counties.

Besides private hunting camps, several WMAs in Florida home good populations of Osceola turkeys. The 48,050-acre Green Swamp is one of the better public hunting areas in the state. It extends over Polk, Lake and Sumter counties about 30-miles Northwest of Lakeland, Florida. This area is protected and controlled and only can be entered through a checking station. Portions of this WMA have been control burned, and cattle are allowed to graze in this region --both practices which help improve habitat for turkeys. Although Green Swamp WMA has a daily quota limit, you do not have to apply for a permit in advance.

Another WMA with turkey hunting is the 3,877-acre Andrews WMA in Levy County. Although this WMA is small, the turkey hunting can be good. However, because it is a quota WMA, a permit is necessary to hunt.

Upper Hillsboro WMA is another small region located in Sumter County Northwest of Lakeland and consists of 5,178-acres with good Osceola turkey hunting on it. It normally is a primitive weapons only WMA. But during spring turkey season, shotguns are permitted on Wednesdays and Thursdays.

Other WMAs with good populations of Osceolas include the 28,000-acre Tosohatchee WMA and the 6,000-acre Seminole Ranch WMA, both in Orange County. However, the highest populations of Osceola turkeys will be found in Osceola, Okeechobee and Glades counties.

Often the Osceola is nicknamed the swamp turkey and some of the Osceola's habitat is swampy. But the Osceola turkeys have modified their behavior in response to their habitat. The Osceolas that live on the dry flatlands of Florida behave in about the same way as any other flatland turkey does. The turkeys that live in Florida's water habitat will wade water when it is not above their knees, a depth of about six inches. This behavior confuses hunters not familiar with the swamp turkey's patterns.

The novice hunter of the Osceola also quickly learns another predator of the Florida turkey competes with him for the toms -- the bobcat. Florida has a large population of bobcats. Considered to be the number one predator of the Osceola, these animals can create problems and surprises for the hunter in pursuit of a gobbler.

THE HISTORY OF THE NAME OSCEOLA

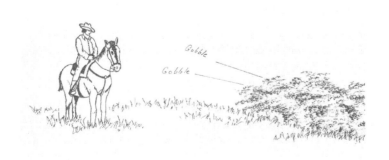

If you can gain access to hunt the Osceola turkeys, you once again will step back into the pages of history and be able to hunt one of the most romantic birds in American folklore. The legend of the Osceola gobblers is steeped in the history of the Seminole nation. Named after the war chief of the Seminoles, Chief Osceola, this turkey is a bird of mystery and is known for his ability to vanish. The very name Osceola rings with defiance since Chief Osceola blazed his name in history by leading his people into battle against one of America's finest generals -- Andrew Jackson, handing Jackson his only defeat in the Indian wars of the early 1800s. So powerful was the Seminole nation they never signed a peace treaty with the American government but chose instead to retreat to the swamps of Georgia and Florida.

Chief Osceola was a guerilla fighter who effectively used hit-and-run tactics to defeat Jackson's army. Because Osceola and his men would appear and disappear just as quickly, many soldiers under Jackson attributed supernatural powers to Chief Osceola. Even today, the turkey that bears his name, Meleagris gallopavo osceola, is believed by many of the Seminole nation to be spirit-possessed.

When I had my first invitation from Allen Jenkins of the M.L. Lynch Call Company in Liberty, Mississippi, to hunt these mystical gobblers with several of Jenkins' friends and Marcelous Osceola, a direct descendant of the legendary chieftain, Osceola, I was quick to seize this opportunity. This hunt was to be special -- a reintroduction for the Seminoles to the old way of hunting turkeys. Jenkins and I were to teach Osceola how to call and harvest the wily Osceola gobbler as his forefathers had. Until Jenkins arrived in the swamp, Marcelous Osceola never had called a wild turkey to within close range as his ancestors once did.

Today on the Big Cypress Swamp Indian Reservation near Miami, Florida, the Seminoles, like native Americans on most reservations, can take game throughout the year in any numbers for subsistence. Through the years, the harvesting of gobblers and hens for food primarily has been a rifle sport practiced around large fields and pastures on the reservation, a technique the Indians ironically have learned from the white man. But Osceola wanted to learn the traditional way of bagging the gobblers bearing his family's name.

THE MYSTERY OF THE SWAMP MAGICIAN

When we arrived on the reservation late in the afternoon, we met friends of Jenkins who had been scouting and had heard and seen a few turkeys. However, the elusive gobblers had failed to respond to calling and had vanished. I unrolled my sleeping bag and donned 100-percent Deet repellent, which would be my shield during the entire trip from the clouds of mosquitos inundating the area just at dark.

That evening as supper was prepared over a Coleman stove, Marcelous Osceola and his wife, Etau, came into camp. We talked about the upcoming hunt. Then Osceola explained the native religion of his people -- the Green Corn Dance, a faith that attributed supernatural powers to the animal life of the swamp.

"If an owl flies through the camp during the annual festival of the Green Corn Dance, many believe the owl will capture someone's spirit, and they will die," Osceola told us. "Also some of my people believe because of tradition that the spirits of our ancestors are reincarnated in the wild turkeys."

When I asked Etau Osceola where this legend came from, she answered, "The wild turkey often appears and vanishes without ever making a sound. Sometimes we will spot a turkey in a cemetery and then it will be gone in the blinking of an eye. The Osceola turkey is a ghost-like creature that moves silently through the swamp. You only hear him when he wants to be heard, and you only see him when he wants to be seen. When an Osceola gobbler spots you, he vanishes. The Osceola turkey is an integral part of our people's history and heritage."

After listening to the Osceolas, I realized how the reputation of the ghost gobbler of the swamps paralleled the reputation of Osceola, the war chief of the mighty Seminoles. Cunning, elusive and mystical, they each dodged their pursuers with almost supernatural skills. When I asked Marcelous Osceola how he felt about hunting the bird many thought might be one of his ancestors, he said, "I eat plenty of wild turkeys. If one of them is dumb enough to get shot, he probably wasn't a very good ancestor anyway."

That night as I attempted to sleep in my tent, I thought about the legend of the Osceola turkey and experienced an uneasy feeling until the chirping of the crickets and the distant moaning of a bull alligator finally lulled my mind to sleep.

THE HUNT FOR AN OSCEOLA

Before first light, the camp was up. Soon Jenkins, Osceola and I were out listening for gobblers. After 10-minutes of silence, a swamp gobbler began to crow. When we determined the direction where the gobbler was, we climbed back into our truck and drove 1/2-mile to get closer to the bird. However, after 45-minutes of calling and listening, we could not find the tom.

In most areas of Florida, scouting is done more from a vehicle than on foot. Much of the land that is hunted is crisscrossed with woods roads and fence lines. Also because the land in many places is very marshy, wading through the swamps or walking through the palmettos can result in a snake encounter. You will be attacked by biting insects. Since you will make so much noise walking through palmettos and the leaves of the hardwood trees, travel by vehicle is a much more effective way to scout for gobbling turkeys. In most areas, these Florida turkeys are not spooked by cars and trucks. They hear vehicles every day on the ranches and in the woods and are not afraid of them. Scouting in a car or a truck will allow you to get much closer to a Florida turkey quicker than if you are on foot. Because the dense foliage, in many areas, you can drive within 150-to 200-yards of a gobbling bird.

"I can't believe I can't crank this gobbler up and make him talk," Jenkins commented with disgust in his voice. "The bird has vanished, and I don't know where he's gone. Let's go see if we can locate another one."

We drove about two miles and listened. Once more we heard a turkey gobble. Again when we went to where a tom should have been, the gobbler was no longer there.

Unlike hunting eastern turkeys, if you hear a bird gobble in Florida, you cannot assume automatically that you will have the opportunity to move to the bird or call the bird. Because the Osceola turkey has a very limited range and plenty of hunting pressure is exerted on most flocks of these birds, they are extremely wary and often call-shy, becoming silent and walking away from a call rather than responding to it.

In many areas of Florida, the best way to scout for turkeys is to use binoculars to look for the birds in fields and pastures from the roads. Often turkeys will fly from their roost over the wet, swampy ground and spend most of their days in fields or on the edges of fields. If you know the particular fields where a band of turkeys feed every day, the likelihood of bagging a gobbler near that field is greatly increased. An effective tool I have used when hunting the Osceola gobbler is to scout other fields after my morning hunt is over. Once I locate turkeys on the edge of a field, the next morning before daylight I will go to the edge of that field and listen for the turkeys to gobble. Many times I will be able to call the turkeys to me because I am set up in a place they normally come to, whether I am calling or not.

"There's a pasture where I always see turkeys in the morning," Osceola mentioned. "Maybe we'll spot a gobbler there."

We drove about five miles, climbed out of Osceola's truck and walked down a raised dirt road between two pastures to reach a back pasture where Osceola had watched turkeys before. After we had walked about 150-yards, Jenkins suggested that we stop and listen for toms.

Within five minutes, a gobbler reported, apparently in the back field where Osceola had thought he would be. We moved quickly down the road to reach the corner of the field. Just as Jenkins, who was out in front, came to the edge of the back field, he motioned for Osceola and me to get down.

Crawling back to us, Jenkins whispered, "A longbeard is out in the field, but we don't have a place to hide. I'm going to set up my portable blind on the edge of the road. John, you can move off the edge of the road into the ditch and up beside the field and watch the turkey with your binoculars. Marcelous, you stay here behind the blind, and I'll try and call the turkey to you."

As I belly crawled to the ditch, I listened to Jenkins quietly telling Osceola how the hunt should go. No question was in Jenkins' mind or mine that if the turkey came into range, Osceola would put the gobbler down. Osceola, who had shot competitively on the trap and skeet circuit for some years, was a certified master with a shotgun. If the bird was in range, years of training and shooting thousands of targets would make Osceola's aim deadly accurate.

Creeping through a small patch of briars to reach a vantage point to watch the drama unfold, I was confident in Jenkins' ability to call and Osceola's skill to shoot. The only unknown factor in the equation was whether or not the turkey would be willing to come to the call.

Peeking over the edge of the ditch and scanning the field with my binoculars, I could not see the gobbler. The tom had quit talking, and the field was empty. Because Jenkins and I were friends and had hunted together for many seasons, I knew what to expect next.

Jenkins is a patient hunter who disagrees with the idea that anyone should hunt turkeys aggressively. Because the birds of southern Florida receive so much hunting pressure, often calling less and waiting more are far more productive tactics for bagging these birds than the aggressive style of hunting commonly utilized in the northern part of the United States. A native Mississippian, Jenkins has been raised to a patient hunter.

Because we were roaming private lands and no other hunters should be competing with us for this bird, the slow, patient, little-calling tactic of the Deep South should prove to be the most effective technique to bring in this Osceola gobbler.

If you have the opportunity to hunt the Florida turkey on private lands, then little calling and tons of patience will be your best allies to take an Osceola tom.

Although I was eager to reach a vantage point to see the action, I was careful not to spook the gobbler. I knew Jenkins would provide a tongue lashing that would make the Seminole Indian War appear to be a minor disagreement between two close friends. For 10-long minutes of silence, the field was empty. Then I spotted a huge, black dot in the very back of the field.

Jenkins recalled later, "John, while you were crawling, the bird in the field gobbled. Just as he did, a second tom gobbled. When the turkey in the field heard the second tom gobble, he hushed and left the field. Apparently the tom in the woods was the dominant gobbler, because he flew into the field after the subordinate gobbler left."

Turkeys have a definite pecking order. Often when a gobbler that has been talking all morning falls silent, you may not have made a mistake in calling, and the tom may not have left the area. The original gobbling bird may be a subordinate tom that has called up a dominant gobbler. Once a dominant gobbler moves into an area and causes the subordinate gobbler to cease his calling, often the older, bigger bird will come to you silently. Knowing this fact of turkey hunting, always expect the turkey to move toward you when he ceases his gobbling. Do not get up to leave, because you will spook the bird coming to you.

However, on this particular morning, the gobbler did not move toward Jenkins and his calling. As I watched through my binoculars and studied this legendary ghost of the swamp, I saw a much darker bird than the eastern wild turkey. Although smaller in body than the eastern, the Osceola turkey was just as proud when he strutted and gobbled. When Jenkins began to call, the gobbler seemed to key in to the sound like a beagle dog locked into the fresh scent of a rabbit. The turkey gobbled, walked a few steps and then strutted. Next the tom ran a few steps, stopped, strutted and gobbled. The bird was coming, and I had a ringside seat for the show.

Back in the blind, Jenkins told Osceola, "That gobbler's coming in quick. Sit on your leg, and get braced to take the shot. When the turkey reaches the edge of that little ditch, I'll make him stop with my calling. He'll then stick his neck up. Shoot for the wattles where the feathers join the neck. By aiming there, you'll put more pellets in the turkey's kill zone."

Osceola waited anxiously as his forefathers historically had to bag turkeys in the palmettos. However, instead of a master-crafted shotgun and high brass shells, they used longbows and wooden arrows they had whittled from sticks. The gobbler continued to close ground rapidly while Jenkins sounded like the sexiest hen ever in the swamp. The bird moving toward us wasted no time trying to court this eager hen. When the gobbler was 20-yards in front of Jenkins and Osceola, Jenkins clucked loudly. The tom stopped and craned his neck.

Boom! The sound echoed throughout the swamp as the gobbler dropped in his tracks. When I arrived at a small wash, Jenkins was holding up a magnificent turkey and congratulating Osceola. Deep hues of burnt bronze and black reflected a green tint when the sun danced off the downed tom's feathers. With an eight inch long beard, this Florida gobbler was a fine trophy for Marcelous Osceola.

"Hunting like this must be the most exciting way in the world to take a turkey," Osceola observed with a big smile as he experienced the sheer joy that came from outsmarting a gobbler and bagging it the old way. "This is the first time I've ever shot a tom that close to me and looking at me. Usually I take them at 100-to 150-yards with my rifle. What a thrilling way to hunt! I want to learn to call and to hunt like this, which is much more fun than taking a bird with a rifle."

How tragic that Osceola and many other members of his tribe took up the ways of the white man and lost many of the hunting skills of their forefathers. The Europeans learned to call and hunt turkeys from the native Americans, like Osceola. But then our civilization enveloped theirs, and they lost many of their traditional skills or gave them up for more modern strategies. How appropriate that now Jenkins and I could reintroduce a native American to the method of hunting his ancestors had taught our ancestors --using calling ability and stalking skills to get in close to turkeys.

As Jenkins, Osceola and I headed back to camp, we discussed the future of the reservation's turkeys.

"Marcelous, if you and your friends want to have plenty of turkeys to hunt, don't take any hens for a year or two," Jenkins counseled. "Don't shoot the young gobblers. Hunt only the longbeards. The reservation has plenty of food and habitat for turkeys. If you'll begin to protect the turkeys and take only longbeards in the spring, then in just a year or two, you'll have more gobblers to hunt than you've ever had. Every morning in the spring when you get up to go turkey hunting, you'll have a longbeard to call."

"That's what I want," Osceola explained. "I'll learn to use this call and teach my brother how to call. Then we'll start hunting the way you guys do. Calling and hunting with a shotgun is a much more interesting way to take turkeys than shooting them at 100-yards with a high-powered rifle."

That night at camp, Osceola treated us to a Seminole feast. We ate fried alligator tail from an animal he just had taken the day before. The meat was delicious, and the conversation around the campfire was even better. We talked about the ways of the Seminoles, their past, present and future. We discussed the Osceola turkey and its future on the reservation. We talked more about the legends, myths and religion of the Seminoles.

The turkey the Seminoles hunt is shrouded in legend and history. The opportunity to hunt the spirit gobblers of the Florida Everglades with a descendant of the man they were named for is a memory that will be treasured as long as I am able to tell the tale of the spirit gobbler of Big Cypress Swamp.

CHAPTER 11 - BAGGING RIO GRANDES

Half asleep in the saddle, the cowboy listens to the light mooing of the herd that has been bedded down all night. His old Winchester 94 30/30 rifle fits snugly in the saddle holster on the side of his horse, and the leather of his saddle squeaks only slightly to the gentle swaying of the horseman as his buckskin mare walks among the longhorns.

Then off in the distance, the familiar sound of the cows wailing to the moon triggers a new sound just before daylight. From the cottonwoods near the creek, the thunderous roars of Rio Grande gobblers reverberate from the tops of the branches. On this day, the cowboy will feast on a turkey dinner.

Just before first light, the leather-chapped rider steers his steed toward the cottonwoods. Walking in the shallow creek bottom, he notices a turkey tail fanned on the edge of the rimrock. As the horse turns to go up a small wash, the Winchester is retrieved from the holster. A coyote howls, and the turkey gobbles.

70-yards out on the plains, three fine gobblers strut with their harem of hens. As the Winchester comes to the rider's shoulder, the cowboy's head lowers as if to pray. But instead, his cheek finds the cool, hard wood of the stock of the Winchester as he cocks the hammer, looks down the iron and lines up the sight on the end of the rifle with the V-notched sight on the receiver. When the aiming point locates the butt of the tom's wing, the hammer falls, the rifle reports, and the turkey tumbles.

Riding at a gallop now, the cowboy-turned-hunter retrieves his gobbler and ties the bird to his saddle horn. Then he rides back to the chuckwagon to present the cook an alternative for beef for the noontime meal.

This style of hunting was and still is the western tradition. The plainsmen of the old West rarely had use for shotguns. A rifle that could be carried on their saddles could take almost any game they encountered. With a rifle, they could defend their herds from rustlers and predators, they could harvest the game they needed to eat, and they could defend themselves from attack. The early frontiersmen saw little need for any weapons other than a pistol and a rifle.

As in most areas of the country, tradition dies hard in the West. The way your forefathers historically hunted has a direct influence on the way you hunt today.

The turkeys in the West never had been considered as much of a prize. Western hunters were beef eaters with an occasional deer, antelope and jack rabbit thrown in when times were tough. Although turkeys were plentiful, they were rarely in high demand by the cattlemen in Texas. Yard chickens provided a Sunday meal, and if you just had to have a turkey for Christmas and Thanksgiving, there were plenty of birds from which to choose.

The Rio Grande turkeys, found primarily in Texas, at times numbered around 500,000-birds just in Texas. These Texas turkeys did not experience nearly the hunting pressure the eastern turkeys did. The Rio Grande gobblers' primary enemies were not man but were the coyote, the fox and the bobcat.

However, today with the removal of many of these predators and the protection offered to these birds has resulted in a tremendous increase in Rio Grande populations. Some turkey hunters view the state of Texas and the other western states that home virgin Rio Grande gobblers as their Valhalla, the place of waiting between life and death where many of the dreams of the Vikings, the great Nordic warriors of ancient times, came true.

The Rio Grande is thought by many to be the easiest turkey for the hunter to take because in many areas of Texas, their numbers are very high, the hunting pressure is low, and large numbers of birds move into older age classes.

A couple of years ago, I had the rare opportunity to hunt on lands in Wheeler County, Texas, where the turkeys never had never been called to or hunted with a shotgun before. These virgin Rio Grande gobblers liked to hear calling and would come to you quicker than you could get your gun up. The two birds I took were four year olds that sported 1-1/2-inch spurs and weighed 22-pounds each.

The next year when I hunted in Sonora, Texas, I could hear thirty or forty turkeys gobble in the morning and saw plenty of turkeys all day. However, two days were required to bag a trophy Rio Grande bird.

HOW DESERT BIRDS ARE DIFFERENT

The Rio Grande gobbler presents a different challenge to the turkey hunter than either the Osceola or the eastern wild turkey does. Because trees are so scarce in the desert, finding one hundred birds in a small group of cottonwoods is not uncommon. Since the land is so flat and dry, the sound of a turkey's gobbling often can be heard from 1/2-to 3/4-mile away.

The Rio Grande turkey wakes up in the morning with his day already planned. This tom knows from the time he gobbles on the limb where he is going all day long. Even though he may answer your calling, if you do not take a stand along the route he plans to travel, you will not be able to bag the bird. I have been in a roost site before where thirty turkeys have been gobbling, and each time I call, a large percentage of those birds have answered. But when they fly down from the roost, every turkey has walked away from me without my ever getting a shot.

Generally the Rio Grande likes to hear more calling than the eastern turkey or the Osceola. Most Rios I have hunted must be called to incessantly to keep their attention and to make them come to me. More than likely, if you are hunting where Rio population numbers are high, you will call in three or four gobblers at one time rather than one gobbler like you will when you are calling easterns or Osceolas.

Usually, when the Rio Grande gobbler flies from the roost, he is going to feed. In desert areas, he most often has a trail he normally walks every day. These trails are often well-defined, just like deer trails. If you set up a calling position near one of these trails, you quickly and easily can call in a tom in the mornings.

After the birds have fed and the sun begins to heat up the floor of the desert, the Rio Grande gobbler searches for shade, which is another unique characteristic of the Rio. If you do not take him immediately after he flies down from the roost or on his way to a feeding site, there are two other places you can catch up to this bird. From 10:00 A.M. until late in the afternoon, the bird will be looking for shade and water. In the desert, taking a stand near a stock tank in the middle of the day often will produce a longbeard.

Allen Jenkins, one of my favorite hunting companions, and I once chased Rios all morning long before finding a stock tank out in a pasture at 11:00 A.M. When we called, several turkeys gobbled. However, no big trees or bushes were nearby where we could take a stand or hide. The only cover on the floor of the pasture was an abandoned, rusty, tin, calf feeder. Jenkins and I climbed inside the feeder, which was located between where the turkeys were and the stock tank. As we called, a flock of fifty turkeys with five or six longbeards in the flock started moving toward us. Three of the longbeards came toward the calf feeder where we were calling. When I finally squeezed the trigger on my Browning 5A three-inch magnum, the report of the rifle rattled around in that stock feeder making Jenkins and me feel like we were inside a bass drum just as a college football team scored a touchdown and an enthusiastic drummer pounded out his delight. Oftentimes, one of the most difficult problems associated with hunting the Rio Grande is finding a place to set up a stand because of the lack of cover.

HOW TO HUNT WHEN YOU DO NOT KNOW WHERE TO HUNT

If you are fortunate enough to hunt Rio Grande turkeys, often the landowner can tell you where he has seen turkeys. However, most Texas ranchers are not turkey hunters. If you are on a piece of property and do not know where to hunt, look for water. Most of the time when you locate a stream or a creek running through the land you are hunting, you will encounter Rios since water is a critical need for Rios because ...

- the turkeys need water to drink,

- much of the food the turkeys eat grows near water,

- the trees the turkeys roost in will be found near water, and

- the trees and the bushes growing along the water's edge will provide the shade the turkeys need to dodge the hot sun and the high temperatures found in the desert.

Hunting near water for Rios helps you be a more productive hunter since ...

- you can walk along the creekbanks or the edge of the water quietly without spooking turkeys and

- you can move through a larger area unseen by the turkeys if the creek has steep banks you stay below the banks.

When hunting for Rios in northern Texas with Preston Pittman, the president of Preston Pittman Game Calls, we found a creek on a piece of property and began to hunt at 1:00 P.M. By 3:00 P.M., we both had bagged longbeard toms, each weighing more than 22-pounds with 1-1/2-inch spurs, and had the opportunity to bag three or four more birds each. We simply stayed in a creek bottom and hunted from the edge of the water.

WHAT ARE THE BEST HUNTING STRATEGIES FOR RIOS

One of the mistakes most hunters make who hunt the Rio Grande gobblers for the first time is traveling to Texas and shooting the first big birds they see. Because of the large number of gobblers you often will find concentrated in one place, you will have a tendency to take the easy tom. However, because Rio Grande turkeys are not pressured nearly as hard as eastern gobblers are, if you will be patient, you may be able to harvest a trophy Rio.

When you hear Rios gobble in the morning, move in close to the roost site, and begin to call. The turkeys usually will gobble as they fly from the roost to their feeding area. One of the most frustrating problems with hunting Rios is that often this feeding region will not be near where you have set up to call the birds. You will want to chase the gobblers and try and catch up to them when they are going away from you. If you can get ahead of the birds, you may call them to you. However, if you cannot move ahead of the birds, take the first day of your hunt to learn how to hunt Rios.

The First Day Of A Rio Hunt

Notice the direction the turkeys fly to from the roost, because more than likely that same direction is where they will fly the next morning. Find the trails they use to go to feed. Try and keep up with the birds all day to learn the shady places they frequent and loaf in after they are through feeding. Look for water holes, streams and creeks where the turkeys can water, and notice the trails the birds use to return to their roost sites. If you take a day to learn how to hunt the Rios in the area where you are, you will be much more successful on the second day of your hunt.

Day Two of Rio Grande Hunt

The first time I hunted Rio Grande turkeys I wanted to shoot the first gobbler I saw. In the East, gobblers are rare and so difficult to take that a sportsman rarely passes up a longbeard. However, in the West, if you are hunting a place with plenty of birds, you may have the opportunity to see from twenty to thirty gobblers in a day, especially if you have taken the first day to scout and learn why and where the turkeys are going.

Hold your shot, use your binoculars, and look at the turkey's spurs before you shoot. In many areas, finding a bird with an 1-1/4-inch to 1-1/2-inch spurs is not too difficult. Instead of shooting the first turkey you spot, take your time, look over the birds, and pick the best gobbler that presents himself.

Also, if you will check fields late in the afternoon, you will see numbers of gobblers and can start to select more carefully the turkey you want to take. Most of the time, the same turkeys will appear in the same fields at about the same time of day. Then they usually will go to their roost along the same route, and you can intercept them.

A few years ago, I hunted with Cecil Carder of Houston, Texas, on the 4-M Ranch near Sonora, Texas. Although we had several opportunities to take turkeys on the second day of the hunt, fate always seemed to deal the birds the winning hand.

Then late in the afternoon about two hours before fly-up time, we spotted a big gobbler on the edge of a field with a harem of fifteen hens. Since a dry river bed skirted the field, Carder and I got into the river bed and sneaked around behind the turkeys. As we neared the spot where the tom strutted with his hens, we saw a natural dirt ramp cutting through the bank of the hill that went down to the river and up the other bank. This ramp looked like a natural place where a turkey could walk from the bank across the river bed and up the other bank. Carder and I decided to take a stand in a small plum thicket on the edge of the ramp. Although calling a longbeard gobbler away from his hens would be difficult at best, we knew this chance would be the only one we would have to bag this big bird this day.

Because the gobbler had so many hens with him, we did not call as aggressively as we normally would but chose instead to call a little and wait a lot. Each time we called, the gobbler answered aggressively. However, as the sun went down, the turkey still had not come to us. Finally in the last rays of light, just before fly-up time, the hens filtered through the plum thicket. The Mossy Oak camouflage Carder and I were wearing prevented the females from seeing us as the hens walked within six or eight feet of where we sat motionless.

I saw the ivory-colored head of a royal Rio moving toward the ramp. The bird was in full strut and about 30-yards from where I was sitting. In the low light, I looked through my Nikon scope mounted on my three inch magnum. Because of the brightness of the scope, I immediately spotted the gobbler's head. When the turkey was directly in front of me in full strut, Carder clucked one time on a pushbutton call. When he did, the big bird dropped his strut and craned his neck to see what had caused a hen to cluck.

At that moment, my crosshairs found the bird's wattles, I squeezed the trigger, and the gun reported. Although the Rio was a huge tom, when I reached him, his beard was only 2-1/2-inches long. I wondered if I had shot the beard off since this gobbler was fully mature with 1-1/2-inch spurs. When Carter saw the bird and looked at the beard, he began to laugh as he said, "Congratulations, John, you've just bagged the world's record jake."

I was convinced the turkey had to be at least three or four years old and was not a jake. After Carder gained his composure from laughing, he explained that sometimes Rios get mites in their beards that eat on these hairlike protrusions. Apparently this turkey had

had a case of mites that had eaten up most of his beard. We both laughed, put the big bird on my shoulders and headed back to camp.

Tips

To bag a Rio in an area where the turkeys have not experienced a lot of hunting pressure, call loud and call often. The Rio Grande gobbler is much more forgiving when you make mistakes in your calling than either the eastern or the Osceola. You can call more aggressively to Rios and even continue to call as the bird moves to you. Actually to keep a Rio Grande coming, you have to call continuously because of the high population of Rios in many regions. If you do not sound like a very aggressive hen, your gobbler will go to one of the six other hens he has close by. You must sound very sexy and be very demanding and enticing with your calling. You almost have to dare a Rio tom not to respond to you.

Hunting Rios is a way to get a novice turkey hunter hooked on the sport, because more than likely you will see numbers of Rios and be able to call to many birds. A beginning turkey hunter can practice his calling and make birds come to him. Also a bowhunter has a greater chance of success with the Rio Grande bird than any other type of wild turkey since Rio numbers are so high.

Traditionally, Rio Grandes have been hunted with rifles. When a western sportsman sees a turkey at 100-to 150-yards, he shoots the tom with his rifle and seldom employs any of the strategies easterners use to hunt turkeys. However, today, more and more Lone Star State hunters are shotgun hunting for Rio Grande gobblers.

To hunt Rios, you must is be in good physical condition. A hunter must cover more ground to locate and call turkeys in Texas than he does in the East. I may walk five miles in the morning looking for a Rio because these toms may travel three or four miles in a day before returning to their roost.

Binoculars are also much more important to successfully hunting Rios in Texas than eastern wild turkeys in states like Pennsylvania and Alabama. You can spot a turkey from much longer distances in Texas than in the more wooded East where you may not be able to see 50-yards. You need to know whether the bird is a gobbler or a hen before you begin the hunt.

Camouflage is another critical ingredient to successfully hunting Rios. Brown camouflage is helpful cover for the desert areas. Unlike hunting for easterns, you will find the western turkey's terrain usually bleak. The sneaking and crawling methods behind bushes and ground cover traditionally used in the East will not work. However, if you are hunting creek bottoms, you still will see some green.

Tactics

A problem associated with hunting Rio Grandes is the misconception that because there is so little cover to set up next to, utilizing a blind is a more efficient way for hunting these desert turkeys. I too adhered to this philosophy until I tested portable blinds for Rios. But if the wind causes your blind to move or flap, you will spook more turkeys than you take. The best place to set up a portable blind, if you intend to use one to bag a Rio, is on the downwind side of a big tree. The more trees and cover you can have around a blind, the less likely it is to flap in the breeze. Another trick to employ when using a blind to hunt Rios is to lean brush and limbs up against it. This practice breaks up the square or round construction of the blind and makes it more natural looking.

Yet another important key to taking Rios is to disregard the obvious. In most areas of Texas, baiting is permitted for turkeys. The obvious place to take a stand is close to a feeder. Then you can bag the birds as they come in to feed. However, many animals will come to the feeder besides the turkeys -- including javelina, deer and coyotes -- and often will spook the turkeys coming to a feeder. Most of the time a large number of turkeys will be at a feeder, which also means more eyes will be looking for you.

A better tactic if you are hunting a place with a feeder is to take a stand along a trail the Rios use to go to and from the feeder. Probably the turkeys have learned that a feeder not only represents food but also a place where danger often is present. Besides man, other predators remain close to a feeder since birds congregate there. Many times turkeys will approach a feeder cautiously and will be looking for anything out of the ordinary near the feeder. If you take a stand 100-to 150-yards away from the feeder, the birds are not nearly as likely to spot you.

For me, sitting close to a feeder and killing a turkey is not the sport of turkey hunting. Bagging a Rio is not nearly as important to me as having the opportunity to hunt the turkey. To make that bird come to me, to convince him I am the sexiest hen he ever has talked to, and to get that bird so excited he performs an unnatural act like coming to a hen rather than making the hen come to him is the purest form of turkey hunting and makes me a turkey hunter. When you learn where the bird wants to go, why he wants to go there and when he will show up, and then take a stand along the route he will travel to call him to you, then you are a turkey hunter. When you sit beside a feeder and shoot a bird that has been baited in to feed on corn, you are a turkey shooter.

Many easterners believe the Rio Grande is an easy bird to bag. But remember, even though the Rio Grande tom has not been hunted for 200-years as eastern turkeys have and has not felt as much hunting pressure, some turkeys in some places in Texas have been hunted heavily. After the first season of shotgun pressure, these turkeys get smart about hunters and often become very difficult to hunt.

The Rio Grande gobbler is the turkey of the West, the cowboy, the cattleman, the sheep rancher and the oil baron. A part of Americana, the Rio Grande is exciting to hunt. To complete your hunting experience, make a trip to the country of the longhorn, and go in search of the bird of Pecos Bill and the other legends of the West.

CHAPTER 12 - HUNTING MERRIAMS

Usually, the hunter will see and hear more turkeys in the West where the Merriams live, be able to call louder and more aggressively to the turkeys in the West and have a much more enjoyable hunt in the West than in the East. However, before any sportsman rushes out to buy a ticket and head to the Big Sky Country, he should realize even the most beautiful rosebush is guarded by prickly thorns. In the desert areas which are part of the Merriams's range, just about everything a hunter sit on, bumps into or brushes up against will stick him. Even though a sportsman finds enough cover to hide behind to call a turkey to him, he must make sure he has some type of pad or cushion between himself and the ground and whatever he leans up against.

If you do not hunt the desert Merriams, your option is the mountain Merriams. These turkeys live at altitudes where flatlanders never should hunt. On some of the Merriams' high range, you must suck in four mouthfuls of air to equal one mouthful of air on flat ground.

I have found the muscles in my body do not like to hunt the Merriams that live at high altitudes. To prepare for a mountain Merriams hunt if you are a flatlander, climb stadium steps daily for at least six to eight weeks before you go on the hunt. Plan to arrive a day or two early at your destination to allow your body to acclimate to the altitude. When you hear a Merriam gobble, plan to take twice as long to reach him as you will if you are hunting Osceolas, Rios or easterns. But Merriam gobblers are one of my favorite turkeys to hunt and have taught me many lessons I have not learned when hunting flat ground turkeys. Also Merriams are beautiful birds and majestic to watch.

To get a turkey hunter fired up about turkey hunting, let him hunt Merriams. He can hear the birds from great distances, and many western states allow you to hunt all day long. In some eastern states, the law requires you to stop hunting at noon. Also, these western turkeys are much more vocal in the afternoon and even up until an hour after dark, which means they are much easier to roost and more fun to listen to than eastern gobblers, which rarely gobble in the afternoon and seldom from the roost at dark.

I suggest when you are hunting unfamiliar terrain that you employ the services of a guide or hunt with a local. Locals know the land in an area and generally have pinpointed where turkeys will be or will go, which can save you hours of guesswork hunting. They also know the shortest distance to travel to get to a turkey as well as the shortest distance back to your car. You will increase your odds for finding and taking gobblers and be able to come out of the mountains once you get into them.

I had been turkey hunting for six weeks straight the spring I went on my first Merriam hunt near Raton, New Mexico. A turkey had gobbled at the top of the hill, and I headed toward him on a dead run. I was in shape. I had been walking and running three to five miles a day and had turkey hunted across 3-to 10-miles a day, three to four times a week for six weeks since turkey season had opened. I thought a short sprint up the hill to get to my first Merriam gobbler should not be difficult. However, after I had covered 50-yards, my breathing was very labored, my legs were weak, my muscles were quivering, and my chest was burning. If I did not get more air, I felt probably would die. I had failed to consider one of the most critical keys to success for taking mountain Merriams -- less oxygen is present, and you tire quicker at high altitudes.

The turkeys we were hunting were at 7,000-feet. The terrain made hunting Merriam one of the most physically demanding hunts of my life. Although Merriam turkeys inhabit a wide range from Nebraska to Minnesota, South Dakota,

Washington, California and New Mexico to Colorado, the Merriams are birds of the mountains in many areas. Merriams love altitude and usually stay high.

TACTICS FOR BAGGING MERRIAMS

I soon learned the best way to find and take Merriams was to stay on the mountaintops and call to the birds below me. However, where I hunted, the Merriams were not as concentrated in large numbers as Rio Grande turkeys generally were but were scattered over vast expanses of mountains. I constantly was having to make the decision of whether to walk the tops of the mountains and continue to call until I found a bird on the mountain I was hunting or cross the mountain to get to turkeys I heard on nearby ridgetops. I always chose to go to the turkeys.

A turkey hunter cannot resist moving to a gobbling turkey, just like a cat must chase a mouse. If you ever have watched a cat chase a mouse in a barn, sometimes the cat is so intent on catching the rat and running so hard that when a rat ducks into a hole in the side of the barn wall, the cat will collide with the wall without being able to stop.

Most true turkey hunters will follow that same course of action when hunting Merriam gobblers. If the only turkey you hear is three mountaintops away, then you feel you must go to that bird, even though the walk severely will test your physical endurance. The bad news is that the Merriam gobbler walks much more than the eastern gobbler, the

Osceola or the Rio Grande. By the time you reach the mountaintop where the Merriam tom is gobbling, often that bird will have walked over two other mountains and be gobbling from another ridgetop.

Climbing Above

To bag a Merriam, get above him. If the turkey is gobbling on the side of a mountain, you may not have to go all the way to the top of the mountain. However, at least reach a calling position above the bird, and try and call him up to you.

The Merriam gobbler, like the Rio Grande, is a fun bird to call to, because this turkey species likes to gobble and generally enjoys hearing plenty of calling. The terrain and the weather are the most difficult problems you will encounter when hunting the Merriam turkey.

Working With The Wind

On another hunt on the Smith Ranch in New Mexico, I encountered another problem with hunting the Merriam. This particular piece of property was very dry and arid with turkeys primarily found in or near the canyons on the property. For three days, the wind blew so hard while we hunted the turkeys we rarely heard a tom gobble. Standing on a rimrock and listening to the howling of the wind reminded me of the song "Moriah" from the Broadway production, "Paint Your Wagon." If ever a bird should have been called Moriah, it was the Merriam turkeys living on this ranch.

The wind on the mountains and in the plains where Merriams are found often will reduce the distance at which you can hear a turkey gobble. On this particular hunt, we remained on the floor of the canyon and waited for the wind to die down. After an hour and a half wait on the third day, the wind finally ceased.

As soon as a calm fell over the canyon, we heard a turkey gobbling from the cottonwoods along the edge of the creek in the canyon. We got down in the creek and walked under the lip of the bank to take up a calling position about 100-yards from the bird. The turkey immediately answered our calling and started coming to us. When the gobbler was 32-steps from us, my Remington 3-inch magnum SP with a Nikon scope reported. The bird tumbled. As if some mystical hand controlled the wind, as soon as the shot was fired and the gobbler fell, the wind strongly blew again --almost blowing the feathers off the downed bird. In three days of hunting, we only had that one hour and a half break from the wind, but that time was long enough to hear and call my Merriam.

Hunting Merriams On Horseback

Because the hunt for the Merriam can be so physically grueling, many westerners hunt these turkeys on horseback. Using a saddle holster for my shotgun and saddlebags for my shells, lunch and water, a horseback hunt for Merriams is my favorite way to go after the mountain gobblers.

Mountain-trained horses can climb steep, rocky paths and walk down into deep gorges without stumbling. If you have to cross three mountains to reach a bird, you can go quicker and easier on a horse than you can by foot. Because the horse is a natural part of the environment where the Merriams are found, usually a horse will not spook a gobbler nearly as quickly as a man on foot will. Another advantage to riding a horse is when you reach an area where you want to call, you can tie up the horse or hobble it and move in close to the birds. Then if the gobbler comes in quickly, you will not be breathing hard, and your muscles will not quiver from exhaustion. You can hold your shotgun much steadier, and you are less likely to miss the bird.

Also if you are riding a horse and take a bird, the tom can be tied onto the saddlehorn by his feet and carried out of the woods effortlessly. Besides, horseback hunting for gobblers is the traditional western way to find and bag the birds.

I enjoy hunting the four major subspecies of gobblers in the United States, learning how Americans in other areas of the country hunt turkeys and then using their styles of hunting. For instance, in the South, I like to hunt swamp gobblers because that type of area is traditional to my concept of the South. In Florida, I prefer to hunt in the palmettos and around the big fields, which is Florida Indian hunting for Osceolas. In the North, I enjoy hunting mountains and croplands -- the traditional turkey hunting for that region. In Texas, the cottonwoods are as much a part of the hunt as the Rio Grande gobblers themselves. Then when I am hunting Merriams, riding horses like the early plainsmen, frontiersmen, fur traders and mountainmen once did adds a sense of history to the hunt that both excites and intrigues me. Too, I have learned from experience that riding a horse up a mountain where the air is thin is much easier than trying to walk or run up that same mountain.

Recognizing The Importance Of Shade And Water

If you are hunting the desert country of Texas and New Mexico, two critical factors associated with finding and taking Merriams are shade and water. Since water is often scarce in the West, turkeys may frequent stock tanks and watering holes to survive.

Because most of the East is heavily timbered, shade is not a primary concern of eastern gobblers. But in the West where the sun beats down hard on the barren ground, and little shade is present, turkeys often will be in some type of shade during the hot times of the day. By hunting stock tanks and shade in the middle of the day, hunters increase their chances to locate and bag western turkeys, particularly the Merriams.

Hiding From Merriams

Utilize a blind when you are hunting open and arid terrain. With no cover to hide behind, you must carry a portable blind with you. Then you will have cover anywhere you want to take a stand.

However, the intense wind may prohibit the use of a blind in the West. Turkeys know the terrain they inhabit, and western turkeys may notice a blind. When the wind blows, and the blind starts moving, often that movement will spook a turkey. A blind may not be the best solution for a lack of cover when a hunter is trying to set up on western toms.

Camouflage clothing is a turkey hunter's best bet to be able to hide from gobblers, whether they are eastern or western. Turkeys are the most intelligent gamebirds in North America and have keen hearing and eyesight that can spot movement and colors.

Coursing A Gobbler

The term coursing refers to how to get from where you are to where you think a turkey is. This critical tool of woodsmanship is one every turkey hunter must learn, especially in the West. In the East, coursing a gobbler is not too difficult. Because of the abundant foliage in the East, often you will not hear a turkey gobble more than 1/4-to 1/2-mile.

But when a Merriam sounds off in the West, he may be standing on the top of one mountain gobbling with you two or three mountains away. Although the tom may sound as though he is close by, you may have to travel two to three miles to where the bird is as well as climb mountains, go down steep hills and travel through ravines.

Too, the sound of a turkey's gobbling may travel differently in the West than it does the East. The air is usually thin and clear, which causes sound to travel further. But the gobble also will bounce off canyons and echo through the mountains. A hunter can be fooled into believing a turkey is where he is not because of the route his gobbling travels.

Generally I listen to a Merriam turkey gobble much longer before I make the decision to go to him than I will any of the other subspecies of turkeys. Often a turkey will turn in several directions when he gobbles. Only when that bird faces more than one direction and gobbles can you tell exactly where he is. You still are operating from a best-guess philosophy.

When you hunt Merriams, wait longer, listen more, and if possible, have a friend listen 20-to 30-yards away from you. Your odds of going to the area where the bird is gobbling will be much greater.

Merriams, which seem to form bigger flocks than eastern turkeys, may have two or more dominant gobblers in a large flock. Calling the toms away from their flock may be very difficult. Your best chance is to work a lone bird rather than a flock. If in the mornings the weather is warm, I anticipate the weather will change drastically, the wind begin to howl, and the temperatures drop. To dress for these unexpected conditions, I carry a lightweight, 10X Gore-Tex camouflage rainsuit in the back of my turkey hunting vest, which is as effective a windbreaker as it is a rainsuit. If you are dressed in lightweight cotton or of chamois clothing for turkey hunting, the fingers of Jack Frost will dig through the cotton and chill your skin. Putting on the outer shell of the rainsuit helps you defend yourself from Jack Frost, remain camouflaged and cover the noise of your movement.

Often in the Northwest you may have to hunt in snow. You may locate a bird one day, get up the next morning to move to that turkey and then not be able to reach him because of an overnight snow storm, which has caused hazardous road conditions. Do not forget to carry extra clothes, since the weather may be very cold, even in the spring when hunting Merriams.

Binoculars and Spotting Scope

Another critical piece of equipment for hunting Merriams is a quality pair of binoculars or a spotting scope. Merriams never seem to gobble close to where I am, and I rarely see a Merriam close to me. Before I have made a 45-minute stalk and then peeked up over the rim of a canyon only to discover I have been stalking a hen instead of a gobbler. If you see turkeys on a distant hilltop, in the base of a canyon or at the foot of a mountain, you will have plenty of time to set up a scope and study the birds.

Spotting scopes and binoculars are especially effective when the wind is high and hearing turkeys gobble is difficult. On a windy day, you probably will see more turkeys than you hear. Your ability to see at a distance is much more essential than your ears and your ability to hear a bird gobble.

Remember when using a spotting scope or binoculars to learn if a gobbler is in a group of turkeys to also wait an extra moment or two to study the direction in which the turkeys are moving. Take a course that will put you slightly ahead of the birds. To make this judgement call, like a submarine captain you must determine direction and speed of travel order to pinpoint the spot where you need to be to take the shot.

Osceolas and eastern gobblers walk somewhat slowly and cautiously since they travel through thick cover that may be dangerous. The turkeys of the West, however, like the Merriams and the Rios, are accustomed to crossing open terrain. They have learned the faster they move across open ground, the better their chances of survival are. If you have hunted eastern turkeys and come West to hunt Merriams, once you spot a gobbler with your optics and decide on a course to take to intercept that bird, double or triple the distance you normally will get in front of an eastern gobbler. The Merriams usually will cover ground at a rate two to three times faster than either the Osceola or the eastern turkey will. Although no statistical data confirms this assumption, the only way to learn this fact is to hunt Merriams enough to know that unless you use this barometer, you always will be taking a stand where the birds were instead of where the birds are.

Compass

Unless you live in the area where you hunt Merriams, getting lost is much easier in the mountains of the West than in the East. The western United States does not have as many fences, roads, fields and firebreaks as the East. In the home range of the Merriams, you may walk all day and never see a sign left by another human. Therefore, the chances of getting lost on a Merriam hunt, especially in the mountains, are much greater than your becoming lost when you are hunting other races of turkeys.

Also since the sound of a Merriam gobbling usually travels far because of the terrain, you often will cross plenty of country before you reach the bird. You may get to a spot where a turkey has been gobbling, find that he has ceased his gobbling, hear another bird begin to talk, start chasing the second bird and forget where you are, how you have gotten there and how to get back. Because I am very efficient at getting lost in the mountains of the West, I know the first assumption you must make when you decide to hunt Merriams --especially without a guide --is that you will get lost. Then you will not fear being lost. Simply carrying a compass in your pocket will not help you find your way home. You need to pick out landmarks on the property where you will be hunting and use your compass to determine what direction of travel you need to take from those landmarks to get back to your vehicle.

Survival Equipment

Take standard survival equipment with you, including waterproof matches, a space blanket, extra food, some lightweight rope or strong string, aspirins for the headache you are sure to incur once you realize you do not know how to reach home and anything else that will make an overnight stay in the outdoors easier. The fear of being lost is much like the fear of having a wreck in your vehicle. If you realize it can happen, you will be much more cautious and more aware of where you are, where you have gone and how to reach home.

Experts agree the two biggest differences between hunting eastern and western gobblers are terrain and the amount of hunting pressure the turkeys experience. Although more gobblers may live in the West, and these birds may be easier to call and take since they are not as familiar with hunters and/or calls as eastern turkeys are, as soon as hunting pressure is applied, the easy gobblers of the West can become just as difficult to call and bag as their eastern cousins. Many tough, old, western gobblers are just as elusive as eastern toms. The calls and many of the hunting strategies eastern turkey hunters have employed successfully for years will produce longbeards when they go West to hunt Merriams.

CHAPTER 13 - BAGGING TURKEYS WITH BLACK POWDER

I was caught as unprepared as a baby on his first birthday. The turkey had gobbled less than 30-yards away. As we stood in the middle of the road, we had no place to run and no place to hide. We dropped to our knees. I quickly put my knees in front of me and my CVA trapper shotgun on one knee. I cocked the hammer and took the plastic nipple protector off the nipple and cap.

"Can you see him, John?" Bo Pitman whispered.

"No, there's a little hump in the road in front of me, I can't see him, even though I can hear him," I answered back quietly.

By now the gobbler was screaming, and the leaves on the trees quivered from the force of his gobble. Pitman had his bow and arrow, and I had my blackpowder shotgun. We had planned this hunt to be a primitive weapon hunt. We had agreed that Pitman would take the first shot offered. If he could not get the shot or if he missed the shot, I would back him up with my smoke pole.

"I can't draw, John," Pitman said in a low voice. "You'll have to take the shot. The bird's at 20-yards. Go ahead and shoot him."

"I still can't see the bird because of the rise in the hill," I quietly explained. "Is the gobbler to the left or right of my gun barrel?"

"He's straight in front of you," Pitman observed. "He's less than 18-yards. Please take the shot."

But because of my position below the hill, I still could not see the bird. Pitman was sitting less than 6-feet from me. Yet he could watch the bird over the hill. "He's in full strut, John," Pitman reported. "Take the shot."

The tom was so close I could hear him spit when he drummed, his feathers drag the ground and snap forward when they caught on a limb and his heavy feet crush the ground. I was so close I almost could feel the bird breathing. I realized he would see us and then be gone at any time.

But finally, just over the top of the hill, I spotted the gobbler's white crown of ivory. Still some brush stood between me and the turkey. I knew the foliage would absorb the lead before it could get to the bird's head if I took the shot.

My cheek was on the stock, the hammer was back, and the bead on my blackpowder shotgun was superimposed over the wattles on the gobbler's neck. Because the turkey knew he should be seeing the hen at this range, he became very nervous. He putted, made two quick steps forward and stopped. His neck went up like a periscope, and I let the hammer fall. When the gun reported, the area in front of my face filled with gray smoke. Pitman was up and running before I could gain my feet and reached the bird before I did. We discovered there had been no need to hurry since the blackpowder shotgun had performed for me like it had for the early frontiersmen.

BLACKPOWDER GUNS FOR HUNTING TURKEYS

Most blackpowder shotguns today are cylinder bore, which means they are straight pieces of pipe that are not choked or narrowed down to tighten the pattern. For this reason, oftentimes taking a turkey at more than 12-to 20-yards is difficult. The pattern may spread out and not be effective at distances any further than this.

However, a blackpowder shotgun on the market that is fitted with screwin chokes is Connecticut Valley Arm's (CVA) Trapper shotgun. You can have a full choke barrel by simply screwing one of these new choking systems into the Trapper, which was designed by CVA for the growing sport of hunting turkeys with black powder. Not only does this single shot blackpowder shotgun have a screwin choking system, it also has posts for a sling and a recoil pad to help take the beating out of a turkey shotgun and allow you to spend more time on the range sighting in the gun.

Although CVA and other manufacturers do produce double barrel blackpowder shotguns, most of these are also cylinder bore. Even though you gain another shot with a double barrel, you still lose the tightness of the pattern.

I prefer the CVA Trapper for blackpowder hunting turkeys. When I aim at the wattles on a turkey head target, seventeen shots will be in the turkey's head and neck area at 30-yards with a full choke screwin tube. Without the tube, only one to three shots will be in this same target at this distance.

I made this discovery by accident when I hunted Osceola turkeys in Florida with Dick Kirby of Quaker Boy Calls. I screwed the choke out of my gun and loaded the gun with 1-1/8-ounces of powder and 1-1/8-ounces of shot by volume. Next I put in a plastic shot cup, poured in the shot and placed the overshot patch over the load. I screwed the choke back in, aimed and shot the target. The charge produced exactly what I had expected -- seventeen shots in the target.

I then reloaded the gun to let Kirby shoot. But when he fired two different times, I could see the pattern begin to lay down at about 15-yards. The shot continued to fall on the ground all the way to the target. When we checked, he only had put two shots in the pattern. He fired the gun three more times but had the same results each time. Finally we realized that after the first time I had shot, we had forgotten to screw the choke back in the gun after we reloaded. Once we returned the choke to the barrel of the gun, it produced the dense pattern it had in the past.

That consistent fifteen to seventeen shot pattern is the reason I choose to black powder turkey hunt with this gun. When I squeeze the trigger on a gun, I want to be sure I have a better than reasonable chance to down the bird. There is no more sickening feeling than knowing you have made a good hit on a turkey and then watching the bird run off because the pattern is so loose you have not hit the vital organs.

LOADS FOR BLACKPOWDER TURKEYS

When you blackpowder hunt, you have an advantage over the conventional shotgun hunter because you can modify each individual load. You can improve the pattern of your blackpowder shotgun in several different ways.

You can use more or less powder. Most blackpowder shotguns can handle 1-1/8-to 1-1/4-ounces of powder. 1-1/8-ounces of Pyrodex is equal to 80-grains of 2F black powder. The 1-1/4-ounce charge of Pyrodex is equal to 90-grains of 2F black powder. You can utilize either Pyrodex or black powder when formulating your charges.

The choice of powder also can be changed according to weather conditions. Generally, 2F black powder is preferred on rainy days or days when the humidity is very high. This old conventional black powder does not seem to absorb as much moisture as Pyrodex does. However, blackpowder hunters often argue about this theory. On clear, dry days, often Pyrodex is preferred because it tends to burn cleaner.

By testing both powder charges, you can determine which charge produces the best pattern for you. For me, the 1-1/8-ounce charge usually yields a denser pattern. Often when I test the 1-1/4-ounce charge, the additional powder tends to blow the pattern out -- spreading the shot over a wider area. The shot does not stay as dense in the target area as it does when I use the 1-1/8-ounce charge. However, each gun shoots somewhat differently, and the combination of wadding and shot may have various effects with each of these two charges.

Another method of improving your pattern without adding or reducing your powder charge is the amount or type of overpowder wadding or cushion you use. If you select a cardboard kind of overpowder wadding, you often can change your pattern by trimming the thickness of the cardboard to increase or decrease the size of the wadding.

Yet another way to tighten your pattern is to use the plastic shot cups like those found in modern day shotgun shells. I prefer this type of wadding because I believe less deformity occurs in the shot when the powder is ignited and the shot travels down the barrel than when using the cardboard type wadding. The modern plastic shot cup seems to have a better cushion in it to absorb some of the shock when the powder explodes. This shock-absorbing feature of the modern plastic shot cup prevents the lead pellets from being smashed together and deformed as much when the powder explodes.

An advantage to utilizing the plastic shot cup is this particular kind of wadding encases the lead shot in a protective covering as it travels down the barrel, which also seems to aid in preventing deformity of the shot by keeping the shot from hitting the sides of the barrel as it travels the length of the barrel before it exits. Once the shot leaves the barrel, the plastic shot cup seems to hold the shot together longer, which I think tends to produce a tighter pattern than if the shot spreads out as soon as it leaves the barrel like a cardboard wadding permits.

However, this opinion of mine differs from many blackpowder hunters who believe the cardboard kind of wadding is more traditional and shoots just as tight a pattern as a plastic shot cup. Use the wadding system that produces the best pattern for you and your gun. Regardless of which type of wadding system you utilize, you must use an overshot cardboard patch to keep the shot from rolling out the end of the barrel.

Another option that determines pattern density is the amount of pressure you use to pack your load. Many blackpowder shotgunners are convinced the overpowder wadding and the overshot wadding must be rammed home and forced down the barrel snugly. However, if you pack the powder and the shot tight in the barrel by adding more pressure to the ramrod, you can decrease the size of the volume of the powder and increase the rate at which it expands. If you ram your shot and cup home too hard, you may create such a tight compression of the powder you may blow your shot pattern out.

I particularly enjoy blackpowder hunting with a shotgun for turkey or any other game because I can customize my loads with powder, patches and shot until I get the type of shot pattern I want for that day of hunting. I have determined that my best load is 1-1/8-ounces of powder, a plastic shot cup, 1-1/8-ounces by volume of No. 6 shot and a cardboard overshot patch.

I have experimented with duplex loads mixing No. 4 shot and No. 6 shot together, and even combining No. 2, No. 4 and No. 6 shot. However, I have found that for the gun I shoot, the No. 6 shot produces the densest pattern at 30-yards. Remember, each gun patterns differently. You may discover that No. 4s or No. 7-1/2s will produce a better shot pattern in your gun. The more pellets you can put in a turkey head target at 30-yards, the better your odds will be for bagging a bird with a blackpowder shotgun.

BLACKPOWDER ACCESSORIES

I have found a few accessories essential for the blackpowder turkey hunter.

Sling

I prefer to have a sling on my shotgun. Just because you are carrying a blackpowder gun does not mean your hunt for the gobbler will be any different. Since often you will have to cover long distances in a day, a sling can make carrying a gun much more comfortable.

Nipple Protector

I also like to use a hard plastic nipple protector, which allows me to carry my gun at half cock with the cap on the nipple without the danger of the gun going off. When I utilize a nipple protector, I also can cock my gun when I sit down to call a gobbler. I leave the nipple protector on the nipple until the turkey is close and then simply slide the nipple protector off the nipple to be ready to fire. This system eliminates my having to cock the hammer and the turkey's possibly hearing the click of the hammer's being cocked, which may spook a gobbler.

Cap Guard

This device is a small plastic ring which secures the cap to the nipple.

Muzzle Protector

I also use some type of muzzle protector and particularly like the rubber finger cots. This soft latex rubber protection can be rolled over the end of the barrel and prevent moisture from getting in the barrel while not prohibiting the smooth flow of the shot out of the barrel.

Recoil Pad

A recoil pad on the butt of the shotgun allows me to shoot without receiving a blue shoulder which often accompanies shooting a blackpowder shotgun many times during one day.

Fiberglass Ramrod

Another modification I believe is an advantage for the blackpowder hunter is the fiberglass ramrod. I probably am the world's worst at breaking wooden ramrods. But a fiberglass ramrod solves this problem for me.

Cleaning Jag and Patch Puller

I also carry an extra cleaning jag and a patch puller with me because I have gotten my cleaning jag stuck before and have lost a patch down the barrel while cleaning it. Without these two accessories, your hunt will be spoiled.

Speedloaders

I also prefer to use speedloaders to carry additional powder charges and shot into the field. The speedloader lets me pre-measure my shot and powder and put these loads in small cylinders I can carry in my shirt pocket with several overshot patterns and the same number of shot cups. Then I greatly reduce the amount of equipment I have to carry in the field if I need to reload while hunting.

Possibles Tool

A problem you face when blackpowder hunting turkeys is carrying all the tools in the field to solve any problems you may have with your shotgun including nipple picks, nipple wrenches, screwdrivers, knives and other equipment. This equipment can weigh you down and be clumsy to carry. My CVA possibles tool folds up like a Swiss army knife and contains several tools in one, compact, knife-like accessory.

Although you can carry many other accessories for blackpowder hunting, this equipment I have mentioned can fit easily in my pants pocket or in a pocket of my hunting vest.

TRICKS OF THE TRADE

Reducing Misfires

One of the worst things that ever can happen to a turkey hunter who uses black powder is to find a gobbling bird, call that turkey up, have him within range, squeeze the trigger and have a misfire. Although this problem does occur, I have found a method to reduce the chances of a misfire. Before I go out in the morning, after I have loaded my blackpowder gun, I remove the nipple and pour a few grains of powder down the nipple hole. Then I take my nipple pick and clean the nipple one more time to make sure I have a clear channel for the fire from the cap to go down the nipple and ignite the powder. Next I place a small plastic ring called a cap guard over the cap, which secures the cap to the nipple.

Understanding Your Effective Range With Black Powder

When I am calling up a turkey I plan to take with a conventional shotgun, I usually think my maximum effective range, even with a 3-inch magnum 12-gauge, is 35-yards. However, most of the time I will not take a shot unless the bird is at 30-yards or less. I generally apply this same extra 5-yard measuring device when hunting turkeys with black powder.

Even though I know I am deadly effective at 30-yards with my blackpowder gun, I prefer the turkey to be at 25-yards or less. Although I have bagged birds with a blackpowder gun at 12-yards, I do not advise your letting the tom get that close. The pattern on your shotgun will not have the opportunity to spread out as much at that close range.

I always wait for a clean shot on the head and neck area. If the turkey does not present that clean shot, I do not take a shot. However, I do not wait for a perfect shot, because many times the turkey will see you and run off before you get a perfect shot. Once the gobbler is within that 25-yards where I have decided to take him, then I take the shot when he sticks his head up and presents a shot.

Realizing The Precision and Thought Involved In Black Powder Turkey Hunting

Blackpowder hunting for gobblers is not that much different from conventional shotgun hunting for turkeys. The primary differences are:

- you must formulate your own shot.

- more chances exist that something can go wrong.

- you usually have to let the bird get closer than you do with a conventional shotgun.

- you have to be able to solve the problem of cocking the hammer.

- you have to be conscious of keeping your powder dry.

- you must have a checklist you go through every morning before you hunt, including...

...am I loading properly, and do I have the right amount of powder?

...have I seated the shot cup properly?

...have I put in the proper amount of shot?

...have I put in the overshot patch?

...have I cleaned the nipple and added additional powder?

...have I put on the nipple protector?

...have I put on the barrel protector?

...have I got speedloaders on hand loaded with the proper amount of shot and powder?

...do I have extra caps?

.. do I have extra shot cups and patches?

...do I have my possibles tool?

...do I have the accessories I need in the field if something goes wrong with my gun?

Turkey hunting by its very nature is a difficult sport. The birds often can be hard to find, difficult to call and practically impossible to get in close enough for a shot. When you further handicap yourself by hunting with a blackpowder gun, some people think you drastically reduce your odds for success. However, I believe just the opposite.

I like the precision of blackpowder hunting and fine tuning my equipment. I enjoy giving a turkey an extra advantage, which causes me to use skills as a turkey hunter better. Blackpowder hunting for turkeys also provides an added challenge and makes the trophy far more valuable and more exciting to hunt than when you utilize conventional weapons.

In most turkey camps I go into, often I will be the only blackpowder hunter present. Usually most hunters begin to tell me why I will not be able to take a turkey with a blackpowder gun. However, if I am fortunate enough to bag a blackpowder bird, many of those same skeptics will decide to take up the challenge of trying to bag a bird with black powder.

Two of the fastest growing sports in America today are turkey hunting and blackpowder hunting. For me, blackpowder hunting is a logical progression in my evolution of being a turkey hunter. A turkey hunter must first learn to call and hunt turkeys with a conventional shotgun and have some success bagging birds before he moves on to a more difficult way to hunt turkeys. Blackpowder hunting for gobblers adds a new dimension to the sport and tests the mettle of the hunter more since he must be very precise, give forethought to the sport and employ all his woodsmanship skills to be successful.

CHAPTER 14 - BOW HUNTING FOR TURKEYS

Bow hunting for turkeys is not a beginner's sport. Primarily two kinds of people take up their bows to pursue longbeards -- bowmen who have shot tournament archery or who have been successful in bagging deer with bows, and turkey hunters who have taken numbers of turkeys and who want to learn to shoot a bow to attempt to bag a gobbler the old way.

A problem with bow hunting turkeys is the bird's small vital area, which is protected by a profusion of feathers and meat. A tom turkey presents an illusion. Although he appears to be a large target, underneath all those feathers he has a small body. You can approach the turkey's vital region, which only is about the size of your fist, in three ways --straight through the butt of the wing, through the back or through the anus. A turkey's head is too small a target and moves too quickly for the bow hunter to have a reasonable chance of placing an arrow there.

Most turkey hunters agree you must call up ten times as many gobblers to get a shot with a bow as you do with a gun. Bow hunting for turkeys requires you to do most of the things you are not supposed to do when you turkey hunt or bow hunt. For instance, when you have a turkey at less than 30-yards, you must not move because the bird can see you move. But when you are bow hunting for gobblers, you must be able to draw your bow when the tom is in that close and can spot you, which requires movement. When you are bow hunting, the quicker you draw, aim and shoot, usually the more effective your shot will be. However, generally when you are bow hunting for turkeys, you have to draw and hold the bow back, often for quite some time before you release the arrow. When you have the bow back at full draw, your muscles must stay contracted, and the more likely you are to miss because of muscle fatigue.

Bow hunters for turkeys utilize tactics that fall into two categories -- with a blind and without a blind. A wide variety of bow hunting equipment for turkeys is available. However, whether or not you use any or all of this equipment is as optional as what bow hunting equipment deer hunters use.

BOWS FOR BAGGING BRONZE BARONS

Although plenty of equipment has been designed specifically for taking turkeys with a bow, most archers believe that accuracy in shooting is the most critical key to bagging a bird. The bow hunters I know who consistently harvest toms every spring change their equipment very little from when they bow hunt for deer to bow hunt for turkeys. Because the target on a turkey is so small, you need every advantage you can have that aids you in shooting accurately. Using the same equipment you have utilized during deer season to set up the same way when you hunt turkeys will help you be more comfortable with your tackle. However, since turkeys are far more sensitive to sound than deer seem to be, here are some additional cautions you can take to quieten your bow even more.

"I take my bow apart, separate the limbs from the risers and put pool table felt between the risers and the limbs to quieten my bow for turkey season," Ronnie Strickland of Natchez, Mississippi, one of the nation's well-known bowmen and master turkey hunters, says.

Strickland also uses large puffs on his string to quieten the string even more. He places felt on his arrow rests and waxes his arrows with furniture polish to keep them from making sounds as they pass across the felt.

"One of the best ways to find out just how noisy your bow is to go into a closed room and draw your bow," Strickland suggests. "Probably you'll be surprised at how much noise it makes. If you can hear the bow's being drawn, the turkey can too."

Most hunters espouse one of two philosophies on what bow weight is best for bagging turkeys. Some believe a heavier bow which produces faster arrow flight decreases the chances of the turkey's moving when the arrow is in flight. Reason dictates that the quicker the arrow is delivered from the bow to the turkey, the less likely the bird will be to get out of the way of the arrow. However, if you pull a heavy bow and have to hold the bow at full draw for some time waiting for the turkey to get into the position for you to shoot, you are more likely to miss the bird. Many turkey hunters feel that a 50-to 60-pound bow is more than adequate for downing a longbeard.

The best yardstick to measure which bow and what pound bow is best for you is to determine which bow at what weight is most comfortable for you. If you have been shooting a 50-pound bow all year long and can hold this bow back for a long time, then probably you should not change the poundage of your bow to hunt during turkey season. If you have been shooting a 70-pound bow in field archery and during deer season, and you feel comfortable holding a 70-pound bow at full draw for an extended time, then a 70-pounder may be the best bow for you.

TACKLE FOR TAKING TOMS

When you have developed a system of bows, arrows, broadheads, sighting devices, releases and anchor points that work for you, you will shoot more consistently if you do not alter any of the ingredients of your tackle.

Broadheads

Which broadhead is best for gobblers is another personal choice. However, consider the shocking power when you are choosing a broadhead. Turkeys are very quick. If an arrow zips through them, more than likely they will fly or run a long way before they expire. Most bow hunters agree that bigger broadheads with the ability to break a gobbler down quickly and disable him produce more success than smaller broadheads do.

"I like the 180-grain Simmons Interceptor with an arrow stopper behind it," Ronnie Strickland mentions. "The bigger broadhead will do more damage quicker than the smaller broadhead will, and the arrow stopper will keep the arrow in the bird and help to prevent him from running off. I believe that shocking power and arrow placement are the keys to recovering the turkey when you are bow hunting."

Probably your ability to shoot straight and accurate is more important than any other factor when hunting turkeys. You may prefer to select the broadhead you have used all season long for deer hunting and give up some shocking power to gain accuracy.

Wasp Archery Products has developed the Wasp Turkey Spur, a six blade Cam-Lok broadhead, specifically for turkey hunting with bows. Three of its interchangeable blades have been technically enhanced with spur-like claws to impede penetration and provide shocking power. The spurs prevent escape by not allowing the broadhead to exit the animal. The three remaining blades are replaceable, razor-sharp, vented carbon blades, fine-tuned for the aerodynamic and precision flight.

String Trackers

Adding a string tracker to your bow and arrow greatly can increase the odds of your finding a gobbler after he has been hit. However, if you plan to utilize a string tracker, practice with this device before you go into the field. The closer a turkey is to the bowman, the more effective a string tracker is. But the further a turkey is from the bowman, the more the string tracker can and will inhibit arrow flight. Once again you must make a decision as to whether you want to shoot more accurately or use a device that will aid in the recovery of your bird.

Before you bow hunt, find out if a tracking dog is in the area where you plan to hunt. Many times a birddog or a dog that has been trained to trail and locate turkeys drastically will improve your chances for finding a tom once he has been arrowed.

NO BLIND OR BLIND HUNTING FOR TURKEYS

I have hunted turkeys from blinds and without the aid of a blind. Both methods work. Where and how you are hunting and your knowledge of the turkeys often dictate whether or not you should use a blind for turkey hunting with a bow.

In many areas, being able to move quickly and efficiently to get into a better position to take a shot at a turkey is critical to your success. Some bow hunters feel they can move quicker and set up faster without a blind. However, without a blind, you do not have a place to hide your movement from turkeys when you are bow hunting.

"Often when bow hunters set up to take turkeys with a bow, they don't think about back cover," Ronnie Strickland explains. "If you're silhouetted without back cover, the gobbler is more likely to see you when you draw. I also prefer to have plenty of cover on either side of me. Then the tom can't watch me draw, and I can wait on the bird to step in front of me. Side cover often is just as critical as back cover when you're hunting without a blind."

In many areas of the East, finding this much cover is not too difficult. But locating turkeys -- enough birds to increase your odds for taking a turkey with a bow -- can be very difficult. However, in the West when you are hunting Rio Grandes, you may have plenty of birds to call to in a day but not discover sufficient cover to hide your movement when you draw your bow.

According to Strickland, "Having a blind is more critical to your success in the West than in the East."

John Demp Grace of York, Alabama, both a master archer and a fine turkey hunter, has wrestled with the problem of bagging eastern birds with a bow for many years. Finally, Grace has developed a blind that totally covers the hunter but has several shooting ports on all sides. This blind allows the hunter to quickly and easily assemble it, get inside and wait for the right shot. This blind provides front, back and side cover, as well as cover from above. The bowman can move around in this blind without being detected, draw when he needs to and have several different holes in the blind through which he can shoot. For some years now, Grace has harvested his limit of six turkeys per season with a bow using this type of blind.

"I've used this blind in the West," Grace reports. "In areas with very little cover, the blind's an absolute must."

Because blinds have a distinctive shape, and the wind can blow the material around that the blinds are made of, most hunters prefer to hang or lean brush against the blind. This brush helps to break up the silhouette of the blind, keeps the material from moving in the wind and makes a region less conspicuous to shoot from than a blind that does not have brush around it.

DECOYS

No one ever has made a foolproof turkey hunting aid that always will produce a gobbler. Remember this when you use a turkey decoy. A turkey decoy may cause a gobbler to come in or to hang up and stay away from you where you will not get a shot.

If a gobbler sees a decoy he believes to be a hen, he knows that according to the rules of God and nature, all he has to do is strut and drum, and she is supposed to come to him. The tom probably will stop 50-or 60-yards away from the hen, perform his mating ritual and demand she come to him. If she does not respond, he may walk away from her. But a gobbler may be so fired-up about mating that when he sees the hen, he will come trotting to her to get close and attempt to mate.

For the bow hunter, utilizing a decoy takes the attention of the gobbler away from the hunter and focuses the turkey's attention on the decoy. Then you may have time to draw the bow without the turkey's seeing you. When the turkey comes in, he will be looking at the decoy rather than searching for you or your blind.

Most bow hunters who attempt to bag birds generally agree that a decoy is a decided advantage in states where hunting with decoys is permitted. Be sure to check your local regulations.

CAMOUFLAGE CLOTHING AND BOOTS

As with all other forms of turkey hunting, the sportsman will want to wear full camo from head to toe. However, where you anchor the bow before the shot often will determine the type of hat and the kind of gloves you wear and the kind of face camo you use.

Hunters who anchor on the tip of the nose, in the corner of the mouth or on the side of the face generally feel a headnet inhibits their ability to anchor correctly or may get caught in the string when they release. For this reason, many archers use camouflage paint for their faces instead of headnets. The bill of the cap also can interfere with the archer's ability to take or make the shot. Some hunters will wear their hats backwards, with the bill off to the side, or choose a short-billed cap designed just for bow hunting.

Hand camo is also a concern of bow hunters who use fingers, tabs or even a release system. Often a bow hunter will choose camo paint for his hands and wrists to give him a better feel for the bow and the string. Once again, the camo you choose should be the camo with which you are most comfortable. If you bow hunt for deer with camo gloves and a camo facenet and you can draw smoothly and shoot comfortably wearing these two items, then there is no reason to change your camo system for turkey season.

Also important is wearing a quality pair of comfortable boots you can walk long distances in without fatigue. I also have discovered that the proper underwear greatly can increase your ability to hunt more comfortably. I prefer underwear which has the ability to wick moisture away from the skin. In the cool of the morning, this underwear keeps me warm. Later on in the day when I'm sweating, my body actually will cool down quicker, because when I'm sweating, the underwear wicks the moisture away from my body causing a cooling process to take place.

OTHER EQUIPMENT FOR BOW HUNTING

Compass

A compass is also an absolute essential. When a hunter hears a turkey gobble, the most important thing in his life is getting to that bird and setting up for the shot. Only after he has encountered the bird does he usually become conscious of where he is and what he will have to do to get back to his vehicle. Most hunters have been lost more times than they care to admit.

Fanny Pack

A fanny pack or a daypack with a few candy bars and a soft drink in a plastic bottle are also a very important part of your bow hunting gear. If you hunt turkeys hard, you will become thirsty and hungry. Some snacks will make your day go much better, especially if you do happen to get lost.

Turkey Carrier

Many hunters do not think about how they will get a turkey out of the woods if they are lucky enough to arrow him. I always carry some type of turkey toter, which is nothing more than a wide leather strap with rawhide at the bottom to use to tie the turkey's head and feet. Most magazines do not tell you when you see a turkey thrown over a hunter's shoulder and he is holding the bird's feet to carry the tom out of the woods that the hunter did not have to carry that bird very far. I have carried turkeys out of the woods like that and soon learned that using some type of strap or even a turkey vest is a much better method of exporting a bird.

Compact Binoculars

I usually take a small pair of compact binoculars with me as well. They will help you see turkeys further and keep you from unnecessary water-wading or belly crawling, only to discover that the gobbler you have been stalking actually is a hen.

HOW BOWMAN CAN CALL TURKEYS

One of the most effective ways to take a turkey with a bow is for one hunter to call while the other hunter takes the shot. Using this system, two hunters can take advantage of their individual expertise and greatly increase their odds for bagging a bird. Take a stand 20-to 30-yards behind a bow hunter, and try to call the turkey into a spot where the bow hunter can get the shot. Then, the caller can concentrate all his efforts on putting the turkey in front of the bowman, while the archer focuses on getting in position and taking the shot. This technique can be productive -- whether you use a blind or hunt without a blind.

If you plan to bow hunt turkeys alone, then learning to use a diaphragm call is almost a must. Even if you only can make a cluck on a diaphragm call, you will be much more effective at calling a turkey into bow range than if you cannot use a diaphragm call. Many times you may need to make a cluck to get a turkey to take one or two more steps closer to make the shot or to get a bird to drop his strut so you can take the shot. The diaphragm call allows for hands-free use.

WHEN TO DRAW AND SHOOT

If you are hunting from a blind, you can draw and shoot whenever you need to most of the time. But if you are not hunting from a blind, you only will be able to draw when the turkey cannot see you. Bow hunting for turkeys becomes very complicated when more than one turkey comes in to your calling. Attempting to prevent one pair of keen eyes from detecting your movement is difficult. When two or three pairs of those sharp eyes are looking for you, drawing unseen can be almost impossible if you are not in a blind.

If only one turkey is in front of you when you are ready to draw, wait for the turkey to step behind a tree or a bush before you make the draw. If no tree or bush is close by for the turkey to step behind or if the bird is in full strut, wait for him to turn away from you with his tail fanned. When a turkey has his tail fanned and his head laid back in his feathers to strut, he cannot see behind his tail. Then you can draw undetected.

The worst-case scenario for hunting gobblers with a bow is if a turkey will not step behind a tree and does not strut. Then your best chance to draw will be when the tom has his head down feeding. But even then, more than likely the bird will see you.

WHERE TO PLACE THE SHOT

Most bowmen who hunt wild turkeys agree the most critical part of a hunt is shot placement. Where the arrow enters the turkey's body will determine whether you will be able to find the bird once it falls. Usually a hit along the backbone will stop the turkey and is the best place at which to aim.

The turkey's spine can be reached from several different routes. If a bird is facing a shooting port of your blind head-on, aim for the place where the beard comes out of the feathers. If the tom gives you a side view, point your arrow at the spot where the wing butt attaches to the body. If the gobbler is standing with his fanned tail to your shooting port, aim for the anus or the upper center of the fan, slightly above the anus. Here is a look at where master bow hunters aim at gobblers with their bows.

David Hale of Cadiz, Kentucky, one of the owners of Knight & Hale Game Calls and a leading turkey hunter with either gun or bow, prefers a shot at the turkey's back when bow hunting. "Since the spine shot in my opinion is the best shot you can make on a turkey, if a bird is going away from me or has his back to me, then I take the opportunity to shoot for the spine. If the gobbler is in the strut, I'll shoot for the spot where the wings join the body -- again hoping to get a spine shot. If you shoot into the turkey's breast, more than likely you'll lose the bird. If the turkey has his tail fanned in a strut with his back to me, I shoot for the spot where the tail feathers join the body."

Dale Faust of Centreville, Mississippi, who has won 3-D silhouette shoots, field archery competition and just about every award the Mississippi Archery Association has, agrees with Hale that, "The best shot to take at a turkey is the spine shot. Because turkeys will not leave a blood trail like deer and other big game animals, you may have a difficult time retrieving the bird, unless you break the bird down."

However, when Faust is aiming at a turkey that is quartering away from him, he does not shoot for where the wings enter the body like most hunters do. Instead, he directs his arrow just above the spot where the drumsticks join the tom's body, because, "This vital area is where you most effectively can get a quick kill. Many times if you're shooting down on a gobbler and you hit the point of the wings, the arrow will go through the breast rather than through the vitals. That's why I use the drumsticks of a bird to point the way to the region I sight in on and then hit."

Brad Harris, public relations director for Lohman's Manufacturing in Neosho, Missouri, has been hunting turkeys with a bow for more than 15-years. Harris is convinced from his vast experience of bow hunting turkeys that shot placement is the most critical part of the hunt.

"If you put the broadhead into the turkey where it should go, you won't need a string tracker or any type of arrow-stopping device," Harris explains.

Bow hunting for turkeys is hands-down the most difficult and challenging of all the turkey hunting sports. This sport is not for the novice. Your best bet for success may include one hunter calling while the other hunter shoots, using a blind to eliminate many problems a bow hunter faces and carefully setting up your shot to enable you to hit a tom's vital organs. However, once you are fortunate enough to take a turkey with a bow, you will move into the most elite class of turkey hunters in the nation.

CHAPTER 15 - SOLVING TURKEY HUNTING PROBLEMS

The sport of turkey hunting has so many variables there is no set way to solve every turkey hunting problem. The best way to learn how to outsmart a turkey is to have a wide variety of solutions to try on each gobbler you encounter.

No hunter can give exact rules for solving problems with any particular turkey because each gobbler has a personality based on his genetic make-up, how long he has lived and how many hunter encounters he has had. Also turkeys are very moody with changes in their likes and dislikes occurring almost daily. One day a turkey may gobble aggressively and come to any type of calling. The next day you go in the woods, he may not gobble at all, and/or he may shy away from calling. Wild turkeys are very complex birds. But the more you hunt them and learn about them, the greater your odds will be for bagging one.

Although most solutions to turkey hunting problems will produce a gobbler sometime, if you hunt long enough, you will encounter toms nobody can take. Because of these gobblers' knowledge of the hunter, their cunning in the woods and their ability to outsmart all those who come against them, they earn the right to survive.

HIGH PRESSURE GOBBLERS

Turkeys that see numbers of hunters and have many hunter encounters become very wary of any human. Many times these toms will gobble very little or not at all and be very difficult to hunt. Try several tactics to take toms where the hunting pressure is intense.

- Hunt when no one else hunts. If you study the hunter movement patterns of any area, you soon will discover that most of the turkey hunting pressure exerted on any woodlot usually occurs from an hour before daylight to two hours after daylight. In many parts of the country, turkey hunting is a three hour sport participated in before work. If a hunter does not bag his bird by 9:00 A.M., he will leave the woods. Gobblers soon learn the safest time to talk and walk in the woods when they are least likely to encounter a hunter is from 9:30 A.M. to 2:00 P.M. in states where turkey hunting is permitted all day. Also after 9:00 A.M. very few hunters are in the woods, which increases your odds for bagging a bird during that time.

- Go to where the turkey has been. Most turkey hunters in high pressure areas hunt the gobblers that are on the roost. After the turkeys leave the roost, and the sportsman has chased the birds, the hunter rarely will return to call at the roost site or the area where the turkey has flown down. However, after 9:00 or 10:00 AM, turkeys often will come back to the same site they have flown down to or near the same spot where they have roosted. Return in the middle of the day to where the turkey has been in the morning. You may be able to take a tom after all the other hunters have left.

- Hunt the strut zones. In high pressure regions, you may increase your odds for bagging a bird by not calling to him in the morning like all the other hunters do. Turkey toms have certain places where they strut and drum and are visible to hens without their ever actually gobbling. The most productive spot to hunt the gobbler is to go to the area where the turkey likes to strut, drum and meet his hens.

Most gobblers will have three or four sections of the woods or fields where they prefer to strut after they leave the roost. Often these strut zones are on hills or ridges where a tom can see all the way down a ridge and on either side of a hill. Then the turkey feels secure. If you can identify these regions and reach them before the turkey does, often you can call him and bag him. Because a hen ready to be bred usually moves in close to a strut zone, when you hunt a strut zone, call about one-tenth as much as you would in an area where the turkeys have not been pressured.

- Take a nap. One of the best ways to bag a bird in a high pressure area is to call a little and wait a lot. However, patience is not a virtue of mine. Often I will take a nap to force myself to slow down my hunting. If I have hunted a turkey from daylight until 9:00 or 10:00 AM, I will return to the last place I have called to the bird, sit down next to a big tree, get comfortable, yelp three or four times and go to sleep. If I wake up 10-to 15-minutes later by my watch, I will yelp one or two more times and go back to sleep. I may repeat this process for an hour. Or, if I am very tired, I may yelp three times, sleep for an hour and then yelp again when I wake up. I have been awakened by the sound of a tom drumming and strutting in front of me that has come in but never has gobbled. The less you call in a high pressure area, the more likely a turkey is to come hunting you.

- Use a different call. If you can determine the type of call -- either diaphragm, slate or box -- that most hunters in the region you hunt are utilizing, then when you use a different type of call, you will increase your odds for bagging a bird. Before I have hunted in areas where most of the hunters used a diaphragm mouth call. Then when I have utilized a box or a slate call, I have been effective in luring in gobblers because the kind of call and the sound it produces is different from what the turkeys in that region have heard before.

- Do not call but hunt instead. In many high pressure places where the turkeys will not gobble or gobble very little at all, your only opportunity to take a bird may be to hunt him instead of calling to him. You must learn where the tom goes, when he goes there and what he does when he gets there. Once you know the bird's routine, take a stand along the route he normally travels every day. Do not call. Wait on the gobbler to appear. Some turkey hunters who feel they must set the moral code by which other turkey hunters hunt may think this tactic is unsporting and is bushwhacking a gobbler. However, just as much knowledge and skill are required to learn a turkey's routine and be able to bag him in a place he wants to go as you must have to call him up.

SNEAKY TOMS

When a gobbler is in close enough for a shot but you cannot make the shot because the bird is behind you, often a turkey will circle the hunter and come up from behind your calling position. You can hear him drumming, strutting, spitting and walking --perhaps less than 15-steps from you. When this situation occurs, you must have nerves of steel and the patience of Job.

A novice turkey hunter will try to turn and shoot before the turkey can get away. 90-percent of the time, he will miss or not be able to get a shot at the gobbler. The most obvious solution to this problem is not the best answer. Only patient tactics will solve this problem.

- Wait for the turkey to walk in front of you. By remaining still and motionless, I have been able to let a bird walk 20-yards in front of me, move behind a tree at which time I can make a slight move to aim, and then when he steps out, bag him. Having to wait for a turkey to walk from behind me to in front of me is the most exciting hunt I ever will experience. When the bird is in that close and screaming a gobble, the hair on the back of my neck usually stands up. Waiting on the tom to come to where you can get a shot is the surest way to take him.

- Remain motionless, and let the bird walk off, if the turkey never walks in front of you. I look at my watch when I think the turkey has left the area and wait an additional 20-minutes or so before I move. Most hunters get up too quickly when they think a turkey is gone and spook the bird.

If you will be still for 20-minutes or longer than you think you should, you will have an extra time barrier to help you prevent spooking a turkey. Then attempt to circle, get in front of the gobbler, and call to him again.

GOBBLING AND WALKING TURKEYS

This kind of turkey is what has inspired the phrase, chasing gobblers. Most hunters will run after this bird, continue to close ground and try and call him to them. But remember, when a turkey walks away from you, he is going somewhere. You either will have to bag him in the place where he wants to be or return to that spot the next day and wait on him to come to you. Do not scare the tom in this safety zone. If you do, the gobbler probably will not return to that same site during turkey season. However, you can take this tom that talks and walks.

Follow the bird through the woods at 100-to 200-yards where he cannot see you. Use crow calls or owl calls to keep the turkey gobbling. Then you can remain in contact with the turkey and know his location. Once the gobbler seems to have stopped, more than likely he is in a strut zone or a place where he feels safe and secure and can see in all directions.

Once you know where this spot is in the woods, take your time as you move as close as you can to the turkey. Once you see the bird, call very little to him. Wait on him to come to you.

Do not call this turkey while he is on the roost the next morning after following the turkey through the woods on the first day and locating the spot in the woods where he wants to go. Instead, move to the location where you have seen the turkey, start calling and wait on the bird to show up.

Trail the bird through the woods at a distance where he cannot see you. Give clucking, light yelping and feeding calls like the purr about every 10-to 20-minutes. Then the gobbler will think a hen is following him through the woods and trying to catch up with him. At some point, the gobbler may turn and walk to meet the hen he feels is pursuing him.

Once you can tell the turkey has turned around and started back to you, take a stand immediately. Give only a few feeding calls, and wait for the gobbler to show up.

Hunting a walking and talking turkey requires the hunter to have an abundance of patience, exert extra effort and plan carefully.

DEFIANT GOBBLERS

This turkey will respond to your calling but will stop 50-to 60-yards from you and refuse to come any closer. This gobbler has decided he is close enough for the hen to see him and that she must come to him. He knows the way of nature dictates that the hen should come to him if she hears or sees him. He will wait to see her before he moves any closer. Oftentimes, continuing to call will make this turkey more defiant and actually prevent him from coming in to where you are. Try these tactics.

- Use your hand to scratch in the leaves like a hen turkey when the turkey's not looking. The hen turkey uses a certain cadence when she scratches -- scratch; scratch - scratch; scratch. By utilizing this same cadence when you scratch in the leaves, you will make a defiant tom believe a hen if feeding in the area that is disinterested in mating. Often the gobbler will drop his strut and move in closer to allow what he thinks is a hen to see him better, and he can see her.

- Change calls. On one hunt I made, I had a turkey at less than 20-yards strumming and drumming behind a palmetto blind. I waited for an hour. However, the turkey would not step out from behind the palmetto and give me a clean shot. When my hunting companion began to call on his slate instead of the diaphragms we had been using, the gobbler dropped his strut, stepped out from behind the palmettos and rewarded us with the shot we had hoped to get.

- Do nothing. Many times when a turkey refuses to respond to you, the best thing you can do is to do nothing. Do not call, move or give any indication a hen is in the region. Then the tom may believe the hen has walked away from him. He may drop his strut and attempt to catch up to the hen.

- Let the turkey walk away from you. When a gobbler refuses to come to you, allow the bird to walk off. Then reposition yourself ahead of the turkey, change calls, and try and call him in once more.

FLYING TOMS

Turkeys do not like to fly except to and from their roost -- much preferring to walk anywhere they want to go. However, in some situations you may encounter, the only way to get a bird to you is to make him fly across a river, a canyon or some other terrain break to where you are. The most effective way to force that gobbler to make the flight is to promise him the most exciting experience he ever has had in his life.

Begin by cutting and cackling like an excited hen. Oftentimes, one excited hen will force a tom that is in the mood to mate to take to the air. However, if the turkey still will not fly to you, bring some more hens to the party. If you are using a diaphragm call, give excited clucks, yelps and cackles on your box call. At the same time you are calling on the diaphragm, call with the box. If the bird does not take to the air, bring in the voice of another hen. Either change diaphragm calls to give your calling another type of voice, or use a slate call.

If you still cannot coax the gobbler to you, begin your excited calling sequence again, gobble, and give the gobbling call. Any time you give a gobbling call, be sure you are sitting with your back up against a tree where you can see in all directions. Then no hunter can move in on you. Although the gobble of the wild turkey will challenge the turkey you are attempting to call, this gobbling call also can lure in other hunters. Use this call with caution.

After you have painted this picture of a group of excited hens in the tom's mind and you give a gobble, the bird will think another tom has moved into his territory and is trying to mate with his hens. Often this pressure is more than the turkey can withstand, and he may fly to you.

If the longbeard still fails to take to the air, you have several choices. Either swim the river, or cross the canyon, or plan to hunt the turkey another day in another place.

SILENT GOBBLERS

Some turkeys refuse to talk. On any given morning, all the turkeys in the woods may give you the silent treatment. When this happens, your knowledge of the woods and the turkeys in that region is all you have to rely on for a successful hunt.

Go to an area where you have heard turkeys gobbling before. Begin to call, and look for and expect a turkey. Do not anticipate that the turkey will gobble before you see him. Constantly be looking for the turkey's white head or any movement in front of you. Patience will be your ally, and very little calling will be your most productive strategy.

If the turkeys are silent in the morning, they may not remain quiet all day long. Try and get a turkey to gobble using an owl call, a hawk call or a crow call later on in the day. Cover plenty of ground, make numbers of calls, and listen from high places.

SHEIKS

A sheik is a longbeard dominant gobbler that already has corralled a harem of hens. Because this bird usually has everything he wants to make him happy, he can be very difficult to call and bag. Like the sheiks of old, he has a large number of lady friends to keep him entertained. In most instances, the hens will lead him to food, water, shade, shelter and the roost. Only by understanding the social make-up and the personality of the individuals in this flock can you possibly bag this tom.

Oftentimes the leader of this flock is not the gobbler but rather is a dominant hen. Like gobblers, hens have a pecking order. Generally one hen will be at the top of the order. All the other hens in the flock are below her and rarely challenge her for her authority.

To get to a sheik, you often must go to war with the dominant hen. By calling aggressively with cuts and cackles, you invite the gobbler to leave his harem and the reign of the dominant hen to come to you. The hen harem leader sees your calling as a direct threat to her leadership and rule. She will cut and cackle back at you to let you know that she is in charge of this group, and the best thing for you to do is to move off.

- Talk directly to the dominant hen as soon as she calls by calling back to her immediately with the same intensity and volume that she calls to you. If the dominant hen becomes upset and decides to come and run the challenger off, she will lead the rest of the flock to you. When you see her coming, cease your calling, and wait. Most of the time, you will have to sit still enough to let all the hens in the flock pass by you. In most situations, the gobbler will be trailing the hens. If you try and ready for the shot before the hens have passed you, more than likely one of the hens will spot you and spook the flock. But if you can sit patiently and let the hens get past you, you may be able to take the gobbler.

- Use the reverse tactic, which also will work. This time when you call, if the gobbler answers, call back to him immediately. Completely ignore the calling of the dominant hen. Instead, speak directly to the gobbler. Even though the gobbler has all the hens with which a sultan can possibly hope to mate, he believes there is something special about that hen over in the bush he cannot see. If the gobbler becomes very excited and gobbles each time you call to him, he may start to herd the hens toward you in an attempt to pick you up and add you to his harem. Once again, you will have to let the hens pass by before you prepare a shot at the gobbler.

- Gobble at the tom. Any time you use a gobbling call, you are in danger of calling up another hunter. Do not utilize this tactic when hunting public lands or private lands with other hunters in the woods. More than likely, they will have heard the same turkey you have heard gobble and may be moving toward that bird to take a shot.

A gobble often will work on a sheik because you offend him and cause him to believe that one of his hens has strayed out of his flock and encountered another boyfriend. His manhood will not permit this to happen, and he may come running to you looking for a fight.

HARD-TO-TAKE TURKEYS

Both man and beast are attracted to a crash and/or a fight and want to see the outcome of a battle. Often when no other strategy will work, simulating a fight will make closed-mouthed turkeys gobble. Turkeys that walk and talk also will return to you running, and even henned-up sultans will leave their lady friends to come and view the contest.

By using two pushbutton-type box calls that produce a coarse purr like the Fighting Purr System developed by Knight and Hale, you can simulate a gobbler fight and pull in toms at which you otherwise may not be able to get a shot. As soon as you begin to give the fighting purr calls, expect the turkey to gobble and prepare for the shot. Many times longbeards will come on the run to see the fight you are simulating. Often if you cannot get a shot, you can call that same gobbler back to that same spot using the fighting purr.

WHAT TO DO WHEN YOU MAKE A MISTAKE

Often the biggest problems in turkey hunting are caused by the hunter. The best way to hide or mask a sound that may spook a turkey is to cover that sound with another sound to make a turkey forget the bad sound he has heard. For instance, if you make a bad call with your caller, do not stop with that bad call. Often turkeys make bad calls. Continue to call to mask or hide the bad sound you have made.

When you are walking through turkey country trying to move in close to a gobbler or a place where you think a gobbler will be, and you break a limb, use a deer grunt call to make the turkey think that you are a deer. Or, brush the side of your coat lightly against a tree to sound like a turkey's feathers brushing up against the side of that tree. By taking an unnatural sound or an alarm sound and converting that sound into a sound the turkey is accustomed to hearing, often you will not spook the turkey.

To camouflage your movement through the woods, walk like a turkey. Take one or two steps, and scratch in the leaves with the toe of your boot. Make one or two more steps, and scratch in the leaves with the toe of your boot.

If you have to swat a mosquito or scratch, move your hand slowly up your body, and either swat or scratch with the tip of your finger. If you spook a turkey, do not assume the turkey realizes you are a hunter. Turkeys are very nervous birds that may be spooked by the natural sounds of other animals that are not predators. When a turkey putts and runs off, he makes the same sound he does when he is excited. If you will cut excitedly on your calls when you spook a turkey, oftentimes you can convince a gobbler that what he has heard or has seen is not danger and that the hen is more excited and has not run off. Then he can return to that same location and once again meet his hen.

If you shoot and miss, do not assume the turkey knows you are a hunter. Often in forests, fields and deserts, lightning will strike, trees will fall, and animals will come crashing from the top of the timber. Immediately after you shoot, begin to give exciting cuts and cackles to convince the gobbler that even though his situation is unusual or exciting, no danger is involved. By continuing to call enthusiastically for a few minutes after the shot, you may convince the gobbler a hen has remained in the area and may have been concerned by the sound but that no danger now exists and he can come back and meet her.

Every time you make a wrong sound or move while hunting turkeys, try and convert that sound or that movement into a natural sound to calm the gobbler down or convince him he has not heard or seen what he thinks he has. Although these problems are not all you will encounter as a turkey hunter, these are some of the most common ones with solutions that have worked for me and other hunters. When you learn to deal with these turkey hunting situations correctly, you will be able to more effectively bag gobblers on every outing.

CHAPTER 16 - HUNTING SAFELY

Each year some hunters will be shot while turkey hunting. One of the problems associated with turkey hunting is the hunter imitates the game he is trying to call in and bag. Oftentimes he will call in another hunter and be mistaken for the game.

But just how safe is turkey hunting? Is the sport more dangerous than deer hunting? To find the answer, I talked with Gene Smith, editor of "Turkey Call Magazine" and director of publications for the National Wild Turkey Federation (NWTF).

"Turkey hunting is much safer than it often is perceived," Smith reports. "About 75-percent of the accidents that occur while turkey hunting are the result of the hunter being mistaken for game. However, when you consider accidents per 100,000, which is the way accidents are judged, far fewer accidents happen while turkey hunting than in many other sports."

In the latest report on turkey hunting accidents, the Erickson Report, twenty-eight states were surveyed. The total survey included more than 10-million days spent in the woods turkey hunting. Those numbers of days spent in the woods resulted in 198-accidental shootings. The deaths per 100,000 participating in the sport of turkey hunting are much less than the deaths from many other sports.

"Accident Facts," a national publication of the National Safety Council, reports that in a typical year, the number of deaths per 100,000 for parachuting is 72.5, 41.3 for hang gliding, 4.5 for scuba diving, 2.5 for boating and 2.5 for swimming, but hunting is only 1.06. The Erickson survey notes only thirteen deaths for the more than 10-million man days of turkey hunting, which means the sport is safer than hunting in general.

However, when a turkey hunter gets shot, the news media usually sensationalizes the accident. Although seven or eight murders may take place in a large city in a day, these deaths only may warrant a paragraph or two in the local newspaper. If a turkey hunter is shot and not even fatally, a half page of the sports section may be devoted to the accident. This sensationalism of turkey hunting accidents by the media makes the danger in the woods seem greater than it actually is.

I do not want to minimize the dangers of turkey hunting. I am convinced we all should hunt defensively. But I think the media attention that has been focused on the dangers in the turkey woods and often overdramatized may cause some sportsmen to be reluctant to hunt.

To have a safe hunt, do not let the gobbler take control of your mind. Do not be so intent on bagging a tom that you forget to be a safe hunter. No turkey -- not even a world's record turkey -- is worth becoming a turkey hunting statistic or causing someone else to become a turkey hunting statistic.

TEN KEYS FOR SAFE TURKEY HUNTING

1. Never stalk a turkey. If a turkey is gobbling in front of you, do not try and sneak up on him and shoot him. A gobbling bird calls in hunters. If another hunter has sat down, started to call to that tom and hears you walking or sneaking in the area, you may be mistaken for game.

   The sound of a man's walking is the same sound a gobbler makes when he walks. A man crawling on his hands and knees is about the same height as a turkey. If another hunter is in dim light and looking for something making the sound you are making and about the same size you are when you are crawling, then you may be mistaken for the gobbler. If you plan to ambush a turkey rather than call to him, learn the direction in which the bird is going and set up far enough in front of him not to be mistaken for the turkey. If you want to call to the bird, sit down. Never attempt to sneak up on a gobbling turkey.

2. Do not wear the colors of the flag-red, white and blue. The colors of a turkey's head are red, white and blue with a white crown on top of his head, blue cheeks and usually red wattles. A turkey hunter searches for these three colors. If you wear these three colors, the chances of your being mistaken for game are greatly increased. Some common mistakes include:

   - Wearing a white tee shirt under your camouflage outfit. If your mask or camouflage gapes open and reveals just some of that white tee shirt, another hunter may mistake you for game.

- Using or wearing a red bandana, a red or white handkerchief or any other red clothing during turkey season. Do not wear a red chamois or wool shirt on cool mornings under your camo shirt.

- Carrying white toilet paper into the woods to be used when nature calls. The movement of that white toilet paper can cause a hunting accident. Some companies make camouflaged toilet paper, which is an absolute must for the turkey hunter.

  I check out my hunting partner before I go into the woods. If I see any red, blue or white on him, I caution him about what may happen. I ask my partner to look me over to see if he can spot any of the three danger colors on me.

3. Do not wave at or continue to call when you see another hunter. If another hunter is approaching your stand, do not wave to him or try and get him away from your hunting position by using your hands. Remember that hunter is looking for any movement to indicate he has found a turkey. If you see another hunter coming to you and you are sitting on the ground, remain perfectly still. Allow him to walk on by you if he is off in the distance.

   If the hunter is close, speak to him in your normal voice and tell him, "Hey, buddy, I'm over here." If he answers you, say, "I'm to your left or your right, and I'm about to stand up. Don't shoot." When some hunters see another hunter approaching, they continue to call, hoping they can call a gobbling turkey to them before the other hunter has a chance to get to the turkey. However, if you keep on calling, even if you are using a mouth diaphragm, you will move slightly, the hunter will know exactly where you are, and he may assume you are a turkey. Even if you are making hen calls, the other hunter may think a gobbler is with that hen and may stalk you.

   Never call when you spot another hunter. Also never move until you have identified yourself with your natural voice, and the other hunter has answered you.

4. Never try and get closer than 100-yards to a turkey on the roost. If the turkey is gobbling from the roost, most hunters will set up about 100-yards from the bird and expect the bird to be coming to them within that 100 yard-range. If you move in closer than 100-yards and walk around, then you are inside the range where a hunter expects a turkey to be walking. Another hunter may assume that what he has seen and heard is a gobbler that has flown down from the roost and is walking to him. Never walk toward a roost tree after fly-down time. Always assume another turkey hunter is set up on that same bird. Consider the area within 100-yards of a roost tree no man's land. If you decide to go there, travel with extreme caution, and expect another hunter is in the region.

5. Never use a gobbler call unless you are in a defensive position. When you make the call of a wild turkey gobbler, you are producing the sounds

159

the turkey hunter is hunting. You entice hunters to hunt you. If you decide to use a gobbler call, make sure you have your back up against a tree much wider than your shoulders. Be certain you can see in all directions and that no hunter can slip up on you.

When you decide to leave the spot from which you have been calling, before you stand up, give an owl call, a crow call or a hawk call, or bark like a dog, or use your natural voice to let someone know where you are. Always utilize sounds that are not turkey sounds to let someone who may have come in behind you know you are not a turkey. Even if you are in a good defensive position, when you move, you will provide the movement to go with the calling that has lured in another hunter.

Using a gobbler call on public lands is one of the most dangerous sins a turkey hunter can commit. I advise using a gobbler call only when you turkey hunt on private lands.

6. Select open calling sites. When you take a stand to call a turkey, do not be so well-hidden you cannot see all the way around you. Do not take a stand in bushes where you will shake the bushes if you have to move a gun barrel or if you have to reposition yourself. If your blind prevents your seeing in all directions, another hunter may slip in near you without your seeing him.

7. Protect your back. The gunfighters of the Old West always sat with their backs to the walls. Then no one could slip in behind them undetected. Anyone approaching the gunfighter had to step into his vision first.

Remember this defensive position when turkey hunting. If your back is protected by a large tree, a bank or some type of barrier another hunter cannot see through, then if another hunter does approach, you should be able to see him. If another hunter shoots at a turkey that walks up behind you, you are protected.

8. Remember camouflage does not make you invisible. Actually an invisible man has an advantage over the turkey hunter because then you cannot see him when he moves. In most of today's camouflage advertisements, camo manufacturers use words like, invisible, vanish, blend in and disappear to cause you to believe you cannot be seen by a turkey if you wear a specific camouflage. Often this idea gives the turkey hunter a false sense of security. You may think if you remain motionless, you may not be able to be seen. However, when you move and you are camouflaged, you may not be identifiable when another hunter spots your movement. When you wear camouflage, you are not invisible but rather may be indistinguishable. Remember, a turkey hunter is looking for movement.

Rob Keck, executive director of the NWTF, explains that, "Statistics seem to indicate the more experienced turkey hunters are often the ones responsible for turkey hunting accidents. An experienced turkey hunter knows what a turkey sounds like moving through the woods, the colors of a turkey's head and where a turkey should be. He has all the puzzle parts he requires to put together a successful turkey hunt.

"His mind may play tricks on him when he hears a sound that's the same sound a turkey makes. When he spots the colors of red, white or blue, he may assume those colors are a turkey's head. When he sees movement like a turkey makes, his brain draws a picture, says, 'That's a turkey,' and he fires."

For example, in a shooting accident in South Carolina a few years ago, a man had been calling to a turkey. Apparently the turkey had left the area. The hunter was sitting next to a large tree and decided to take a smoke break. He reached in his pocket and took out a white cigarette. He lit the cigarette, brought it to his lips, took a smoke and lowered the cigarette. He brought the cigarette up and down to his lips for a few minutes which was the same motion a turkey's head would make. Another hunter came in, saw that patch of white moving up and down like a turkey's head and fired.

The hunter taking the smoke break had depended solely on his camo to hide him from the turkey and other hunters. He forgot that the movement of his hand going up and down resembled a turkey's head as did the small patch of white on his cigarette. Although camouflage can break up your silhouette and cause you to blend in with your environment, it does not hide your movement. Be conscious of the way you move. Before you move in turkey woods use sounds that are not turkey sounds to announce your presence.

9. Do not shoot at sound or movement. Being the victim of a hunting accident is bad but often no worse than being the cause of a hunting accident. One of the reasons an experienced turkey hunter may be involved in a hunting accident is because he feels he must shoot a turkey.

   In a turkey hunting camp the night before a hunt, a sportsman with some turkey hunting reputation may have to endure some ribbing from his buddies, who will say, "Hey Joe, how come you haven't gotten a gobbler this season? You usually have bagged one or two by now. What's the matter? Are you losing your touch?"

   When one hunter puts that kind of pressure on another hunter, the sportsman doing the teasing is cocking the hammer on a loaded gun. Then the other hunter thinks he has his reputation to uphold and that to regain his stature in camp, he must return to camp with a bird. If he sees something that looks or moves like a turkey, he may shoot much quicker than usual.

   Instead, talk in your hunting camp about the number of hunters in the woods. Emphasize to all that each must be careful when hunting turkeys.

10. Assume every sound is a hunter. Paul Butski of Niagara Falls, New York, hunts public lands in his home state and always practices defensive hunting. When I hunted with Butski, he explained, "John, when hunting public lands, always think every call and sound is made by a hunter. Assume each piece of red, white and blue you see is a hunter's clothing, and don't fire a shot until the bird proves to you he's not a hunter.

"Look for a tom's beard first. Next try to see his wattles. Search for his eyes. Then see one feather clearly before taking a shot. When I'm hunting public lands, I always assume I'm calling another hunter. I make the turkey prove he's not a hunter before I shoot." Butski's philosophy is defensive turkey hunting. If we practice this way of thinking, we will eliminate turkey hunting accidents.

Hunting private lands may give you a sense of false security. When you and your buddy are the only two hunters on private land, you may assume you cannot run into each other in the woods. However, if either of you starts moving on a gobbler and repositions yourself, you may walk into each other's territory. Or, a hunter may accidentally walk off his land and onto your land. A poacher may be sneaking through your woods. Do not be trapped into believing that just because no other hunters are suppose to be in the woods that you can shoot any sound or movement you think is a turkey.

Once a friend of mine and his son were hunting private land and had separated to hunt two different turkeys. Later in the morning, the man, who was an experienced turkey hunter with many seasons to his credit, spotted what he thought was a gobbler. He raised his gun, fired and shot his son.

Accidents can happen. But if you hunt defensively, never shoot at movement or sound and always clearly identify a turkey before you squeeze the trigger, you can prevent accidents.

SAFETY WITH DECOYS

Many states now permit the hunter to use a decoy when calling in a turkey. These lifelike replicas of both hens and gobblers move in the wind and give the appearance of a live bird. When a hunter spots a decoy, has heard what sounds like a turkey, sees something move that resembles a turkey, he may fire -- even though the beard and the red, white, blue on the turkey's head are not present.

When you utilize a turkey hunting decoy, do not take a stand immediately behind the decoy but on one side or the other of the decoy. Then if an unsuspecting hunter does see and shoot your decoy, you will not be in the line of fire.

SAFETY WHEN TAKING A TURKEY OUT OF THE WOODS

Although hunters mistaking dead gobblers for live gobblers is rare, the best way to carry a turkey out of the woods after you have harvested him is to place him in a hunter orange vest or put a hunter orange flag on the vest once you are through hunting. Never leave a turkey's head hanging out of your game bag. If possible, try and put the tail feathers inside the bag, also. By hiding anything that looks like a turkey, you are more likely to prevent accidents from occurring.

OTHER SAFETY TIPS

Although the chances of becoming bitten by a snake while turkey hunting are remote, still a chance does exist. Do not be foolish. Since snakes often like to lie beside logs, before you step over a log, look carefully. If possible, step on the log, look down, and then step over. Be careful if you are wading the edge of a creek or a stream, . If you see a snake, do not play with it but rather avoid it.

Some years ago I wrote a column in my local newspaper about an encounter I had with a water moccasin. The snake was beside my canoe when I beached it on a whitewater trip. In the article, I mentioned I killed the snake. The animal rights activists in our area wrote letters to the editor explaining why I should not have killed the snake. I began to reevaluate my action and thought perhaps I could have moved the snake out of the way. Perhaps it would not have bitten me or anyone else. Maybe I should have gone against my instincts and permitted the snake to live.

Later on that spring when I was turkey hunting, I was walking along a dark woods road beside flooded timber. In the middle of the road was a cottonmouth water moccasin. I had no way to walk around the snake without getting in water over my thighs. But I remembered my critics and decided to locate a long stick and move the snake out of the road. Then I could pass.

After I found a stick, I attempted to move the snake off the road. However, this water moccasin had decided this was his road. Not only would he not give any ground, he began to strike and come toward me. At that moment, my survival instinct replaced my conservation ethic. This snake met the same fate as the other one. Although I would have walked around the snake if I had had the option, I still should not have gotten as close as I did to the snake. Avoid snakes when possible, but when a snake poses danger, dispatch the snake.

I have known some turkey hunters who have been calling turkeys and noticed a snake lying close to them or next to them. They have continued with calling the turkey -- hoping to take the bird without spooking the snake. However, given the chance to take a gobbler or put myself in harm's way with a snake, I always will let the snake have my hunting place. Do not become so intent on taking a gobbler that you forget common sense.

Carrying a survival pack into the woods for yourself and your hunting companion always is a good idea. Matches, candy bars, lightweight rope and band-aids can make a bad experience more bearable and comfortable until you can get out of the woods.

MOSQUITOES, TICKS AND REDBUGS

Although a quality insect repellent can keep these creatures away, if you have chased a gobbler through the woods or have had to walk a distance to get to a gobbling bird, your protection will break down or be washed away by perspiration. Always carry insect repellent with you. No matter how much repellent I have put on before I hunt, before I start moving toward a gobbling bird or sit down to call, I spray my entire body with insect repellent.

Insect repellent will keep mosquitoes, ticks and redbugs from attacking you while you are calling a turkey. osquitoes buzzing around your eyes and ears and lighting on your gloves can distract you and cause you to not get a shot. Also, if you have to swat at mosquitoes or scratch insect bites, you will be making movements that may resemble a turkey to another hunter.

If I am bitten by redbugs or have them imbedded in my skin, I paint the wounds with a substance called Chigger Rid. Although some hunters use fingernail polish and other forms of medication, Chigger Rid not only seals the wound and cuts off the air to the little red mites but also has a substance in it that helps prevent intense itching. Another good product is Afterbite made by the Tender Company, which has an antiseptic-type solution that also prevents itching from insect bites.

GETTING LOST IN TURKEY WOODS

The number one accident that occurs to hunters is becoming lost in the woods. The gobble of the bronze baron has such a hypnotic effect on you when turkey hunting that often you may be so intent on bagging a bird you may lose your way in the woods. Even hunters who carry compasses still get lost in turkey woods. Always take a small emergency blanket to keep you warm if you do have to spend the night in the woods. Carry waterproof matches, a few candy bars, a knife and other items to make your night's stay safe.

Remember, no one plans to get lost, but if you do become lost, wait to get found. Once you realize you are lost, do not panic. Build a fire, and wait for someone to find you. A fire not only can provide light at night but also is a signal to would-be rescuers. If you decide to walk out, follow drainages until you find a bridge or some type of crossing, or walk ridgetops where you can see a long way. Always tell someone where you will be hunting, and when you will be back. Then if you do get lost, someone will know to look for you.

CHAPTER 17 - CARING FOR YOUR BIRD

The gobbler stands 20-yards away, your shotgun is resting on your knee, your cheek is on the stock, you have just pushed the safety off, and the bead on the gun comes to rest on the turkey's wattles as your fingers slowly and gently begin to caress the trigger. The gun explodes and carries its swarm of pellets to the target. What happens next determines whether or not you will have a fine gobbler to eat or mount.

When a turkey is hit, very rarely will he fall motionless. Often a turkey will flop and begin to bounce around on the ground. Even though the bird is dead, his body does not know that yet. The tom may begin to furiously beat the ground with his wings and his body -- actions which will knock beautiful feathers off him and create bald spots which may or may not be repairable by a taxidermist.

Generally as soon as I fire, I get up quickly and hurry to the turkey. I grab the bird by his feet and legs and lift him off the ground, allowing him to beat the air with his wings. This process prevents the turkey from bouncing around on the ground and knocking many of his feathers off. Once the turkey quits flopping, the next decision to be made is whether or not I will mount the tom. Also this is the time to quickly capture your gobbler on film with your camera.

If you plan to eat the bird, you need to field dress the gobbler. Begin by cutting a small hole around the anal area. Reach inside the turkey. Pull out all the entrails, being sure to remove all the red, spongy lung material, which can spoil very quickly. Do not wash the inside of the carcass since water will increase the bacteria build-up inside the bird. After you have removed the entrails, the bird is ready for transport out of the woods.

Decide now whether you will pluck or skin the bird to prepare it for cooking. Pluck the turkey as soon as you arrive home. However, if you choose to skin the gobbler, do it in the woods when you are field dressing him. With either method, you still can save the prized parts of the bird for mounting such as the tail, the spurs and the feet.

Although the classic turkey pose is to throw the turkey over your shoulder holding him by the feet and walking out of the woods, after you have walked 100-to 200-yards, you quickly will realize those round, bony legs supporting 16-pounds plus of weight severely will cramp your shoulder, weaken your muscles and be a clumsy way to carry a bird. If you have some type of strap, tie a noose around the turkey's head and feet and put the turkey on your shoulder using the strap. If for some reason you do not have on hand a turkey toter or a turkey vest, use the sling on your shotgun to carry out the bird. The best method is to put the turkey in a turkey vest, being careful to fold his wings and not damage his tail feathers.

If the bird is to be mounted, do not remove the entrails. Take care folding the wings and protecting the tail feathers if you will carry the gobbler out in a vest. If any feathers are loose on the ground -- especially wing feathers or tail feathers -- be sure to pick them up, and carry them with you.

When you get the turkey to the car, be conscious of the temperature. If you are hunting in the spring, the temperature reaches 60-or 70-degrees, and you put the bird in the trunk of your car, the temperature inside the trunk will be even hotter, causing the trophy to spoil. Instead, put the turkey on the floorboard of the back seat, and leave the windows down. Then air can circulate.

The best method to get a turkey home from the field is to take a 100-quart cooler with you. Whenever I hunt or fish, I always carry a 100-quart cooler in my car. With a cooler this size, I can take cold drinks and food as well as have plenty of storage space for my bird. I also keep on hand 30-gallon trash bags. Then I can put the turkey inside a trash bag, pull the drawstrings tight around the tom's legs, and place the bird in the cooler. Using this technique, the bird will stay cool and dry with little or no chance of him spoiling, even if I am in the field for a day or two.

If you plan on mounting the bird, the sooner you can get your bird to the taxidermist, the better your chances are of having a quality mount. If you want to eat the bird, the quicker you can get the turkey plucked and on ice, in a refrigerator and/or in a freezer, the better the meat will be. Whether you plan to eat a turkey or mount him, never leave the gobbler in the trunk of your car, and drive all over town for a day or two showing him to your friends.

GETTING YOUR GOBBLER READY TO COOK OR FREEZE

After field dressing the gobbler before you leave the woods, then pluck the turkey as soon as you arrive home. If the bird is still warm, the feathers will probably come out quite easily. But if the bird has cooled, a wet plucking is preferable.

The simplest way to pluck a turkey is to dunk your turkey into steaming hot water. Allow it to soak a minute or two. Slosh it around to make sure it gets completely wet. Remove it from the water. Then begin to pluck it in the same direction the feathers grow -- from the neck toward the feet. Do not pull the feathers backwards, which may tear the skin. Next, singe your turkey to make sure you have removed all the pinfeathers. A pair of tweezers may be needed to do this properly.

You also can skin a turkey, a chore you can complete before you leave the woods. The breast and the legs, which are the main edible parts of a wild turkey, take up minimal space in a cooler. Some hunters, especially those who intend to be in camp for a day or two before returning home, debone each side of the breast to make the turkey cool quicker, thereby also conserving their cooler space.

To skin a turkey, tie one or both feet to a limb, and use your fingers to tear the feathered skin away from the flesh. The cut made in the anal area where you removed the entrails is a good place to begin the skinning process. Use a trash bag carried for that purpose to hold unwanted parts of the bird to keep the woods clean. Use another garbage bag to provide a container for parts you may wish to save such as the tail, the wings, the lower legs, and the beard - parts you may want to mount.

The turkey's skin is tender when the bird is freshly dead and will come away in large tears. Once the skin and feathers are removed, use a knife to cut the breast away from the back, and cut off the wings at the joint. Cut off the legs, as well. (In some areas, you may be required to leave a tag on the leg of your gobbler until you reach home. Some regulations also may require the beard to stay on the carcass of a spring turkey).

If you plan on cooking the turkey in one or two days, then store the bird in the refrigerator. However, be sure to cover the bird, and put it in the meat cooler, if possible. If it is to be frozen for cooking later, triple wrap the parts of the bird using clear plastic, then foil, then freezer paper, packing each layer very tightly to eliminate any air and any chances for freezer burn. On the outside of the package, write the turkey's weight and the date it was put into the freezer. The turkey tastes best if cooked within two months of the kill, but it can last as long as one year in the freezer.

TAKING CARE OF THE TROPHY FOR MOUNTING

Besides writing, I also operate a part-time taxidermy business. I never will forget the day a proud hunter brought a big, 22-pound eastern gobbler that sported an 11-inch beard and 1-1/4-inch spurs into my office.

"I want to get the bird mounted because he's the biggest bird I've ever taken," the customer told me. "But I don't know where I'm going to hang him once he's mounted. My wife's an artist. She says we're not having any dead bird hung in our house. I either may have to put him in my office or in my basement, but he's too fine a bird not to mount." I agreed with the hunter. When he left, I began to mount the bird. The mounting and drying process took several months. When the turkey finally was completed, he was mounted flying and was a fine bird. I called the man's home to notify him his turkey was ready. But he was out of town. His wife agreed to come and pick up the turkey. I heard some reluctance in her voice at having to perform a task she was not eager to do. However, when the woman arrived at my shop, I saw a drastic transformation in her attitude as though a worm had crawled out of a cocoon and become a butterfly.

Talking non-stop she was very excited as she said, "That's the most gorgeous bird I've ever seen. I never have realized a turkey's feathers contain so many iridescent colors. Look at how the bird seems to change colors when you change its position or the lighting. I can't believe something as ugly as a turkey can be so beautiful and that this is what a wild turkey looks like. I'll surprise my husband. He'll be gone for two weeks."

I helped the lady load the turkey into her van and was excited that someone else had discovered the rare beauty of the wild turkey. After a couple of days, I had forgotten about the artist and the gobbler. Three weeks later, my telephone rang. On the other end of the line was the hunter whose wife had picked up his turkey.

He told me, "John, you're not going to believe what happened. When I came in from a business trip, I walked into my living room. In the center of the wall where my wife's favorite painting once hung was my gobbler. The bird almost seemed to glow. When I looked up into the ceiling, I realized my wife had called in an electrician and had special lighting put in to hit the bird from different directions and cause his iridescent feathers to shine. The turkey seemed to change colors as I moved around the bird.

"As I stood there looking at my turkey, my wife came in, and said, 'Isn't he beautiful, honey?' I never would have believed my wife would have hung the turkey in the house, put the bird in a place of honor or seen the beauty in the bird and gone to the expense of having special lighting put in the house just to show off my turkey. Although I was proud of the gobbler when I bagged him, I've never been as pleased with any trophy as I am that gobbler hanging in my living room."

DECIDING ON HOW TO MOUNT THE TURKEY

There are several reason for mounting a turkey. If ...

- you have hunted long and hard and bagged your first gobbler, then he represents a trophy to you.

- the tom has an exceptionally long beard or lengthy spurs or is very heavy, you will want to mount the turkey.

- you are trying to collect all subspecies of wild turkey and want to have one of each kind of turkey mounted in your office, trophy room or home, these are reasons for mounting a gobbler.

However, I like to mount gobblers because they are so beautiful. What a shame we only can see them for a few weeks each season. The beauty of the feathers, the majesty of the head and the representation of all that is wild are preserved in the mounted wild turkey.

The wild turkey also gives me a sense of history when I look at a mounted bird. This turkey's ancestors fed my forefathers. He was a major source of life to the early native Americans. At one time, he was considered to be the national bird. He was the bird most prized by Ben Franklin, and his tail feathers were used to pen the constitution and the Bill of Rights that gave us all the freedom we enjoy today. When I look at a wild turkey, I think of the freedom that is America and the hunting heritage Americans always have had. A mounted turkey is part of our heritage.

After all the time and trouble you have gone to hunt and bag a gobbler, if you plan to mount the turkey, you do not want to trust your prized possession to just anyone who claims to be a taxidermist. They may not be skilled in taking a pile of feathers and a dead head and making a lifelike recreation of the wild turkey you hunted. The best way to select the taxidermist you will use is to look at a finished product done by him or her before trusting them with your own gobbler. Actually the best time to make this choice is prior to turkey hunting season when you have plenty of time to look around, and evaluate your options. Remember, allow your taxidermist time to do a good job. Taxidermy is an art.

How To Mount The Turkey's Head

Once you arrive at the taxidermist's with your gobbler, you must decide on how you want the turkey's head, the most colorful and noticeable part of the mount to be prepared. Through the years, I have observed the evolution of many ways of mounting a wild turkey's head. The first taxidermists' only option was to skin the head and neck, remove the meat, preserve the wattles and skin as best as possible and pray the head's skin would not crack for at least two or three years.

Later, polyurethane and latex rubber heads, which could be easily and unnoticeably attached to the turkey's body, became available to taxidermists. Oftentimes these heads could fool even the most keen-eyed hunter if skillfully painted. However, many of these heads looked artificial, although they prevented the cracking which occurred with natural heads.

Another choice, which I consider to be the best, now is available for preserving the turkey's head -- freeze drying. In this process, the gobbler's neck and head are removed, posed in a lifelike position and placed in a freeze-dry machine, which removes all the moisture from the head without shrinking it. The process keeps the head intact, preserves it and eliminates cracking.

The number one complaint of hunters about their turkey mounts usually is the color of the gobbler's head. Seldom can a gobbler's head be restored to the same exact color it was when the turkey was bagged. The turkey's head must be painted to restore the color that is lost once a tom is killed.

A turkey's head changes according to his emotional state, his sexual state, the time of year when he is killed and the area where he is found. Turkeys' heads can range in color from white or blue to shades of red or any of these colors in various mixtures. Most often, the turkey's head will be white on top, blue or violet around the eyes, and either red or white on the wattles. But this coloration is not true of every tom. To insure your turkey's head is the color you want, clearly understand what your taxidermist intends to do, and be sure he knows what you want.

How To Determine Your Turkey's Pose

Another factor to consider in mounting is where the mount will be displayed and what the turkey's posture will be. Where the mount will be displayed will dictate the pose of your gobbler. If the room where you will hang your mounted trophy is small, a turkey in a large, flying position may not be a good choice of mounts because of the bird's vast wing span. However, this pose is the perfect selection for a large room. For a smaller display area, a walking, sneaking or strutting mount may be a better choice. To make your decision on which mount to use, measure the area where you will stand the mount or hang it. Check these measurements with your taxidermist to be certain your trophy and mounting position will suit the place you have chosen for it to be displayed.

How To Make A Skin Mount

If you do not want the entire turkey mounted, mounting the turkey's skin on barnwood makes a beautiful display. This type of mount does not require an artificial body and does not use the turkey's head or feet.

Begin by skinning the turkey along the stomach as you will for any turkey mount. Remove the head just above the beard, split the underside of the wings, and remove the meat from between the bones. Using Instant Mounting Fluid from Touchstone Taxidermy Supply, inject the tail butt and the tips of the wings where a small amount of meat may remain. With a knife, razor blade or scissors, remove all excess meat and fat from the turkey's skin. Rub powdered borax into the skin and into the cavity in each wing where the meat has been removed.

Next, stretch the skin out with the fleshy side down and the feather side up. Then place a nail in the skin on either side of the back. From this base nail, run string to other nails around the edge of the wings in such a way that the string forces the feathers to lie down flat on the wings. Also place nails between each of the spread tail feathers. Run a length of cord from one nail to the next, making a loop around each, to hold the tail feathers down and in place.

Once the wings and the tail are secured, allow the skin to dry in a warm, dry place for three or four weeks. During this time, look around for an old barn door or siding on which to mount the skin. Then when the skin is dried, nail it to the wood. Use the feathers to hide the nails. You can easily fashion a loop hanger with a length of clothesline to suspend your skin mount from the wall and have an attractive mount for a den or office.

What Other Mounts Are Available for Turkeys

Oftentimes a hunter may not have his gobbler mounted but still will save the feet, beard and tail. He may spread the tail and let the tail, the beard and the feet dry. Usually these types of trophies are discarded or packed away after a few years. But you can preserve the tail and feet with little effort to ensure that decay and insects will not destroy them.

Fill a large hypodermic syringe with a preservative solution like Instant Mounting Fluid. Inject it into the fleshy part of the tail. Spread the tail on a large piece of cardboard or wood, and use either pins or nails to hold it in place. Store the tail in a warm, dry area to insure its drying in the proper position. Inject this fluid into the feet, along the tendon on the back of the leg, into the palm of the foot and in each toe. Lay the feet on their sides, curling the toes together the way your hands look when cupped and all the fingers are touching. Let the feet dry until rigid. Rub borax into the meat on the beard, and put it in the same place to dry.

As soon as the specimens dry, make a covering for the butt of the tail using velvet or leather. A velvet skullcap, can be purchased from the San Angelo Company, Inc., or from some outdoor catalogue houses.

Design a panel with your own woodworking skills, or purchase one from a taxidermy supply house. Attach the gobbler's tail to a panel using nails and hot glue. Place the tail in the center somewhat high on the panel with the velvet covering over the butt. Then put the feet on either side of the mounted tail, using a strong, instant glue which can be purchased in most hardware and discount stores. Mount the beard just below the tail. You may wish to glue small pieces of rawhide over the butts of the legs and the meat of the beard to make the mount more attractive.

Wings also can be added to this type of mount. To preserve the wings, make an incision on the underside, and pull the skin back, exposing the muscle and bone of the wing. Remove the muscle from the bone, leaving the skin intact. Sprinkle borax into the incision, and then rub it into the skin and along the bone below the incision. Use cotton to replace the tissue that has been removed, and sew it up with braided nylon casting line or quilting thread. Inject fluid into the rest of the wing from the incision to the tip before stretching the wing out and letting it dry.

When both wings are dry, dust them, place the tail on the mounting panel, and attach the wings by running wires from the back side of the panel over and around them and back through the panel. Twist the wires firmly to secure the wings. Then mount the tail in the center of the panel and slightly high, overlapping part of the wings. Flank the tail with the preserved feet. A small incision can be made in the velvet covering to glue in the turkey's tail and beard.

Another possibility is to mount only the beard and feet, since the real trophies of a gobbler are his beard and spurs. Inject the feet with the preserving fluid. Arrange the toes together, and curve the feet into the desired position. Apply borax to the meat on the beard.

Once dry, use a piece of rawhide or deerskin to cover the ends of the legs and the meat on the beard. Shellac the feet to make them shiny, or leave them natural. Use hot glue or instant glue to attach the feet to a small wooden panel. In the center of the panel, glue the beard above the feet, and then attach an engraved plate with the information about your trophy -- how much he weighed, where he was bagged and the date he was taken.

Another way to preserve the spurs is to remove them from the legs, and coat them with shellac or clear gloss to make them shiny. Then they can be used for tie tacks, cuff links, tips for bolo ties, centerpieces for belt buckles, necklaces or earrings. Another part of the gobbler, the beautiful feathers, can be used for feather jewelry such as earrings and crafts.

COOKING THE WILD TURKEY

In these days of eating healthy for our hearts, most all of us are aware of the merits of eating turkey, a meat low in cholesterol and fat but packed with protein. Today's grocery stores feature turkey steaks, ground turkey and turkey sausage as well as turkey breasts and whole turkeys for cooking. As with all wild game, the wild turkey is much healthier for you to eat due to its lower fat content than domesticated turkey.

Unlike domestic turkeys, the wild turkey is not bred for its breast meat. This lack of breast meat may disappoint most first-time wild turkey eaters. The meat also will be more dry than a domestic turkey's, due to the wild bird's lack of fat. If you plan to roast the turkey, plan to baste it generously to keep the meat moist and flavorful. A cheesecloth placed over the breast and kept moist with a buttery sauce is a good choice. The recipe you use for cooking the turkey will determine the kind of basting sauce you should use. One of my favorite basting sauces is made from 1/2-cup of orange juice, 1/2-cup of butter and a small amount of grated orange peel for added flavor.

If you separate the legs from the turkey, the meat usually will cook more to your liking since the legs take longer to cook than the breast. Often the breast will dry out while the legs are still cooking if they are cooked together. I often cook the legs and wings separately from the breast, sometimes using a different recipe.

Historical Wild Turkey Cooking

The wild turkey has played a major role through the years in the foods of the United States. Brillat-Savarin, who fled to exile in America during the French Revolution, was considered the world's greatest authority on gastronomy by his contemporaries. In America, he was a close friend of our gourmet President, Thomas Jefferson. The colonials' roasted wild turkey was the American dish that made the most impression on Savarin. Europeans had domesticated poultry, but wild turkey was indigenous to the Americas.

Also President Andrew Jackson's favorite food was turkey. He preferred it be made into a hash, which was more of a gruel than a hash. It would be called a thin fricassee of turkey today and probably be much too plain for modern tastes.

However when President Franklin D. Roosevelt was newly elected he visited Jackson's estate, the Hermitage, in 1933. Because the chef wanted to serve something elegant to F.D.R., he added Worcestershire sauce to spruce up the original recipe for Andrew Jackson's turkey hash.

Andrew Jackson's Turkey Hash

Prepare a medium-sized (8-to 10-pound) turkey for a roaster; add sufficient water to make stock: put celery, onion, a bay leaf, salt and a pod or two of red pepper in the water. Cover; allow to cook slowly until tender; do not brown.

Then pour and strain off stock; allow to cool. When the fat rises to the top, skim off but do not use. When turkey has cooled, pull apart, discarding all skin, bones, and gristle; cut in fairly large, bite-size pieces.

Make the sauce by heating 4-tablespoons butter in a large skillet or saucepan and blending in 2 tablespoons flour until smooth. Heat until bubbly. Stirring constantly, add gradually a quart of the turkey stock. Bring to boiling, and cook 1-to 2-minutes. Season with Worcestershire sauce, and add white pepper, if needed. To each quart of sauce add 2-quarts of cut-up turkey. Serve very hot from a double boiler.

NOTE: To prepare less than 2 quarts, cook a smaller portion of sauce and cut up enough turkey in proportion to the amount of sauce used and the desired number of servings. This leftover turkey may be used for other food preparation.

During President Ulysses Grant's administration in 1869, a forward-thinking turkey entrepreneur hit upon the idea of sending a turkey to his neighbor in the White House. Grant received a 36-pound Rhode Island turkey from the state famous for its poultry. Mr. Vose, the turkey grower, sent Christmas turkeys to all of the presidents from Grant through Teddy Roosevelt. Roosevelt's was a more modest 26-pound turkey. The White House released this recipe for stuffing a 19-pound bird.

Teddy Roosevelt's Christmas Turkey

1 dozen large oysters, minced very fine; 2 cupfuls of fine bread crumbs, a tablespoonful of chopped herbs (parsley, thyme or sweet marjoram), and a sparing amount of salt and pepper. Stuff turkey; roast.

Another traditional turkey recipe that has been popular through the years is turkey with johnnycake stuffing.

Roast Turkey With Colonial Johnnycake Stuffing 4 cups crumbled johnnycake (cornbread) turkey giblets, neck

>3 chicken bouillon cubes 1 quart water
>
>celery leaves 1/2 teaspoon salt
>
>1/4 teaspoon dry mustard
>
>1 pound chestnuts
>
>1/2 pound small pork sausage links
>
>1/2 pound butter
>
>2 tablespoons lemon juice 1 cup chopped onion
>
>1 cup chopped celery
>
>1/4 cup chopped parsley
>
>1/2 cup whole sage
>
>1 teaspoon crushed rosemary
>
>1 teaspoon crushed marjoram
>
>1 teaspoon crushed basil
>
>1 teaspoon crushed thyme
>
>salt and pepper 1 cup turkey stock
>
>1/2 pound unsalted butter
>
>parchment paper 14-pound turkey

Combine ingredients for the turkey stock (giblets, neck, bouillon cubes, water, celery leaves, salt, and mustard), and bring to a quick boil. Then reduce heat, and simmer, covered, until giblets are cooked tender. Discard turkey neck; reserve giblets for gravy if you wish. Strain stock through cheesecloth or fine sieve and reserve.

Cut a gash in the tough outer skin of the chestnuts; boil them. When cooked, peel, and chop them fine. Parboil sausages until cooked, but do not brown them; cool and crumble. Melt 1/2-pound butter in a large skillet, add 2-tablespoons lemon juice, and saute onion and celery until soft but not browned. Combine the crumbled johnnycake with parsley, herbs, and seasonings; toss lightly. Add chopped, cooked chestnuts and sausage meat. Stir mixture into skillet with celery and onion, and stir until all the butter is absorbed. Moisten dressing with 1-cup of turkey stock.

Loosely pack stuffing into turkey cavity. Skewer or sew up opening, and truss bird. Rub skin with some unsalted butter. Melt the remaining butter, and liberally butter the parchment paper. Place turkey on a rack in a shallow roasting pan. Lay buttered parchment paper on top of turkey. Roast in a 325-degree oven until done. (During roasting period, brush turkey with the melted butter, and re-cover with the parchment paper.) About 14 servings. (This recipe is particularly good for wild turkey, which will be a more dry meat. The combination of the butter and the parchment paper will keep the meat moist.)

Smoked Wild Turkey

Rub a 10-to 15-pound wild turkey with curing salt. Refrigerate for five days in a plastic bag. Then wash turkey thoroughly inside and out, being careful to remove all the salt. The turkey must be smoked in a covered barbecue pit using dampened hickory sawdust. Add sawdust to the fire from time to time to keep the smoke going. Smoke for 36-hours, turning now and then. Baste every hour during the daytime with a mixture containing equal parts of cola beverage, vinegar and white wine.

Recipes

How to Prepare Wild Turkey for Cooking

Dry pick, and singe a wild turkey. Wash with warm water (4-teaspoons soda to the gallon). Remove the tendons. Soak the fowl in salt water (4-tablespoons salt to gallon of water) for 3-to 3-1/2-hours. Pour off the salt water, wash the turkey, and rub well with lemon juice. Then proceed with any recipe for roasting and baking a turkey. You can make a paste of butter and flour -- 8-to 10-tablespoons butter to 1-cup flour --spread the paste over the turkey. Place the bird in 475 degree to 500 degree oven, and brown quickly for 30-minutes to set the paste. Stuff bird with dressing, and cook as directed.

Oven Fried Turkey

8 cups packaged herb-seasoned stuffing mix 12- to 16-pound turkey, cut up

salt

pepper

3/4 cup butter or margarine, melted

Crush stuffing finely. Sprinkle turkey pieces with salt and pepper. Brush with melted butter or margarine; roll in stuffing crumbs. Place pieces, skin side up without crowding in greased, large, shallow baking pan. Drizzle with any remaining butter or margarine. Cover pan with foil. Bake in moderate oven, 350-degrees, for 1-hour. Uncover, and bake 30-to 45-minutes, or until tender.

Turkey-Noodle Bake

Blend 1-1/2-cups milk into a 10-1/2-ounce can condensed cream of mushroom soup; stir in 3 beaten eggs. Add 3-ounces (about 2 cups) fine noodles, cooked and drained; 2-cups cubed cooked turkey; 1-cup soft bread crumbs (1-1/2-slices); 4— ounces sharp processed American cheese, shredded about 1-cup; 1/4-cup chopped green pepper; 1/4-cup butter or margarine, melted; and 2-tablespoons chopped canned pimiento. Turn into 13x9 baking dish.

Bake in moderate oven at 350-degrees for 30-to 40-minutes, or until knife inserted in center comes out clean. Cut in squares to serve.

Ham-Turkey Pie

Rice Shell:

2 1/2 cups cooked long-grain rice 2 beaten eggs

1/4 cup butter or margarine, melted

1/8 teaspoon pepper

Pie Filling:

1/4 cup butter or margarine

5 tablespoons all-purpose flour 1/4 teaspoon pepper

2 cups chicken broth 1 cup chopped fully cooked ham

1 cup chopped cooked turkey

1/2 cup chopped mushrooms

1/4 cup chopped green onion

3 tablespoons snipped parsley

To prepare rice shell, thoroughly combine cooked rice, beaten eggs, 1/4-cup melted butter or margarine, and 1/8— teaspoon pepper. Press rice mixture firmly into an ungreased 9-inch pie plate. Set aside.

In a saucepan, melt remaining 1/4-cup butter or margarine; blend in flour and 1/4-teaspoon pepper. Add chicken broth all at once. Cook over medium heat, stirring constantly, until mixture thickens and bubbles. Remove from heat. Stir in chopped ham, chopped turkey, mushrooms, green onion and snipped parsley; mix thoroughly.

Pour ham-turkey mixture into prepared rice shell. Bake in a moderate oven at 350-degrees for 40-minutes. Let pie stand about 5-minutes before serving.

Turkey Hash-Oven Style

1 1/2 cups coarsely ground cooked turkey

1 cup cubed cooked potato

1 small can evaporated milk (2/3 cup)

1/4 cup finely snipped parsley

1/4 cup finely chopped onion

1 teaspoon Worcestershire sauce

1/2 teaspoon salt

1/4 teaspoon ground sage

dash pepper

Crumb Mixture:

1/4 cup finely crushed saltine crackers (about 7 crackers)

1 tablespoon butter or margarine, melted

In a mixing bowl, stir together turkey, potato, evaporated milk, parsley, finely chopped onion, Worcestershire sauce, salt, sage and dash of pepper. Turn mixture into a greased 1-quart casserole.

Toss together saltine cracker crumbs and melted butter; sprinkle crumb mixture evenly over hash. Bake in a moderate oven at 350-degrees until heated through, about 30-minutes.

Turkey-Tomato Bake

1/2 cup chopped onion

1/2 chopped celery

1 tablespoon butter or margarine

1 15 ounce can whole kernel corn, drained

1 1/2 cups chopped cooked turkey

1 10-3/4-ounce can condensed tomato soup

1/3 cup catsup

1 ounce processed American cheese, shredded (1/4 cup)

1 9-ounce package frozen French-fried crinkle-cut potatoes

In a skillet, cook onion and celery in butter until vegetables are tender but not brown. Stir in the corn, turkey, soup, catsup and cheese. Turn into an 8x8x2-inch baking dish. Arrange potatoes over top. Bake, uncovered in a hot oven at 425-degrees for 25-minutes.

Turkey Spoon Bread

1/2 cup chopped onion

1/4 cup chopped green pepper

1 clove garlic, minced

1 tablespoon salad oil

1 15-ounce can tomato sauce

2 cups diced cooked turkey 1 1/2 teaspoons chili powder

1 teaspoon sugar

1/2 teaspoon salt

Prepare spoon bread (see below). Cook onion, pepper and garlic in hot oil just until tender. Stir in remaining ingredients. Simmer, covered, 15-minutes. Serve over wedges of spoon bread.

Spoon Bread:

In a saucepan, gradually stir 2/3-cup yellow cornmeal into 2-cups milk, and cook until thickened. Add 1-cup shredded process American cheese, 1-tablespoon butter, 3/4-teaspoon baking powder, 1/2-teaspoon salt and 1/4-teaspoon paprika.

Stir until cheese melts. Gradually add a moderate amount of hot mixture to beaten egg yolks; beat well, and return to hot mixture. Beat 2 egg whites till stiff; fold into cornmeal mixture. Turn into greased 9-inch pie plate. Bake at 350-degrees for 40-to 45-minutes.

Turkey Puff Casserole

3 cups turkey stuffing 2 or 3 cups sliced, cooked turkey 1 tablespoon minced onion

2 tablespoons butter 2 tablespoons flour 2 cups broth made from giblets 1/2 teaspoon ground ginger

1/2 teaspoon nutmeg

salt and pepper 2 beaten eggs

2 tablespoons bread crumbs mixed in 1 tablespoon butter 1/2 teaspoon thyme

Grease 2-1/2-quart casserole. Line bottom with a layer of stuffing. If packaged, mix according to instructions for 3 cups of dressing. Arrange slices of turkey in a layer over stuffing. Set aside and make sauce.

Sauce:

Saute onions in butter. Stir in flour, and gradually stir in broth and seasonings. Pour into beaten eggs, stirring well. Cool. Pour carefully into casserole and sprinkle with crumbs.

Place casserole in a pan of hot water and bake, uncovered, at 375-degrees for 45-minutes, until top is set. Can be cut in squares to serve on the plate, or served buffet style.

Turkey Stew

20 pound turkey

6 pounds onion, diced 6 pounds potatoes, diced 1 No. 2 can corn

1 1/2 pounds fat back, diced

1 bottle Worcestershire sauce

1 quart tomato juice

1 1/2 jars mustard

1 1/2 pounds butter

Cook turkey in water until meat leaves the bone—about 3-1/2-hours. Remove from water, and cut in bite-size pieces.

Return to the turkey stock, add all other ingredients, and cook until vegetables are tender. Salt to taste.

Leftover Turkey Terrapin

2 cups turkey, cubed 3 tablespoons margarine 1 1/2 tablespoons flour 1/4 cup chicken broth (use bouillon cube)

1 1/2 cups heavy cream or evaporated milk

8 ounce can sliced mushrooms 2 hard-cooked eggs, chopped salt

pepper

paprika

1/4 cup cooking sherry

Dust turkey with flour; lightly brown in melted margarine in large skillet or pan. Blend in broth, and add cream, mixing until smooth. Add mushrooms, eggs, salt, paprika and pepper to taste. Heat thoroughly. Add cooking sherry. Serve on toast points or in pastry cups. Add pimiento if desired.

The wild turkey offers many trophies, including a tasty dinner. This bird is prized by those who hunt him, and the preservation of the memory of the hunt is a treasure most hunters want to keep forever -however they chose to do so.

CHAPTER 18 - TEACHING THE SPORT OF TURKEY HUNTING

I had rather hunt a turkey with someone else than hunt the bird by myself for several reasons.

- An outdoor experience is twice as good if it can be shared.

- Two heads are better than one when trying to outsmart a turkey.

- I either learn or teach when someone else hunts with me, and I like to do both.

- I double my odds for getting the bird.

Most of what I know about turkey hunting I have learned from other people. I have been fortunate enough to have hunted with some of the best turkey hunters in the nation. In preparation for this book, I hunted eight states with 22-different hunters and took the four major races of wild turkey in the United States.

Although I have hunted turkeys for more than 30-years, each time I go with someone I never have hunted with before, I learn more about the sport of turkey hunting. Each man has his own style of chasing gobblers and has been generous in teaching me more about how to hunt.

FRUSTRATION OF TEACHING

Turkey hunting is a very intense sport with a hunt often over due only to a slight error. However, when you assume the responsibility of being an instructor, these kinds of mistakes will happen. To solve this problem, assume that when you are teaching you will not get to shoot a turkey. Teaching and hunting at the same time is difficult but it can be done, as long as the instructor is more concerned about is student than he is himself. If killing a turkey or satisfying your own need to hunt becomes more important than teaching your friend how to hunt turkeys, then frustration and aggravation will result from the hunt.

Because turkeys are not forgiving, if either of you makes a mistake, the bird will be gone. But never relinquish the joy that comes from watching a newcomer to the sport get eyeball to eyeball with a big gobbler.

I remember one such occasion when I took a friend of mine on her first turkey hunt. She was enjoying the walk through the woods and learning about nature when we spotted a big gobbler in the field. As we slipped through the woods, waded creeks and reached the backside of the field, her intensity grew.

When we finally took a stand 10-yards off the edge of the field, and the bird began to move toward us, I watched and listened as her breathing became labored. When the gobbler approached our stand, she started to pant with excitement like a marathon athlete who just had finished a race.

With the longbeard gobbler at 40-yards, I whispered, "Get your cheek on the stock and your head down, see the bead on the end of the shotgun, and put that bead on the turkey's wattles. Just relax, and let the bird come closer. I'll tell you when to shoot."

As the tom closed ground to us, the intensity of the hunt continued to speed up her breathing. When the bird was 10-yards away, I whispered, "Shoot," but she was breathing so hard and was so excited she did not hear my instructions.

Once again I instructed her to, "Shoot." This time the turkey heard me, stuck his head up, putted two times and started to run off. When the bird had made about eight steps, and my friend still was concentrating on the spot where the turkey had originally stood, I brought my shotgun to my shoulder and quickly tumbled the gobbler.

Although the turkey was a fine, three year old bird with a 9-inch beard and 1-1/4-inch spurs, it was not nearly as fine a trophy as the memory of how excited my friend got when she saw the beautiful bird in all his splendor. This first-time hunter was completely mesmerized and captivated. The joy and pleasure that comes from seeing someone get that excited at a gobbler coming in makes teaching the sport of turkey hunting more than worthwhile. In the beginning, the sport is best taught from the living room of your own home.

LESSON 1

If you plan to take someone turkey hunting for the first time, invite them to bring all their equipment, and come to your house the week before the hunt. If they do not have any equipment, let them try on the camouflage clothing you plan for them to wear. Also explain the other equipment they will need on the hunt, why each piece of equipment is important, and how and why you use that equipment in the field.

Have the fledgling hunter sit on the floor, pull his knees up, and aim his shotgun to make sure he knows to place his cheek on the stock, keep his head down and look straight down the barrel at the bead. Review with him how to bring his gun up and prepare for the shot, how to move when the turkey moves, how to sit, how to scratch if he gets an itch, how to use one finger to swat a mosquito, how to walk in the woods and how to carry his gun. Teach him hand signals you will need on the hunt for getting down, moving to the left or the right, "I hear a turkey calling," "I hear a turkey walking," "I hear a turkey drumming," "The turkey's behind us," "Don't move," "Let's go," "Slow down," and other information to enable the two of you to communicate without the spoken word.

Explain to the student why you may have to scratch in the leaves, what you are doing when you purr, why you may have to let a turkey walk off without getting the shot, why you do not want to let a turkey get too close, why you will set up so far away from the turkey, why not moving once you have set up is critical to your success, why you should do the calling at first and that you will let him call some if possible. Review every problem the two of you may encounter on the hunt. Then talk with the student hunter about any other questions he or she may have or problems you think the two of you may find. I have found that having a typed-up list of problems and/or instructions to go over with the newcomer to the sport is the most productive way to teach. Then after reviewing the list, I send it home with him.

After equipping the fledgling turkey hunter, explaining the whys of using each piece of equipment and reviewing the problems you may have to face, take the fledgling hunter on his first hunt by showing him turkey videos. Videos allow a novice to learn how much time passes from when you begin to call a turkey until the bird comes to where you are. He will understand that masters of the sport of turkey hunting often do not get their birds but may spook the gobblers and miss them. Then he will not feel so badly if the same thing happens to him.

Explain to him why the hunters on the video are taking a stand where they sit, why they do not shoot as soon as they see the tom and why they get up quickly and go to the bird after shooting him. Utilizing the visuals of videos and your careful explanations, you can give the fledgling hunter a vast amount of knowledge in a short time besides implanting mental pictures of the hunt to give the beginner useful experience.

After watching a couple of turkey hunting videos together and your explaining what is going on in each of the videos, watch the third video. Encourage the beginner to tell you why the hunt proceeds the way it does and why the sportsmen on the video do what they do.

Next, give your beginning hunter a box call or a pushbutton call, and teach him how to use it. Use an audio cassette to enable the novice to imitate these sounds on the call. Let him take the audio cassette home with him to watch and practice.

This training before the hunt serves several purposes. You. . .

- teach safety before the lesson's needed,

- build excitement for the hunt,

- let the beginner go on a hunt and learn tactics without ever setting foot in the woods,

- explain in the living room why you will do what you will be doing on an actual hunt, which will save valuable time in the woods,

- prepare the hunter for the moment of truth when the turkey comes into range,

- teach valuable hand signals that you will use in the woods, and

- will give the beginner the best understanding of the sport and experience in the sport before he ever enters turkey country. Take as much time to plan the hunt of the beginner as you do to plan your hunt for a trophy gobbler. Then your first experience with this novice will live in his

184

memory as long as the memory of any trophy bird you either have taken or missed exists.

PHYSICAL CONDITIONING

One of the most critical keys to making that first hunt successful and enjoyable for the beginner is to be sure he understands that turkey hunting involves plenty of walking, sitting and maybe some jogging to get to a tom. A beginner will have his confidence crushed if he is not in shape for the hunt.

If you will be hunting mountainous terrain, encourage the beginner to start exercising a month before the hunt by walking up hills or climbing steps. Also, make sure a novice has a pair of quality boots with proper support for hunting. Encourage the beginner to participate in his exercise wearing the boots he will have on when he hunts. This plan of action gives a new hunter the chance to prepare for the hunt and get his body in condition for the demands that may be put on it. If he does not get into condition, cannot perform the tasks that are required to get to the birds and performs poorly, then he may never turkey hunt again.

For a successful first turkey hunt, evaluate the physical conditioning of your hunter and the amount of walking or climbing required to get to a bird. If I am taking an older hunter or a person not in good physical shape turkey hunting for the first time, I try and locate gobblers close to the road that are easy to reach. I also allow plenty of time to get to the turkeys before they start gobbling in the morning. If you plan your hunt so that you can walk slow and take rest breaks whenever needed, then you can reduce the amount of physical strain put on the newcomer.

I firmly believe a beginner's having a bad turkey hunt is not the beginner's fault but instead is the responsibility of the instructor who has planned poorly or has not prepared the student properly. The beginning turkey hunting student's having a good experience on his first turkey hunt is far more important than bagging a gobbler. If you prepare the student properly, if you are more concerned with his well-being and his enjoyment of the sport than your own, then the novice will have a good time. You may have a hunting buddy for life. If you are so obsessed with taking tom that shooting the turkey becomes more important than your student, you run the risk of ruining the sport of turkey hunting for the student.

TEACHING CHILDREN TO HUNT

Nothing is more rewarding than taking a youngster on his first turkey hunt. You can approach this task in two ways. I believe the easiest is to find a turkey hunting guide and pay the price to have him take your child on his first turkey hunt. The guide understands he is to be the teacher and probably will be more patient, understanding and willing to work with the student than you will be. A guide or a turkey hunting instructor who is being compensated for the task of teaching will put teaching first and his hunting second.

Often we expect more of our children than we do of someone else's child. We may be so intent on making sure our child bags a bird that we forget about his feelings. If we are short and curt with him, we will ruin the experience. A stranger may be nicer to your child when turkey hunting than you are. If you enjoy the sport of turkey hunting, and are intent on taking a gobbler, often this intensity supersedes the love and affection needed to teach the sport to someone very close to you.

Although my son, John, is my best hunting companion and nothing would have pleased me more than to call his first gobbler for him, I understand how intense I am when I hunt turkeys. A good friend of mine, Harold Knight of Knight and Hale Game Calls, took John on his first turkey hunt where John not only bagged his first gobbler, he watched three other toms die. Because Knight was patient and caring as he taught the sport to John, he gave me a little boy excited about the sport who will be my turkey hunting buddy for life. When I teach someone else's child to hunt, I try and use the same patience and concern that has been shown to my son. Remember when you are teaching a child to hunt turkeys, whether he is your child or someone else's, that children ...

- cannot walk as far, as long or as fast as you can.

- need plenty of stops and breaks.

- have bottomless pits for stomachs.

- are always hungry - often at inopportune times.

- have to go to the bathroom at the worst possible times -- maybe when you are close to a turkey.

- have an enormous amount of energy. (Carrying a blind with you will mean they can move behind the blind and not spook the turkey).

- enjoy talking. Set up specific times when you and the youngster can talk, and be certain the child knows this before you hunt

- may be unruly, undisciplined and not willing to take instructions. Taking an undisciplined child into the woods to try and hunt a gobbler is much like teaching a pig to sing. All that possibly can happen is you irritate the pig and waste your time. Turkey hunting cannot be fun for a child who will not obey his hunting companion and can create an unsafe situation. I am totally convinced some children do not need to turkey hunt. These same children often grow into adults who should not hunt turkeys. If you have a friend or an acquaintance who wants you to take him turkey hunting, has a know-it-all personality, will not listen to instructions, talks incessantly or is very nervous, you may be better advised to not take this individual turkey hunting. The sport of turkey hunting only can be learned by someone willing to give up his rights to be the authority figure, to learn from others and to do what is required to learn the sport.

If a person does not have these qualities, you will find yourself trying to teach a pig to sing. The experience will be unpleasant for both of you.

TEACHING LADIES TO HUNT

Often women will learn to turkey hunt quicker than men, but probably not if the woman is your wife. Husbands usually expect more of their wives, get more frustrated with their own wives than another woman and are often less patient and understanding with them than they will be with another female. Having a friend or a hunting guide teach your wife or girlfriend how to hunt turkeys is much less stressful than performing the same task yourself.

Generally women follow directions better than men. If they have a cushion to sit on, they will sit longer and be more still than most men. Patience also is more of a characteristic of women than men. When a turkey comes in, they will remember your instructions, not become nearly as excited and often will shoot straighter than men. Women are also usually are more emotional than men after the shot as they express more excitement and more sheer joy of the hunt than men do.

Too, many women are in better physical condition than men. Ladies also may become more addicted to turkey hunting quicker than men. Because the sport is so stimulating and so emotionally rewarding, oftentimes a lady will be hooked for life the first time she hunts turkeys. Once a lady has learned the sport of turkey hunting, the chances of her becoming a good turkey hunter are good. If I have to bet on who will bag a bird when a male hunter and a female hunter both have the same experience, I must bet on the lady.

TEACHING YOUR BUDDY TO HUNT

Often the easiest way to develop a hunting buddy is to take one of your best friends into the woods and teach him to turkey hunt. A friend who cares about you will be more understanding and easier for you to teach than someone you do not know as well. A good friend already has developed a relationship with you. He knows your strengths and weaknesses, and you understand his. You often will be more patient with a good friend than with someone else. Turkey hunting together can strengthen and build a solid relationship into an even stronger friendship.

You and your longtime friend have learned to sacrifice for each other. Often some self sacrificing is required to ensure both hunters have an enjoyable and rewarding hunt when the two of you go after a tom. A buddy will be just as quick to let you take the shot as he will to shoot himself.

Often a friend will learn quickly as much to please you as to satisfy his own need to know. He will realize you are a knowledgeable and experienced hunter and that by listening carefully and doing exactly what you say, he can learn from your experience and become a turkey hunter much quicker.

When you teach a good friend to turkey hunt, you now have a close companion you can relive the experience with over and over again. You will enjoy spending your time hunting with your friend and can heighten the enjoyment of your turkey hunting experience.

TEACHING YOURSELF TO BE A BETTER TURKEY HUNTER

The sport of turkey hunting is a continuing education program. The more you learn, the more you will discover you to do not know. To improve your turkey hunting skills, go with a turkey hunter you believe to be better than you are. To learn from this woodsman, let him conduct the hunt. Assume the role of student. Let the other person

187

make the decision as to when to call, where to set up, when to move and when not to move. Dedicate this hunt to your continuing education program. Go on this hunt with an expert to learn how this hunter hunts not to bag a bird. Any time I am in the woods with another hunter more experienced than myself, I always take the position of student. Then I continue to learn.

If my teacher becomes stumped and asks my opinion, I will give him several options I think may work. However, I always let him pick the option he believes will work best. I learn how he thinks and why he selects the strategies he does. I never have hunted turkeys with any man without learning something. Adopting this attitude will help you gain volumes of turkey hunting experience and deepen your enjoyment of the sport.

Going one-on-one with a gobbler is an exciting sport, and learning new techniques from veteran hunters is even more enjoyable. Once you enroll in a turkey hunting course, continue to learn until you hear the last gobble and fly to that great roost tree in the sky.

APPENDIX I: GLOSSARY OF TERMS

BEARD: A hair-like growth that protrudes from a turkey's chest. Both male and female turkeys can have beards, but the beard is the primary sexual characteristic of the male. Beards generally grow at a rate of four to five inches a year. Growth begins when turkeys are about five months old.

BOX CALLER: A thin-walled box with a wooden paddle lid attached to one end. With this box, most all turkey calls can be imitated. To create the friction-based sounds, the lid and two sides of the box are usually chalked.

CACKLING: An excited call given by the hen turkey and made up of a series of fast yelps.

CALLING: Sounds made by the hunter to lure a gobbler into gun range. Calling is not limited to the use of hen or gobbler voice imitations. To mimic other sounds made by turkeys, many hunters scratch in the leaves, beat a turkey wing against tree limbs and bushes or slap the sides of their legs with their gloved hands.

> **Sweet Calling:** Any turkey voice imitation performed with a smooth, clear, crisp tone.

> **Raspy Calling:** A call made by a hen that sounds as though she has a sore throat or the beginnings of laryngitis.

CALL-LESS HUNTING: Attempting to bag a turkey without calling to him. To be a productive call-less hunter, you must know where and when you can meet a tom in the woods during his daily routine. This type of hunting requires much more knowledge of the turkeys, their movement patterns, and their likes and dislikes than does hunting with a call.

CALL-SHY: A term describing a turkey that will not come to conventional calling. Often this bird has been called to by hunters and perhaps shot at and spooked. A call-shy gobbler may not come to a hen but will gobble and wait for her to come to him, as she's naturally supposed to do. If he gobbles and she does not come, some hunters think he will walk off because he assumes the calling is coming from a hunter.

CARUNCLE: Small, fleshy, reddish growths of skin at the base of the turkey's throat.

CEDAR BOX WITH STRIKER: A cedar box caller is similar to the box and paddle box caller with which most hunters are familiar. However, instead of a paddle for the lid of the box caller, the hunter has some type of striker he holds in his hand and freely passes across the lid to produce the calls of a wild gobbler.

CLUCK: A hen turkey's sound that is much like a woman talking to herself.

Contented Cluck: The sound a hen turkey makes while walking through the woods when everything is great in her world.

Excited Cluck: A hen turkey's sound that can mean, "I think there's something over there we'd better look at. Hang on, I'm on the way."

CONTROLLED BURNING: The act of setting fire to the woods to burn away the litter on the ground. The fire releases nutrients into the soil and causes a new growth of young plants without damaging or destroying the timber. Controlled burning is a key management tool for improving turkey habitat.

CROW CALL: The sounds that crows make when they notify one another of their positions. The crow call is used by turkey hunters to cause a tom to gobble instinctively. Many times when a turkey hears a high-pitched noise like a crow call, he reacts as you do when someone jumps out of a dark closet and shots, "Boo!" You may scream, because that is the first vocalization that you give to the emotion you feel when you're frightened unexpectedly.

CUTTING: Very fast, loud stutter yelps and clucks much like the beginning of a cackle, but no going all the way through a cackle. Cutting often means, "If you're looking for a date, I'm the lady who can satisfy."

DECOY: An artificial reproduction of a hen turkey. Many hunters use a mounted hen or a plastic replica as a decoy. Some tough gobblers will come in to a hunter only if they see as well as hear what they perceive to be a sweetheart.

DIAPHRAGM CALLER: A caller made of tape, lead, and latex rubber that is inserted into the roof of the hunter's mouth. When air passes over the rubber diaphragm, the hunter can make many of the calls of the hen turkey and the gobbler.

DISPLAYING: The strutting of a gobbler.

DOMINANT GOBBLER: The gobbler whose strength, size, age, and intelligence put him at the top of the pecking order in a flock. Sometimes called a boss gobbler. Many times a dominant gobbler will keep subdominant toms from gobbling. He claims the right to breed the hens because of his superiority.

DOMINANT HEN: The female boss of a flock. Often the dominant hen determines which way a flock will travel, and she is generally the one that calls a scattered flock back together.

DOUBLE CALLING: Calling done by two hunters at the same time, to imitate a number of turkeys in the same area.

DROPPINGS: Turkey excretion in a stool form. A gobbler dropping has the shape of a fishhook or question mark. A hen's stool is round and resembles a small cow dropping.

DRUMMING: The sound a tom turkey makes when he struts. This sounds much like the shifting of gears of an 18-wheel tractor-trailer truck.

EASTERN WILD TURKEY: (*Meleagris gallopavo silvestris*) One of the subspecies of the North American wild turkey found mainly in the eastern United States.

FLY-UP/FLY-DOWN CACKLE: An excited call the hen turkey makes when she jumps off a limb in the morning and flies down to the ground to greet a new day, or when she jumps off the ground to fly into a tree to welcome a night's rest. The cackle usually begins with a series of excited clucks, followed by a series of fast yelps.

FRICTION CALL: Any type of call consisting of two objects rubbed together to produce the sounds that turkeys make. A slate and peg, a box call, or a Twin Hen (a call made of aluminum and wood with a peg striker) are all examples of friction callers.

GOBBLE: The sound made by a tom that gives away his location, calls hens to mate and notifies other turkeys he is in the area.

GOBBLER: A male turkey.

GOULD TURKEY: A turkey once found in Arizona and New Mexico as well as Mexico that biologists have been helping to make a comeback.

HAWK CALL: The sound a hawk makes as it flies overhead. This is the same call turkey hunters use to cause turkeys to shock gobble.

HEN: A female turkey.

HUNG-UP: What happens when a turkey stops just out of gun range and refuses to come closer to the hunter.

IMPRINT: The process by which baby turkey poults at birth immediately follow their mother and learn to do as she does.

INTERGRADE: A turkey produced by the interbreeding of two different turkey subspecies. Intergrades of the eastern turkey and the Florida turkey are common in a narrow zone across the South.

JAKE: A one-year-old gobbler.

KEE-KEE RUN: A young gobbler's squeal and call. This is the call most often given by young gobblers before they learn how to gobble and the call that turkey hunters imitate mostly in the fall, though sometimes in the spring. In the fall, the jakes (one-year-old gobblers) have not matured enough to be able to gobble. So their sound resembles, "Peep, peep, peep, yelp, yelp, yelp," which is the kee-kee run.

LONGBEARD: A dominant or boss gobbler, usually more than two years old.

LOST CALL: A call given by hunters to pull a turkey flock together or to locate a gobbler. Another name for the lost call is the assembly call.

MERRIAM TURKEY: (*Meleagris gallopavo merriami*) One of the subspecies of North American wild turkey found in the western United States.

MEXICAN TURKEY: (*Meleagris gallopavo gallopavo*) One of six subspecies of North American wild turkey that was originally located in the central part of Mexico and is the forefather of the domestic turkey.

MOUTH YELPER: A diaphragm caller.

OCELLATED TURKEY: (*Meleagris ocellata*) One of two species of turkeys, the other being the North American wild turkey, *Meleagris gallopavo*. Having some blue coloration, the ocellated turkey is found in the Yucatan of Mexico and nearby central American states, and is considered to be by many the loveliest wild turkey.

OSCEOLA TURKEY: (*Meleagris gallopavo osceola*) The Florida turkey, which lives only in the Sunshine State, primarily in the southern part of the state, is named for the Seminole Indian chief, Osceola.

OWL HOOTER: A caller that reproduces the voice of the barred owl. The owl hooter is used to locate turkeys, which will shock gobble in response.

OWLING: Hunter calls that imitate the sound of an owl.

PATTERN BOARD: A sheet of plywood or metal that catches the shot from a discharged shotgun shell. On the pattern board, the hunter can see the density and size of the pattern of shot expended from his shell. Shooting at a pattern board tells him how effective his shotgun will be at various ranges with different loads.

PECKING ORDER: The social hierarchy of the turkey flock; the order of dominance of the individual turkeys within a flock.

PEG: A wooden stick or a round piece of plastic that is stroked across a slate box, a piece of slate, or an aluminum-covered box to imitate the sound of a turkey. The peg is a part of a friction call.

PIPPING: Short, high-pitched tones the mother hen makes to encourage her poults to break out of their eggs while they are in the nest. Soon the poults in the eggs make their own pipping noises as they imitate their mother.

POULT: A baby turkey.

PREDATOR: An animal that feeds on other animals. Some of the predators of turkeys include wild dogs, bobcats, foxes, raccoons, eagles, coyotes, wolves, crows, skunks, and snakes.

PURR: A contented sound made by a hen, much like a woman's humming.

PUSH-BUTTON CALL: A simple friction call that requires the hunter only to push a peg with his finger to produce hen calls.

PUTT: An alarm sound given by a turkey.

RIO GRANDE TURKEY: (*Meleagris gallopavo intermedia*) A turkey in the western U.S. Usually is larger in weight than most other North American turkeys.

ROOST: A particular tree where a turkey perches during the night for sleeping.

SCOUTING: Taking inventory of the area you plan to hunt. Looking for turkey sign, listening for turkey sounds, and becoming aware of the terrain and habitat can help in determining a hunt plan.

SET-UP: An area where you determine a turkey should come, and where you will take a stand to call and wait. A good set-up will generally be in clean woods with no natural barriers the turkey must cross to get to you.

SHOCK GOBBLE: The instinctive reaction of a turkey in response to some type of loud sound. A tom may shock gobble when he hears a car door slamming, a train whistle, a clap of thunder, a crow call, or any other loud, high pitched noise.

SLATE CALL: A caller consisting of a peg and a piece of slate. The peg is stroked across the slate to produce the sound of the turkey. The slate is sometimes enclosed in plastic, wood, or any substance like a turtle shell.

SNOOD, SNOOT OR DEWBILL: A bump on the forehead of a turkey that changes size according to how excited the turkey is.

SNUFF BOX: A caller made from a snuff can. The bottom and half of the top are cut away, and latex rubber is stretched over par of the open half of the top. To operate the snuff box caller, the hunter rests his bottom lip against the rubber and blows air across it. The sound made from the air rushing across the rubber is amplified within the snuff can. The snuff box was the forerunner of what is commonly known today as the tube caller.

SPUR: A horny growth on a male turkey's leg, which sometimes also occurs on a hen's leg. At two years of age, most gobblers have one one-inch spur on each leg. However, some gobblers have no spurs, and some have multiple spurs.

STRIKER BOX: Either a slate-covered or an aluminum-covered wooden box used by rubbing a wooden peg across it to imitate the call of a wild turkey. This type of caller is also known as a friction call.

STRUTTING: The action seen when a turkey coils his neck, causes his feathers to stand up, spreads his tail, and drops his wings to impress a hen. A strutting turkey is much like a man on the beach who flexes all his muscles to draw attention to himself and impress any ladies who may see him.

STRUT ZONE: An area where a turkey goes on a regular basis to strut and meet a hen for breeding.

SUBDOMINANT GOBBLERS AND HENS: Turkeys subservient to the dominant birds in a flock. A subdominant turkey may become dominant if the dominant turkey is removed from the flock.

TIGHT PATTERN: A shot pattern in which the pellets are close together at the point on the target where the hunter is aiming. A tight pattern is much more effective for turkey hunting than a loose pattern.

TRAVELING TURKEY: A gobbler that will answer a call but moves farther away from the call each time he hears it.

TREADING NOTE: A call known today as a cackle.

TREE CALL OR TREE YELP: A very soft series of yelps given by a hen before she flies down from her roost. The tree yelp may be best described as a quiet yawn.

TUBE CALLER: A caller made of plastic and resembling a miniature megaphone. The tube caller has a piece of latex rubber over its end that the hunter blows against to make the sounds of the turkey. The tube caller is the modern descendant of the snuff-box caller.

TURKEY MANAGEMENT: The manipulation of habitat, predators, turkeys, and hunters to produce the optimum number of turkeys on a given piece of land.

TURKEY SIGN: Anything left on the ground that indicates that a turkey is in the area. Signs include droppings, feathers, scratches, dusting areas, and tracks.

WATTLES: The fatty tissue around a turkey's neck.

WING-BONE CALLER: A caller made from a turkey's wing bone. The hunter sucks air through the eh bone to make the sound of a wild turkey. There are also artificial wing-bone caller that resemble pipes.

YELP: A call that varies in rhythm from turkey to turkey.

> **Contented Yelp:** A call a hen gives when she is walking through the woods with nothing in particular on her mind.
>
> **Excited Yelp:** A call a hen gives when she is either frightened, looking forward to meeting her gobbler or excited for some other reason.
>
> **Prospecting Yelp:** A call that says, "I'm over here. Is there anyone out there to talk to?"

APPENDIX II - HOW TO USE MAPS TO HELP YOU HUNT TURKEYS

Various maps are available to help you hunt more effectively as well as have an inexpensive place to camp that are nearby. Here is a list of some of the places you can write to learn that information.

1) U. S. Geological Survey

> U. S. Geological Survey
> Federal Center, Building 41
> P. O. Box 25286
> Denver, Colorado 80225

Purchase indexes and order forms for the maps of states West of the Mississippi River, including Alaska and Hawaii, from this address. The U. S. Geological Survey, which has mapped the entire United States, has topographical maps to scale available at $2.50 each that contain line and symbol representations of natural terrain and manmade structures. These maps will aid a hunter in determining where roads, rivers, firebreaks and property lines are on a specific piece of property. Most outdoorsmen prefer the 22" x 27" maps, which depict on a large scale the amount of land a hunter usually can walk in a day. The indexes of the topographical maps name the region covered by each map, the scale available and the year the area was surveyed. These indexes also include lists of special maps that have been made of a place as well as the names and addresses of map dealers, map reference libraries and federal distribution centers.

"Topographical Map Symbols," "Topographical Maps: Silent Guides for the Outdoorsman" and "Maps for America: Cartographic Products of the U. S. Geological Survey and Others" are pamphlets available from either of the U. S. Geological Survey centers that help explain the various kinds of maps as well as the meanings of the symbols, lines, etc. on the maps.

2) U. S. Geological Survey

> U. S. Geological Survey
> 1200 South Eads Street
> Arlington, VA 22202

Use this address to order topographical maps for states East of the Mississippi River.

3) Local libraries

Many local libraries have sets of topographical maps available as well as order forms and indexes for the maps. Also the library near the place where you plan to hunt may contain maps of that county that are not accessible in other parts of the state.

4) Division of Wildlife Refuges

Division of Wildlife Refuges
% U. S. Fish and Wildlife Service
Department of the Interior Room 2343
Washington, D. C. 20402

This department distributes free maps, which will help hunters determine the best places to set up on nearby lands, of the more than 400-wildlife refuges under federal protection.

5) National Wetlands Inventory Office

National Wetlands Inventory Office
% U. S. Fish and Wildlife Service
Department of the Interior
Washington, D. C. 20204

Approximately 10,000-acres of wetlands are mapped by this group.

6) Water and Power Resources Service

Water and Power Resources Service
% Office of Public Affairs
Department of the Interior
Washington, D. C. 20240

Write for free recreation maps of the facilities of this group, formerly the Bureau of Reclamation, across the United States at 333-reservoirs, including camping areas, etc.

7) "Field Offices of the Forest Service" Pamphlet

"Field Offices of the Forest Service"
% Office of Public Affairs
Forest Service
Department of Agriculture
South Building, Room 3008
Washington, D. C. 20250

This free pamphlet lists the locations and addresses of all national forests and grasslands. Write the National Forest Service office nearest you to order maps of any of the 122-national forests, and indicate what types of activities you are planning, since the Forest Service sometimes produces different maps for hikers, hunters, campers, etc. The maps generally cost $1 - $2 each.

8) U. S. Government Printing Office

U. S. Government Printing Office
% Superintendent of Documents
Washington, D. C. 20402

By writing the above address or visiting the GPO nearest you, you can find many helpful pamphlets and maps.

"National Parks of the U. S. - Guide and Map" is a map available that shows the locations of the national parks and includes a chart listing the services, facilities and activities in each park.

"Maps and Atlases - SB-102" and "Surveying and Mapping - SB-183" are two subject bibliographies available free from the GPO too.

9) U. S. Army Corps of Engineers

U. S. Army Corps of Engineers
% Office of Public Affairs
Department of the Army
2 Massachusetts Avenue, N. W.
Washington, D. C. 20314

The Corps of Engineers produces and distributes maps of the recreation areas it manages, but each map must be ordered from the district where the recreational area is located. By writing the above address, you can learn the Corps' districts and addresses.

10) Office of Public Affairs

Office of Public Affairs
Federal Energy Regulatory Commission
825 North Capital Street, N. E.
Washington, D. C. 20426

This commission can give you information about various maps available on the hydroelectric projects licensed by the U. S. Department of Energy where there are public facilities for hunting, camping and other activities.

11) National Cartographic Information Center

National Cartographic Information Center
507 National Center
12201 Sunrise Valley Drive
or
345 Middlefield Road
Menlo Park, CA 94025

This center is the part of the U. S. Geological Survey that is the main source for maps that are produced or distributed by federal agencies, as well as by commercial publishers. Some of the free publications include, "Types of Maps Published by Government Agencies," "Finding Your Way With Map and Compass," and "Popular Publications of the U.S. Geological Survey."

12) Defense Mapping Agency

Defense Mapping Agency

Office of Distribution Services
Department of the Army
ATTENTION: DDCP
Washington, D. C. 20315

Write this source for information on topographical maps of the U. S. as contained in the "Catalog of Maps, Charts and Related Products."

13) Bureau of Land Management

Learn the addresses of the BLM offices nearest to the land you plan to hunt by visiting your library and studying the "United States Government Organization Manual." The BLM offers access to some fine outdoor recreation in the western states and has a series of 60-minute quadrangle maps at a cost of $4 each that show land contours, roads, streams, lakes and manmade structures along with color codings to indicate whether the owner of the land is federal, state, private, etc.

14) Federal Depository Libraries

Federal Depository Libraries
% Consumer Information Center
Pueblo, CO 81009

By contacting this center, you can receive a list of the public, college and government libraries throughout the U. S. that receive copies of most federal government publications, including maps.

15) Large landholding companies in areas you plan to hunt

Including timber companies, steel corporations, mining concerns and power companies will have maps available to show where permit hunting can be done.

APPENDIX III - ADDRESSES

Florida Game and Fish Commission
620 South Meridian Street
Tallahassee, Fl 32399-1600
PH: (904) 488-1960

(For information about public hunting lands for Osceolas)

National Wild Turkey Federation
770 Augusta Road
POB 530
Edgefield, SC 29824-0530
PH: (803) 637-3106

(For information on managing turkeys)

San Angelo Company, Inc.
P.O. Box 984
San Angelo, TX 76902

(For skullcaps to use on turkey mounts)

Touchstone Taxidermy Supply
Rt. 1, Box 5294
Bossier City, LA 71111

(For Instant Mounting Fluid to use in preserving a turkey)

About the Author

John E. Phillips is recognized as one of North America's leading authorities on turkey hunting, because, as John says, "I've learned just about everything that doesn't work to take a gobbler. I've made the mistakes that hunters make when turkey hunting, and I've learned from those mistakes."

Phillips credits the turkey hunters he's known and the life he's led for most of his turkey-hunting knowledge and skill. His love for the outdoors was nurtured by his hunting and fishing family - particularly by John's father, W.A. Sr., whose time afield with his family came first, and by John's older brother, Archie, who allowed John to tag-along in the woods with him almost as soon as John could walk. Today both brothers are professional outdoorsmen.

John's turkey-hunting education began in earnest at college in the mid-1960s at the University of West Alabama in Livingston, Alabama. The university was located in the heart and soul of southern turkey-hunting country. Many of the counties Phillips hunted never had known a closed season for turkeys. The rumor was that some of Phillips' college buddies who helped him learn how to turkey hunt could call gobblers before they could say, "Daddy."

Not only did Phillips' fascination with hunting elusive gobblers begin in college but also his desire to become a writer. As Phillips remembers, "A friend in law school had an article published in 'Outdoor Life Magazine.' After reading that article, I believed that if he could write and sell an outdoor story to a major magazine like that, I could too. I knew I didn't have the background or training to be a writer, since I was a physical-education major with a history minor. However, I'd always enjoyed hearing and reading stories about the outdoors. And, my dad was a spellbinding story teller."

After service obligations and running YMCAs for several years, Phillips made a decision that would change his life forever. "I decided that being an outdoor writer couldn't be any more difficult than becoming a carpenter and learning how to build a house. I felt I'd have to serve a 5-year apprenticeship to learn my craft, and that there would be hurt, discouragement and disaster along the way to my goal. Just like most carpenters learn to drive nails straight by smashing their thumbs two or three times and falling off ladders, I figured that my course in becoming a writer would follow a similar pattern."

And sure enough, Phillips wrote and sent off 48-magazine manuscripts, before the first article ever sold. During that time, he was also writing a weekly outdoor column for several newspapers in Alabama and producing a daily syndicated outdoor radio show for more than 30 stations in 1973.

Phillips has paid his dues as a writer. Since that time, his work has been published by such magazines as "North American Hunter," "Outdoor Life," "Sports Afield," "Field & Stream," "Bassmaster," "Fishing Facts," "Deer & Deer Hunting," Turkey and Turkey Hunting," "Turkey Call," "Mother Earth News," "Progressive Farmer," all the Harris Publications' hunting and fishing magazines, all the Grandview hunting and fishing magazines as well as Game & Fish Publications, "Louisiana Sportsman" and "Mississippi Sportsman" to name a few. The author of more than 30 outdoor books, Phillips feels that his greatest assets to his writing career have been his wife, Denise, who not only serves as mother to children Kate, John and Hunter, but also as housekeeper, editor, business manager and best friend; his mother-in-law, Marjolyn McLellan, who has been his secretary, receptionist and tireless source of encouragement over many years; and his editors, who have helped mold and shape not only his work but also his talent.

If Phillips has any talent for turkey hunting, he believes it comes from hard work. "Any skill is more the result of hard work, failure and learning from your mistakes than anything else."

In 1988, Phillips hunted for 49-consecutive days for turkeys in a number of states. He harvested eastern, Merriams, Osceolas and Rio Grande gobblers. But Phillips' goal in turkey hunting isn't strictly the bagging of the bird. "If I call-up a turkey and can take him but choose not to, or if I call-up a tom that someone else takes, then I'm just as satisfied, and often more satisfied, than if I squeeze the trigger myself. The real sport of hunting turkeys for me is to outsmart the gobbler and get him close enough to be taken. What happens from that point on doesn't really matter to me.

"I enjoy seeing another sportsman get excited, nervous and anxious as a gobbler starts to walk in to where we are, and then watching that hunter gain control of his emotions, settle-down into a shooting position and harvest his first tom. Those memories last longer and mean more to me than the ones of the turkeys I hunt and take myself. The excitement of the hunt - more than the taking of the tom - is what calls me into the woods each spring when the trees begin to bud, and the gobblers sing their love calls."

A Conversation with Author John E. Phillips

Question: John, why did you write the "Turkey Hunter's Bible?"

Phillips: When I wrote this book, I considered calling it "The Gorilla-Getter's Bible," because at that time, most of the people I knew hunted turkeys as if they were gorillas. There were very-few turkey hunters back then, and only a select group of outdoorsmen even would try to take a turkey. The legends of turkey hunting told everyone how difficult taking a turkey could be, how many hours you had to spend chasing them, how quiet you had to be, and how long was required to master a turkey call. Most people thought when you were hunting a turkey you had to use all the same cautions as if you were trying to capture a wild gorilla with only a throw-net. I wanted to write a book that would explain to any newcomer the equipment and the tactics they could use to take a wild turkey. I wanted them to realize that a wild turkey wouldn't bite you or kill you, you didn't have to be afraid of making a bad note on a turkey call and spooking your turkey, and that really and truly, turkey hunting was a lot of fun. And, once you got into the sport, you'd really like it.

Question: John, have you ever had anyone who's gone out hunting a turkey and didn't really like the sport?

Phillips: Yes, I have. This story is one of the craziest ones I've ever been told, when I was still doing taxidermy more than 25-years ago. I know it's the truth. I had a fellow who came into my taxidermy shop about 2-weeks before the turkey season. He asked me to tell him everything he needed to know to hunt a turkey that upcoming spring. So, I went into great detail about how to hunt turkeys on public lands, since he planned to hunt a wildlife management area close to his home. I told him, "Go into the woods right away, and start looking for scratchings, droppings, feathers or anything else you can find that will indicate there are turkeys using a certain area." He came back and reported that he'd found a place he thought he could hunt on opening morning. I told him the next thing to do was to return to that place before daylight and listen for a turkey to gobble. He said he'd found a place near where the scratchings and feathers were where he could hear a turkey gobble. Next, I taught him how to use a slate call, because that was one of the easiest calls to use. I felt certain he could be successful with it. I also explained that he needed to wear camouflage from head to toe and told him how to build a makeshift blind. On opening morning of turkey season, this hunter was standing at the door of my taxidermy shop with the turkey he'd taken. I was really excited, because I knew he'd never taken a turkey before. I felt successful, since I'd been able to introduce him to the sport. When I asked him what he thought about turkey hunting, I couldn't believe his answer.

"I didn't think too much of turkey hunting; there wasn't anything to it, as far as I could tell," the man said. I just about passed-out. "Tell me about the hunt," I said. "Well, there's not really much to tell," the new turkey hunter said. "I went to the place where I'd found all the turkey sign, made a makeshift blind out of branches and brush and got ready to start calling. But before I could get my slate call out of my pocket, a hen flew-down, landed right in front of me and started yelping, clucking and carrying-on, and every time she'd make a sound, the gobbler would gobble back to her. She walked right past my blind yelping and cackling, so I didn't think there was any reason for me to use my turkey call. The hen wasn't even out of sight when a big gobbler flew-down right in front of my blind, and I shot him. For me, the hunt was over before it even got started. I really can't believe that people think turkey hunting is all that hard."

I was blown away, and I told him, "I can't believe you were that lucky. If you hunt turkeys for the next 5-10 years, you'll probably never have an experience like that again." I saw this fella 3-years later, and he said, "You were right about turkey hunting. I've only taken one gobbler since that first morning when the bird flew-down in front of me. I've found out that I've still got a lot to learn about this turkey hunting."

Question: What do you think is the most-difficult aspect of turkey hunting?

Phillips: Learning patience and learning to hunt on "turkey time." One of my best turkey-hunting buddies is Bo Pitman, who for many years, guided turkey hunters every day of turkey season at White Oak Plantation. When you hunted with Bo, he hunted on turkey time. When I asked Bo what he meant by turkey time, he explained, "You live your life according to time. You know what time you're supposed to get up, go to bed, eat lunch, eat dinner, go to an appointment and leave to get to work on time. But that turkey doesn't live by the same time you do. He does what he wants to do, when he wants to do it, and where he wants to do it. If you want to take him, you have to be willing to stay with him, go where he wants to go and then sit there and wait on him to show-up. Just because you want to eat lunch at 12:00 noon doesn't mean you'll be through turkey hunting then. To take a turkey, you have to commit to staying each day as long as is required to give yourself the best chance to bag that bird. During that day of turkey hunting, there's no other time that can be important to you. I've learned that the turkey dictates when he'll be where he'll be, and if you don't hunt on his time or if you've got other things scheduled, you're not as likely to take a turkey. That's what I like about turkey hunting - that turkey doesn't care what you want to do, or when you want to do it. He'll do what he'll do, and if you don't do what he does, you won't take him."

This may sound like a rambling explanation about how to hunt a turkey, but the sportsmen who consistently have been successful taking turkeys rarely get back to the pick-up point on time, and they'll often miss lunch and even dinner. They can't take a phone call at a certain time, and they don't plan any-other activities on the days they're hunting. The turkey has all of their time, from before daylight until after dark.

Question: What do you think is the biggest mistake most turkey hunters make?

Phillips: I think there are two mistakes. They call too much, and they walk too much. I can honestly say that these are the two biggest mistakes, because I made both of them quite often when I first started turkey hunting. A friend of mine once said, "Patience kills more turkeys than fancy calling," and he was absolutely right. The thing we often forget when we're hunting turkeys is that these birds have short strides. When they take a step forward, they'll often move less than a foot. Often you'll have a turkey coming to you and decide, "If the turkey was going to come within gun range, he should already have been here by now." So, you get-up to move. You either flush the turkey that was coming to you, or walk off and leave the bird before he gets to you.

Question: What are the toughest turkeys for you to hunt?

Phillips: All of them. In Alabama where I live, the turkeys are hunted so hard and so long that the late Ben Rodgers Lee, a friend of mine and a nationally-known turkey caller, said, "Alabama turkeys are the toughest turkeys in the world to take, because every season, all the good gobbling gobblers are taken. So, the only turkeys left to breed are the ones that don't gobble very much." I think there may be some validity to this reasoning. I also have a difficult time with Osceola turkeys, especially when I'm hunting them in the swamps, because the foliage is so thick that when they gobble they sound like they're much-further away than they really are. For this reason, I have a tendency to get too close to the turkeys and spook the birds I'm trying to take.

The Merriam's gobbler is probably the bird I hate the most - not that he's sinister or a bad bird. But you can call to a Merriam's from one mountaintop, and he'll answer you from another mountaintop. After a while, you'll decide the best strategy is to circle around off the mountaintop you're on and get on the mountaintop where the turkey's gobbling. But when you get close enough to call that turkey and start using your turkey calls, that turkey now will be on the mountain where you've been. Merriam's turkeys often have run me up and down more mountains than I can count. The real truth may be that I haven't learned to stay put long enough when I call to these birds.

The Rio Grande gobbler is an altogether-different bird. You may hear 10 to 50 Rio Grande gobblers gobbling from the same roost tree and think to yourself, "This will be an easy hunt." You call to the turkeys, and all 50 of those gobblers will answer you. But what you don't know is that while those turkeys are on the limbs of those trees, they're deciding where they'll go when they fly-down. And, most of the time they won't fly to where you're calling. I've been most successful taking Rio Grande turkeys on the second or the third day that I've hunted them, when I've had time to determine where they want to go when they leave the roost tree, or which way they're coming back in the afternoon. Then I can set-up a blind and do very-little calling, and sometimes get lucky. In my entire turkey-hunting career, I can remember very-few gobblers that I've taken that I classify as easy.

Question: What does the future hold for you and your turkey hunting?

Phillips: I think I'm getting better. Age has allowed me to be much-more patient than I was when I was a teenager and a young man. Wisdom has taught me that if I stay on a stand for 30-45 minutes after I think I should've left, I'll take 20-to 30-percent more turkeys. I've also learned that taking a nap in turkey woods is not an unpardonable sin. I've woken-up several times from a nap to see a gobbler strutting and drumming in front of me. I'm excited about hunting turkeys in the future, because I know I've still got lots to learn, and that you can never truly master the sport.

DEDICATION

There are silent giants who pass through our lives who never walk in front of us yet always stand behind us. They are always available in times of need. In their daypacks, you will find encouragement, hope, love, patience and an overwhelming abundance of understanding. Most of these people pass through life never recognized until the time is too late. But when their presence is gone, their spirit is still felt.

Someone who always has been a quiet source of encouragement, help in time of need and a willing ear is my sister, Betty Sue Jackson. Sis, you may have walked in the shadow of your two brothers at times, but you always have been tops in my book.

Where to Find More Turkey Hunting Information

As Well as More Hunting and Fishing Information

Thank you for purchasing the "Turkey Hunter's Bible." John E. Phillips also has another turkey book in print, "Outdoor Life's Complete Turkey Hunting." See www.nighthawkpublications.com and click on the left side of the splash page on Hunting Books and Fishing Books. This book has 313 pages and a number of black-and-white pictures of some of the greatest turkey hunters ever, including: Sylvia Bashline; Jim Beam; Hugh Blackburn; Jay Brown; Paul Butski; Nathan Connell; Kelly Cooper; Charles Elliott; Ray Eye; Charles Farmer; J. Wayne Fears; David Hale; Dale Harbour; Doug Harbour; Bill Harper; Brent Harrell; Seab Hicks; Rob Keck; Tom Kelly; Harold Knight; Ben Rodgers Lee; Billy Maccoy; Walter Parrott; Aaron Pass; John E. Phillips; Wilbur Primos; Jim Radcliff Jr.; Terry Rohm; Dan Speake; Gary Stilwell; Lewis Stowe; Glenn Terry; Lovett Williams and Jim Zumbo.

Phillips also has Kindle eBooks: "PhD Gobblers," "Turkey Hunting Tactics," "The 10 Sins of Turkey Hunting with Preston Pittman" and "How to Hunt Turkeys with World Champion Preston Pittman," as well as 47 other books on hunting, fishing and cooking, with more planned. See www.amazon.com/kindle. Type in John E. Phillips, and click on the second choice, his author's page, to see the names and descriptions of the available books.

Phillips is a student of the outdoors. For more than 40 years he's been interviewing, photographing and writing about some of the greatest outdoorsmen of our time.

Made in the USA
Middletown, DE
26 April 2019